Home Chefs

of the world

Rice and Rice-Based Recipes

COMPILED BY
Inderjeet K. Virmani

IRRI

INTERNATIONAL RICE RESEARCH INSTITUTE
P.O. Box 933, Manila 1099, Philippines

and

SUHAY

INTERNATIONAL WOMEN'S ORGANIZATION
Los Baños, Laguna, Philippines

The International Rice Research Institute (IRRI) was established in 1960 by the Ford and Rockefeller Foundations with the help and approval of the Government of the Philippines. Today IRRI is one of the 13 nonprofit international research and training centers supported by the Consultative Group on International Agricultural Research (CGIAR). The CGIAR is sponsored by the Food and Agriculture Organization of the United Nations, the International Bank for Reconstruction and Development (World Bank), and the United Nations Development Programme (UNDP). The CGIAR consists of 50 donor countries, international and regional organizations, and private foundations.

IRRI receives support, through the CGIAR, from a number of donors including the Asian Development Bank, the European Economic Community, the Ford Foundation, the International Development Research Centre, the International Fund for Agricultural Development, the OPEC Special Fund, the Rockefeller Foundation, UNDP, the World Bank, and the international aid agencies of the following governments: Australia, Belgium, Brazil, Canada, China, Denmark, Finland, France, Germany, India, Iran, Italy, Japan, Republic of Korea, Mexico, The Netherlands, New Zealand, Norway, the Philippines, Saudi Arabia, Spain, Sweden, Switzerland, United Kingdom, and United States.

The responsibility for this publication rests with the International Rice Research Institute.

ISBN 971-22-0023-X

Contents

Foreword

Food has many meanings: sustenance, security, hospitality, home, life. As one of the chief foods of the world, rice especially occupies a rich and varied place in many cultures. *Home chefs of the world*, compiled by Mrs. Inderjeet K. Virmani, should be especially appreciated by those who are fond of the cuisines of different countries, particularly of the rice-based dishes of cultures dependent on rice.

Mrs. Virmani is an excellent cook in her own right, a skill developed while living in many countries, and a fine writer, as you will discover in reading the articles preceding the recipes collected in the book. She took great pains to select recipes of exceptional representative dishes to include in this compilation, conducting personal interviews and working in the kitchens of many friends.

A major section devoted to rice and rice-based recipes reflects Mrs. Virmani's special interest in rice, developed while living in the IRRI Staff Housing compound. The International Rice Research Institute focuses on increasing the efficiency of rice production and the sustainability of rice-growing environments. Scientists from all over the world conduct research at IRRI and in collaborating countries to meet that objective.

Members of several charitable international women's associations, such as Suhay in Los Baños where IRRI has its headquarters and organizations of women connected with the Asian Development Bank and the United Nations offices in Manila, contributed to the cookbook.

I hope publication of this book will foster increased understanding and cultural exchange among many international groups. Its publication is a joint endeavor of IRRI and Suhay.

Klaus Lampe
Director General

Preface

This book is the outcome of a joint effort by the International Rice Research Institute and Suhay, the international women's organization of Los Baños that supports charitable projects related to food, medical care, shelter, and education for the downtrodden.

The extent of the activities Suhay can support depends on the availability of funds collected voluntarily by members of the organization. During my term as president 1989-1990, I proposed compiling a cookbook, to sell for raising much needed funds to support Suhay's expanding activities. The members agreed.

Consequently, I started compiling and writing this book. Many recipes were submitted by my friends in Suhay and by other colleagues from overseas and members of the United Nations Women's Group and the Asian Development Bank Women's Group based in Manila. My interest in rice has been enhanced by my life in the rice environment of IRRI, and I have devoted a special section to stories about rice in the religious and sociocultural activities of different countries.

I am grateful to the members of Suhay and other international women's organizations who generously shared directions for their favorite vegetarian and non-vegetarian dishes. Without those recipes, this book would not have been completed. (Each recipe bears the name of the contributor and the country where the recipe originates. When two countries are given, the one in parentheses is the native country of the contributor and the other is the country represented by the recipe.)

My special thanks go to Mmes. Fauzi Bhuiyan and Ilse Zandstra. The secretarial help of Ms. Leonida Nazarea is gratefully acknowledged. I would also like to thank Dr. Thomas R. Hargrove, head of IRRI Information Center, for fostering the collaboration with Suhay that made this project possible. Thanks are also due Ms. Gloria S. Argosino for editing and Mr. Ramiro Cabrera for production supervision. I am grateful to Mrs. Marie-Luise Kürschner for the illustrations.

I hope this book will foster international friendship and cultural exchange among people of different nationalities. It can further serve as a souvenir for those who have lived in or visited Los Baños, Laguna, Philippines, and who would like to assist in the continuing, extensive charitable activities of Suhay.

Inderjeet K. Virmani
October 1991

Preface

Rice

Rice

Origin and Distribution

The ancient Indian name for rice—
"Dhanya," meaning "sustenance for the
human race"— indicates the crop's age-old
importance. Man has cultivated rice since
prehistoric times. Specimens of rice
discovered in China date back to 5000 BC.
Rice as a cultivated crop in Asia originated
in tropical India. All Hindu scriptures
mention rice and all offerings to God
include rice, an indication of the antiquity
of the crop.

Rice was introduced into Indonesia by
Deutero-Malayans that immigrated to this
region about 1599 BC. Indonesia is the
land where a race of rice called javanica
originated. In fact, the name Java is said to
mean "island of rice."

Rice came to Japan by way of China.
Japan has long been famous for the
excellence of its rice and rice cultivation
methods. Rice has also been grown in Sri
Lanka (formerly Ceylon) since time
immemorial. Much later, rice cultivation
spread farther west. The Greeks learned of
rice from the Persians and medieval
Europe got it from the Saracens. The crop
was introduced in northern Italy in the
15th century. The Malays brought rice to
Madagascar and Indians introduced it in
the East African islands. The Moors
brought rice to Spain and the Turks
introduced it over much of the
southeastern part of Europe. The
Portuguese introduced rice in Brazil and
the Spaniards in Central America and parts
of South America. The crop was
introduced in Hawaii in 1853. The French
brought it to New Caledonia and the
Germans to New Guinea.

Rice cultivation in the United States of
America dates back to about 1646 AD. The
cereal was introduced in Virginia but was
first cultivated in South Carolina. Presently,
rice is cultivated on a commercial scale in
California, Arkansas, Louisiana, Mississippi,
Texas, and South Carolina.

Rice has been grown commercially in
Australia since 1924. The North Island of
New Zealand also grows rice successfully.

Rice grows from 55 °N latitude to
37.5 °S, from an altitude of 3,000 m in the
Himalayas to places below sea level. It
grows on slopes of mountain ranges to
areas with 2 meters deep standing water.
Thus, rice is the most versatile food crop
cultivated in the modern world.

Food Value

About 85% of the rice kernel is
carbohydrates, most of which are in the
endosperm. Freshly harvested rice
contains 72-75% starch. The protein
content of milled rice is low (8-9%), but its
digestibility is high, being 96.5 for the
whole grain and 98% for milled rice. The
fat content of rice is low (2-2.4%); about
85% is removed in the process of milling.
The amount of fat-soluble Vitamins A and
D in rice is negligible, but the Vitamin E
content is considerable. Husked rice has a
high Vitamin B content, at least one-tenth
that of dried yeast. The riboflavin content
is low and Vitamin C is practically absent.

Rice loses considerable nutrients
through milling and polishing.

Before cooking, it is customary to wash rice, often with several changes of water, to remove dust, insects, husk, and other impurities. Washing dissolves some of the nutrients from the grain, the amount removed depending on the degree of milling and the amount of washing.

Methods of Cooking

Methods of cooking rice vary in different countries. Habitual rice-eaters say there is no one way to cook rice; some varieties of rice and rice grown in certain localities require different treatments.

There are four main methods of cooking rice (FAO 1948)[1]:

1. Large amounts of water are used and the excess is drained away, carrying with it much starch that has been rendered soluble.

2. Rinsed raw rice is immersed in water, just enough to swell the grains properly, and cooked in a double boiler or over a slow fire—to avoid charring at the bottom—until the water is fully absorbed.

3. The cooked rice is often rinsed to ensure the complete removal of the films of soluble starch on the surface of the grains.

4. Rice is sometimes half-cooked by boiling, after which the water is drained off and the rice is steamed to a state of tenderness in a pan or basket in an enclosed space over freely boiling water.

In many countries, rice is sautéed in butter before it is cooked for any kind of dish.

Rice is always eaten with vegetables, pulses, meat, fish, or seafood. A variety of dishes around the world are made with rice.

---

[1]FAO [Food and Agriculture Organization] (1948). Rice and rice diets. Nutritional Studies No. 1, FAO, Washington.

Rice

Asia

Bangladesh

A proper Bengali meal always includes rice. In rural areas it is customary to have rice in all meals.

In Bengali, the word for partaking of a meal is "having rice." The language uses different words for the different forms of rice: for example, dhan is unhusked rice; chaul, husked rice; bhat, plain boiled rice; and pullao, fried rice. Parboiled chaul is common for regular consumption; however, pullao and rice flour are made from rice that is not parboiled.

Major rice dishes are bhat, pullao, kichuri, kheer, and zarda. Bhat is eaten daily, but pullao is served on special occasions. Pullao is a mixture of fine-grained, aromatic rice and other ingredients such as vegetables, fish, chicken, shrimps, and coconut. Pullao, chaul, and goat's meat are the main ingredients of a spicy, delicious dish called Biryani. This dish is served at wedding receptions in the urban areas.

Typically, bhat is served with a vegetable dish along with fish, meat, and pulses. Kichuri is pulses and rice cooked together. This constitutes a light meal and is eaten after several consecutive heavy meals. On a rainy day, the Bangladeshi relish kichuri instead of bhat.

Rice desserts in Bangladesh include kheer, firni, and zarda. Different varieties of snacks are made from puffed rice (muri), parched rice (chivara), and popped rice (khoi). Roasted fried chaul, whole or ground, is also used for making many kinds of snacks.

Rice flour is used for various kinds of sweet and salty dishes. The most popular rice flour dish is pitha, a generic name for different kinds of rice cakes. During rice harvest time, pithas are made from new rice flour. Some pithas are salty with filling, while others are sweet and served in a syrup or with milk.

Special pithas are made by friends and relatives of participants in a wedding, circumcision, etc. For such occasions, nakshi pithas with various artistic designs are made a few days before the ceremonies and are served to the guests, or distributed among relatives and friends. Nakshi pithas are mentioned in many wedding songs. The fresh flavor of certain chauls is suitable for the pithas. Nowadays, the frequency of pitha-making is reduced because of the pressure of urbanization and the increasing cost of labor.

Bhuna Kichuri (Spicy Fried Rice)

1/2 c mongo, skinless
2   c aromatic rice
1/3 c oil
1   c onion, thinly sliced
1   tbsp ginger, grated
1   tbsp coriander powder
    Salt to taste
4   bay leaves
4   1-inch cinnamon sticks
4 1/2 c hot water
4   green chilies (optional)

Roast mongo beans in heavy frying pan for a few minutes. Let it cool. Wash rice and mongo together and let stand in a strainer.

In another pan, heat oil and sauté half of onions until golden brown and crisp. Remove from oil and drain on paper towel. To oil in pan, add the rest of the onions and all spices except green chilies. Sauté for 2-3 minutes. Add rice and mongo, and fry for about 5 minutes more. Add water. When mixture boils, reduce heat and cook until grains are done. Add green chilies and half of fried onions. Stir carefully. Keep covered for at least half an hour before serving. Garnish with the rest of the fried onions.

Serve with vegetables, any beef or chicken curry, salad, and pickle.

Nargis Zapata

Firni (Sweet Rice Pudding)

1/3 c aromatic rice
8   c milk
1   c sugar
1   tsp rose water
2   tbsp raisins
1   tbsp thinly sliced pistachio nuts
1   tbsp thinly sliced almonds

Wash rice and soak in one cup water for at least 30 minutes, then drain in a strainer for one hour. Put some grains, a little at a time, on a chopping board and crush into small pieces by pressing them lightly with a rolling pin.

In a heavy pot, bring to a boil 4 cups milk; reduce heat to medium and continue boiling, stirring from time to time until milk is reduced to 2 cups.

In another pot, boil 4 cups milk. When it starts boiling, add rice. (It is good to wash rice before adding it to milk.) Cook over medium heat, stirring occasionally until rice is done. Add 2 cups thick milk, sugar, and raisins, stirring constantly. When the mixture starts boiling, remove from heat, and add rose water. Pour firni in a dessert bowl. Garnish with almond and pistachio slices.

Fauzi Bhuiyan

Patishapta Pitha

2 liters milk
2 tbsp sugar
3 cardamom seeds, crushed
1 tsp corn flour
1 c rice flour
1/4 c sugar
   Pinch of salt
1/2 c water
1/4 c white all-purpose flour
1 tsp rose water (optional)
1 tbsp oil

Boil milk; when it starts boiling, reduce heat and continue boiling (stirring occasionally) until milk is thick. Add sugar and cardamom. Dissolve corn flour in 2 tbsp milk; add mixture to the thick milk, stirring continuously. Remove from heat and set aside.

Mix rice flour, sugar, and salt. Gradually add water and mix well. (If batter is too thick, add more water.) The batter should be moderately thin. Set aside for 2-3 hours. Just before using the batter, add all-purpose flour and rose water.

Heat a frying pan (nonstick frying pan will be good) and brush it well with oil. Pour 1/4 cup batter in it. Immediately rotate the pan until the batter spreads to form a thin crepe. Reduce heat and cover the pan. When the surface dries, place 1 1/2 tbsp thick milk along one edge of the round pitha. Roll the pitha and press it a little, using a spatula. Transfer pithas to a tray and keep covered. Serve for breakfast, hot or cold. Pithas can also be served for snacks.

Fauzi Bhuiyan

Poa Pitha (Rice Cake)

1 c rice flour
1/2 c sugar
1/2 c milk
1/2 c water
2 c oil

Mix rice flour and sugar in a bowl. Add water and milk to make a smooth batter. Cover and set aside at least one hour. Heat oil in a cooking pan. Deep-fry 2 tbsp batter at a time until the pitha turns brown on both sides. Drain pithas very well. Serve hot or cold.

Nargis Zapata

Sweet Fried Muri (Puffed Rice)

8 c puffed rice
1 c sugar
1 tbsp water
1 c grated coconut

Mix water and sugar in a cooking pan and bring to a boil. Add coconut and cook for 5 minutes. Add puffed rice, mix very well, and cook for 5 minutes, stirring constantly. Transfer to a plate and allow to cool.

Nargis Zapata

China

Rice is the major staple food of the Chinese, although wheat is also used in the northern part of the country. Rice is boiled, steamed, or fried and served along with numerous meat, seafood, and vegetables. Since they eat with chopsticks, most Chinese prefer varieties cooked soft-moist and somewhat sticky. Glutinous or sticky rice is used to make sweets: rice pudding, rice cake, moon cake, etc.

To the Chinese, rice symbolizes life and fertility. They respect rice so much that they do not waste it. It is considered bad luck to upset a rice bowl. Children are taught to eat every bit served to them.

Rice figures strongly in a variety of rituals. In some parts of China, it is the practice to present a wooden bowl full of rice to the family ancestors on New Year's day. Rice is also served to give thanks for the gifts of the previous year and to pray for favors in the New Year.

The Chinese make wine from rice. Shao Shing wine is served on festive occasions such as weddings and special family get-togethers.

Fried Rice (Chinese Style)

4   c cooked rice
1   c diced pork
1   tbsp soy sauce
1/2 tbsp cooking wine
1/2 tsp cornstarch
2   eggs, well-beaten
1/4 c cooked green peas
2   spring onions, chopped
1/2 c oil
     Salt to taste

Marinate pork in soy sauce, wine, and cornstarch at least 10 minutes. Heat 2 tbsp oil in a pan and pour eggs; stir quickly to make a fluffy omelet. Remove from pan and set aside. Again heat 3 tbsp oil; add marinated pork and cook on high heat; keep stirring until well done. Add green peas and cook for a minute. Set aside. Heat 1 tbsp oil; add green onions, sauté for a while, then add cooked rice. Mix well. Add salt, cooked eggs, pork, and peas. Mix again. Serve immediately.

NOTE: Ham, roast pork, barbecued pork (leftover), and cooked shrimps can be substituted for pork.

Sophie Ling
Taiwan

Eight-Treasure Rice Pudding

1	c glutinous rice
1/4	c sweet red bean paste
10	lotus seeds
5	red dates
10	peanuts
10	white raisins
5	walnuts
10	brown raisins
1/4	c candied orange peel
2	tbsp shortening
3	tbsp sugar
1/2	tbsp cornstarch
1/2	tbsp cold water

Clean and wash rice; cook until done. Set aside. Chop walnuts, raisins, and candied orange peel. Make a paste with cornstarch and cold water and set aside.

Grease the bottom of 4 bowls. Divide all ingredients except rice and sweet red bean paste among the bowls. Divide rice and bean paste into 4 portions. Place 2/3 of each portion of rice in a bowl to cover the nuts and fruits, then put sweet red bean paste in the center. Cover the bean paste with remaining rice; flatten it. Steam at least 2 hours. Unmold on serving platter.

Boil sugar in 1 cup water. Thicken with cornstarch paste. Pour syrup on pudding. Serve immediately.

Nancy Chang
Taiwan

Steamed Rice-and-Chicken Pudding

3	chicken legs	1	tbsp green onion, diced
6	tbsp soy sauce		
2	tbsp oil	1/2	c black mushrooms
1	tbsp wine	3	tbsp ham, diced
1	tsp sugar	3	tbsp dried shrimp, soaked and diced
1/4	tsp black pepper		
1/2	c soup	3	c cooked glutinous rice

Brush chicken legs with soy sauce, then deep-fry in hot oil over high heat. Debone chicken when cool. Place one chicken piece, skin side down, in the bottom of a large bowl. Lay 2 other pieces flat against the sides.

Prepare seasoning sauce; mix wine, sugar, black pepper, and soup. Stir-fry green onion, black mushrooms, ham, and dried shrimps for 30 seconds. Pour 2/3 of seasoning sauce, then turn off heat. Add cooked glutinous rice. Mix thoroughly. Spoon glutinous rice on top of chicken in bowl. Push down to make sure rice is tightly packed. Add remaining seasoning sauce. Steam 30 minutes over high heat.

To unmold, place a serving plate over the bowl and carefully turn both plate and bowl over so that the chicken pudding is on the serving plate.

Nancy Chang
Taiwan

Radish Rice Cake

2	c radish
4	tsp salt
4	tsp oil
8-10	strips bacon or ham
1 1/2	c rice powder
2	c chicken broth or water

Shred radish; add salt. Heat oil, add radish and cook until half done. Add the rest of the ingredients. Mix well and pour mixture into a round or square baking pan. Steam for 40 minutes.

Nancy Chang
Taiwan

India

India is a large country in terms of both people and land. From the mountainous Himalayas in the north, through the fields of Punjab, the deserts of Rajhasthan, the plains of Uttar Pradesh and Bihar, and the coasts of the south, India is inhabited by people of diverse cultures and religious backgrounds.

Regardless of this diversity, rice is eaten all over India. In the south and in the east, rice is a staple food. It is a supplementary dish in the north and the west, but is eaten as a staple in northernmost Kashmir and Jammu. Rice is cooked in various ways in each of the regions, but there are a few common preparations: plain boiled rice, khichri (rice cooked with mungbean), pullao (fried rice), and kheer (rice pudding).

India is one of the centers of origin of rice and therefore has a multitude of rice varieties and grain types. There is the long-grain rice that plays a traditional role in the making of sweets and puddings. Parboiled rice is equally important in southern India, where it is used in an array of meals: semiglutinous rice is used for breakfast and snack dishes such as idli (steamed rice muffins), dosai (rice pancakes), chagoni (rice pretzels), kozhakkhatta (a steamed pastry made of rice flour with a sweet or salty filling).

In the south, rice is eaten at all meals. For breakfast, dishes common at the table are dosai, idli, and ada (a kind of pancake). Lunch and dinner feature a simple preparation of plain boiled rice. But during festive occasions, meals boast of lemon rice, coconut rice, tamarind rice,

yellow rice, pullao, and biryani. During some specific festivals, such as Pongal, the main dishes are cooked from newly harvested rice. These are Venn Pongal rice (salty rice with beans) and Sakkran Pongal (sweet rice with jaggery syrup). Rice panicles are also hung at the entrance of homes and temples during these festivals.

In the east, rice is the main course in two meals of the day. In the rural areas, poor people have pantha (leftover rice with onions, salt, and green chilies) for breakfast. The common daily meals consist of bold-grain parboiled rice, which is preferred to fine-grained parboiled rice because it is more nutritious.

On special occasions, fine aromatic rice such as Badshah Bhog and Gobind Bhog are used in preparing dishes such as pullao, murighantta (rice cooked with fish or fish head), biryani (rice cooked with meat), and the like. Desserts such as payesh (rice pudding made of rice, milk, cardamom, raisins, and coconut) and crupa (a dessert cum snack made of rice flour, coconut, and sugar) are common delicacies in the region.

The northwest prefer plain boiled rice known as bhat as well as wheat chapatis, a staple consumed with beans and vegetables. Rice pullao and biryani are cooked along with vegetables. This shows the slight variations in different areas. Khichri is a favorite because of its taste and medicinal value; it is eaten by people suffering from indigestion and those recovering from sickness. The favorite dessert, on the other hand, is kheer. Some desserts, which are also eaten as snacks, are chivra, baara, and laddoo (rice balls).

Farther north, in Jammu and Kashmir, rice is the staple food. Kashmiris eat plain boiled rice for lunch as well as dinner. Special preparations are tahar, khajach mavas (rice with dal), biryani, and zardah (sweet rice with saffron).

In the west, wheat is the main staple. Nevertheless, rice is faithfully eaten daily. In general, lunch or dinner begins with rice, dal, and ghee, followed by chapati, puri or parathas, all of which are wheat dishes. These are eaten with dal and vegetables. Rice is also taken with yoghurt to give a finishing touch to lunch or dinner. The main rice dishes are plain rice, pullao, anarasa (sweet, fried rice patties), chakli (pretzels made of rice flour), thalipeeth (chapati bread made of rice flour with shredded cucumber, onion, green chilies, and spices), and pohe (pressed rice with potato and peas). Breakfast and snacks may consist of chivra and murmura (puffed rice with peanut, dal, peas, and cashews). Kheer, as usual, is a dessert.

Rice is an important factor during rituals and festivities throughout India. The Hindu scriptures mention the use of rice in offerings to the gods in order to express the people's gratitude and happiness. The religious use of rice has existed not only in India, but in China, Thailand, Indonesia, Sri Lanka, and Malaysia. Rice is of chief importance during the Pongal festival in southern India. During wedding ceremonies, rice plays an important role as well. For instance, during a wedding, a mound of

raw rice is kept, surrounded by coconuts and oil lamps. As the newlyweds take their vows, a handful of rice is tied to the corner of the sari of the bride. Upon arrival at the groom's house, she is made to step on a pan full of rice, causing the grains to spill out of the container; the spilled rice is kept by the family as a remembrance.

Rice is both a major component of the life and culture in the east. A thick mixture of rice powder or paste is used to make artistic decorations (alpana) on the floor of the main entrance of the house on every occasion when divine favor is sought.

In the north, rice is used during a ceremony in which a child is endowed with a name. The rice is used to make an array of dishes, each of which is tasted by the child. Another ceremony, called the thread-wearing ceremony, involves the presence of rice. During this Hindu ceremony, the rice is kept as auspicious food. During prayers, rice is offered to the holy fire and given to the priest. During the Bhai Dhooj festival (sister-brother day), the sister places a holy mark with saffron and rice on the forehead of the brother and he, in turn, swears to protect and aid his sister throughout her life. Then he gives her a gift as a token of his affection. During a wedding ceremony, rice is thrown on the newly wedded couple as a sign of blessings. The bride is requested to cook her first rice dish when she joins her husband's home. This dish is distributed among the elders. During the Diwali festival (festival of lights), popped rice is used during worship. On Makar Sakranti, a festival which falls on January 13, the day commences with the preparation of a rice dish, which is usually khichri.

In Jammu and Kashmir, rice is used in Nav-Reh (New Year) ceremonies. The eldest member of the family places raw rice grains in a big plate, on top of which are placed the image of the family god or goddess, one pen, an ink pot, salt, an earthen lamp, and sindur (red powder that married Indian women use at the center of their forehead). When the members of the family awake in the morning, they pray before this plate to ensure a prosperous, meaningful, and blessed New Year. Special rice dishes are prepared during birthdays and wedding ceremonies. Rice pindas (rice balls made of mashed, boiled rice pulp) are offered for the departed soul when there is a death in the family.

In western India, rice is used during both daily and special worship. During a wedding ceremony, rice and a special red powder, kumkum, is marked on the forehead of the bridegroom and rice grains are showered on the bridegroom by his sisters.

During a birthday ceremony, all members of the family put rice and the sacred red powder on the forehead of the birthday celebrant. The lady of the house holds this sacred mixture between the thumb and index finger, and touches the celebrant's feet, knees, shoulders, and hands. She repeats this five times and finally touches the forehead of the birthday celebrant.

Rice also has a significant role during the namkaran (naming) ceremony of a child. All the relatives and friends offer rice grains and coconut to the child and the mother as a token of their best wishes.

Indeed, rice has its own value and place in the life and culture of the Indian people.

Fish Pilau with Mushrooms

1	lb fish	1	tsp salt
2	tbsp oil	1/2	c mushrooms
1	oz pea flour	1/2	lb rice
1/4	c lemon juice	1	crushed cardamom
1/2	tbsp paprika	2	sticks cinnamon
1	onion, sliced	1/4	tsp nutmeg
3	cloves garlic, crushed	1/4	c roasted almonds
		1/2	cucumber, sliced
1	c yoghurt		
1	tsp ground fennel seed		

Wash, clean, and dry fish. Cut into serving pieces. Rub pieces with pea flour, oil, lemon juice, and paprika. Set aside for 15 minutes. Wash fish again and set aside. Put butter in frying pan, add onions, stir-fry for a while. Add minced garlic, 1/2 cup yoghurt, and fennel seeds. Pour mixture over the fish and let stand for 15 minutes. Heat oil and fry fish till pieces are brown. Sprinkle with salt. Slice mushrooms, sauté in butter, and then sprinkle with 1/4 cup water. Cover and simmer for a while. Cook rice in another pot. When half done, add remaining yoghurt and cover. Cook until tender. Place fish in a casserole; top with rice. Sprinkle with cardamom, cinnamon, and nutmeg. Dot with butter. Add salt according to taste. Cover and leave on low heat for 30 minutes. Garnish with fried almonds and sliced cucumber.

Malvika Dadlani

Mixed Vegetable Pullao

1	c rice	1	green chili, chopped
3	tbsp butter	1 1/2	c mixed vegetables, chopped
1	onion, thinly sliced	4	c water
1	tsp chopped ginger	1/4	c cashew nuts, roasted
1/2	tsp cumin seeds	2	sticks cinnamon
2	cardamoms	1	tbsp raisins, sautéed
2-3	cloves		

Clean, wash, and soak rice for 1/2 hour. Heat butter, add onion and sauté till golden brown. Add ginger and sauté for a few minutes. Add cumin seeds, cardamom, cinnamon, cloves, green chili, and mixed vegetables; stir, cover, then simmer for a while. Add drained rice and salt and stir for 5 minutes. Add water, bring to a boil, then reduce heat. Cover and cook on low heat till done. Garnish with cashews and raisins.

Usha Ladha

Rice with Cauliflower

2	c rice (preferably Basmati)
1/4	c butter
2	onions, sliced
4	cloves garlic
1/2	kg cauliflower, cut into pieces
1/2	tsp black cumin seeds
1	stick cinnamon
1/2	tsp curry powder (without turmeric powder)
	Salt to taste
1/2	tsp ginger, chopped
2	green chilies (optional)
1/4	c sour cream
4	c water
1/4	c roasted almonds
2	crushed cardamoms
	Fresh coriander leaves
1	tomato, sliced

Clean and wash rice; soak for 30 minutes. Heat butter; sauté one onion and then set aside for garnish. In same pan, sauté cauliflower till half-cooked. Remove from pan; set aside. Sauté another onion and garlic, then add all dry spices. Drain rice; add to onion mixture and sauté for a minute. Add cauliflower, ginger, green chilies, and salt. Continue sautéing for 5 minutes. Add water and sour cream. Cover and cook on low heat till done. Garnish with sautéed onion, roasted almonds, fresh coriander leaves, and sliced tomato. Serve with yoghurt, curry, sweet and sour chutney, or pickles.

Indu Virmani

Tamarind Rice

1	c rice
1/4	c ripe tamarind
2	tbsp gram dal (optional)
3	red dried chilies
1/4	c oil
1/2	tsp mustard seeds
1/4	tsp turmeric powder
2 1/2	tbsp coriander seeds
1	tsp sesame seeds
	Pinch of asafoetida
6	fenugreek seeds, roasted
1/4	c roasted nuts
	Salt to taste

Cook rice. Soak tamarind in 1 cup hot water for 30 minutes. Extract pulp; add 1/2 cup more water. Mix very well and strain pulp. Soak gram dal in 1/2 cup water for 30 minutes; drain and dry on paper towel. Chop red chilies. Heat oil, add mustard seeds. As soon as seeds start to split, add dal and sauté till light brown. Add chilies, sauté for a minute; add tamarind pulp, turmeric powder, and salt. Boil until mixture is like tomato paste. Add all spices that have been ground into powder; mix well; stir in the rice. Leave on low fire till rice is done. To serve, garnish with roasted nuts.

Geetha Prasad

Coconut Rice

2	c rice
1/2	c ghee or 1 c butter
6	cloves
3 3/4	c boiling water
2	c grated fresh coconut
3	c jaggery or sugar
6	pc cardamoms
1/2	tsp nutmeg powder
1/4	c raisins
1/4	c almonds, sliced
	Yellow food coloring

Wash rice and set aside for an hour. Heat butter or ghee in pan; add cloves and washed rice, and sauté 5-10 minutes. Pour 3 3/4 cups boiling water on rice. Cook rice till done. Spread it on a flat dish to cool. In another pot, cook grated coconut and jaggery or sugar until coconut becomes soft (say, 10 minutes). Add rice, food coloring, cardamom, nutmeg powder, raisins, and almonds.

Vijji De Datta

Lemon Rice

2	tsp black gram dal
1	c cooked rice
2	tbsp oil
1	tsp mustard seeds
1	tsp chopped ginger
3	pc chopped dried red chilies
1	tsp turmeric powder
	Curry leaves
5	tbsp lemon juice
	Salt to taste
1	tbsp roasted nuts

Soak dal in water for 30 minutes, then drain and dry on paper towel. Set aside. Spread rice on a plate, and sprinkle with a little oil. In frying pan, put oil and sauté mustard seeds, chopped ginger, black gram dal, and chilies, then add turmeric powder and curry leaves. Remove from fire. Add lemon juice and salt to taste. Add rice and mix well. Top with roasted nuts.

Vijji De Datta

Kheer (Sweet Rice Pudding)

4	c fresh milk
1/4	c rice
1/2	c sugar
2-3	cardamoms
	Dried nuts (almonds, cashew, raisins, etc.)

Soak rice in water for an hour. Boil milk and add rice to it. Stir constantly over low fire till rice is fully cooked and a thick consistency is reached. Add sugar, cardamoms (partly ground), and dried nuts. Stir for a few more minutes. Serve hot or cold.

Veena Ish Kumar

Yellow Sweet Rice

2   c rice
6   c water
2   drops yellow food color
2   tbsp butter or ghee
4   cardamoms
1/2 c sugar
1/2 c dry chopped nuts

Boil water with food color. Add rice; let boil until rice is half done. Remove from fire and drain. Heat ghee or butter in a pan; add cardamoms, boiled rice, and sugar. Cover and leave on low heat until done. Garnish with nuts. Serve hot.

Anita Chachra

Rice with Molasses

4   c molasses   5   pc cloves
2   c milk and   1 1/2 c rice (preferably
     pinch of cream   very old)
     of tartar   1/4   c sliced roasted
1   c butter   coconut
1/2 tsp cumin seeds

Boil molasses in a pan. Add milk and cream of tartar. Let boil again for a while. Remove foam. Remove pan from fire. Heat butter in a skillet, add cumin seeds and cloves. Add rice; stir-fry for a while. Add molasses; cover and cook till done. To serve, garnish with nuts and roasted coconut.

Promila Ranjhan

Deharodi (Sweet Rice Balls)

2   c rice   3   c sugar
100 grams butter   4   c water
1   c curd   250 grams vegetable oil

Soak rice for 3 days. Dry it in the sun for 1 or 2 days, then grind. Combine ground rice and butter in a bowl and mix well. Add curd and make a hard dough. Take little pieces of dough and form into round balls. Heat oil and deep-fry balls until golden brown. Soak fried balls in syrup for 1 hour.

Syrup for Deharodi
Boil sugar and water in a big pan (1 1/2 liters). Cook for 10 minutes, stirring the liquid occasionally.

Kiran Sahoo

Rice with Baked Mangoes

1   c rice   2   tbsp sugar
4   tbsp milk   1/4 tsp ground saffron
1   c sweet mango   1   tsp rose water
     purée   Butter
1/2 c Nestlé cream

Clean rice and soak overnight. Boil milk and stir over medium heat until reduced by half. Mix mango purée, Nestlé cream, and boiled milk in a bowl; add sugar, saffron, and rose water. Boil rice separately until very soft. In a casserole, alternate one layer of rice and a layer of creamed mango. Repeat until all rice and creamed mango are used. Dot with butter and bake in a slow oven until set and lightly browned. Serve hot or chilled.
NOTE: Mango purée can be replaced with peaches or apricots, also puréed.

Asha Tikku

Idli

1 1/2 c rice (preferably parboiled)
1/2 c urad dal (without skin)

Soak rice and dal separately for 6 hours. Drain. Grind dal fine with 1/2 cup water till foamy. Grind rice medium fine with one cup water. Mix ground dal and ground rice; let rise for 6 to 10 hours. Add salt to taste. Add more water if necessary to make the dough creamy enough to pour. Pour in oiled molds. Steam over boiling water for 5 to 10 minutes. Do not oversteam, or else the idli will be hard. Makes about 24 idlis.

NOTE: a. There is a special mold for making idlis, but cupcake pans can be used.
b. Idlis can be served with coconut chutney and sambhar.

Mercy Dale

Dosai (Rice Pancake)

3 c rice
1 c black gram, without skin

Soak rice and black gram separately in water for 4 hours. Then wash with water several times. Grind black gram in a wet grinder with 1/4 cup water. Grind rice in the same manner. Mix both flours, then add a little salt. Allow the mixture to ferment for 12 hours. After fermentation it is ready for making dosai.

Heat a nonstick pan over medium flame. When the pan is hot, brush it with vegetable oil. Spread 1/2 cup of the mixture on it, then cover it with a lid. After 2 minutes, collect the dosai.

Masala Dosai
1 tbsp oil
1 onion, chopped
2 tomatoes, chopped
1 big potato, boiled and cut into cubes
1 carrot, cut into cubes
Salt and pepper to taste

Heat oil; add onion and sauté for a minute or until transparent. Add tomatoes; stir for a minute; add potato, carrot, salt, and pepper. Cover and cook on low heat for 10 minutes. Spread 1 tbsp of this mixture in the center of a dosai. Roll and serve with coconut chutney and sambhar.

Mercy Dale

Rice Flour Omelet

2   c rice flour
1/4 tsp chili powder
2   tsp coriander powder
1   tsp cumin powder
    A pinch of baking powder
    Salt to taste
3   onions, chopped
5-6 chilies, chopped
1/2 c water
1   tbsp oil

Mix rice flour with dry spices and baking powder; add onions and chilies. Add water; mix, and knead dough well. Heat a heavy skillet and pour oil on it. Make pingpong-size balls of dough; in the pan flatten each ball into a pancake. Cook both sides of pancake on medium heat. Serve with butter or tomato sauce.

Smita Gadgil

Kozahakkhatta

4   c rice
2   tsp cumin seeds
2   c grated coconut
    Salt to taste

Soak rice for 6 hours, then drain. Grind all ingredients together, without adding any water. Form dough into small balls and set aside. Bring water to a brisk boil. Drop rice balls one by one in boiling water and cook for 20 to 30 minutes. When balls are done, scoop them up. Serve with sugar, coconut chutney, or pickles for breakfast.

Latha Pillai

Sweet Kozahakkhatta (Steamed)

6   c rice flour
1/2 c water
    Pinch of salt
1/2 c sugar or jaggery
1/2 c ghee
2   c grated coconut
1   tsp cardamom powder
1   tsp dry ginger powder

Combine salt and rice flour and make a thick dough by adding water. Form dough into small balls and set aside. Combine sugar, ghee, coconut, cardamom powder, and ginger powder. Flatten each rice ball, spoon a little coconut mixture over dough, then form into a ball again. Steam for 15 to 20 minutes.

NOTE: This can be served with evening tea.

Latha Pillai

Pohe (Pinipig with Potato and Peas)

2	c pinipig
1/2	c water
2	tbsp oil
	Pinch of asafoetida
1	tsp mustard seeds
1	onion, sliced
1	potato, cubed
	Few curry leaves
2	green chilies, chopped
1/4	tsp turmeric powder
1/4	c green peas, cooked
1	tsp sugar
	Green coriander leaves
1	lime
	Salt to taste

Wash pinipig, and soak in 1/2 cup water for 30 minutes. Heat oil; add asafoetida, mustard seeds, onion, and potato. Sauté for a while on low fire. Add curry leaves, turmeric powder, and chilies; stir. Drain pinipig and add to mixture in pan; stir, then add green peas, sugar, and salt. Cover and cook for 10-15 minutes on low heat. Transfer to a platter, garnish with green coriander leaves, and sprinkle with lime juice.

Satnam Taneja

Baare

1	c rice
2	c sugar
2	c butter or ghee
1	c chopped nuts

Roast rice in a pan on slow fire for 15 minutes. Set aside. Grind rice and sugar together. Heat butter and mix with rice and sugar very well. Pour mixture on a platter and flatten. Sprinkle with chopped nuts. Cut into pieces and serve.

Meena Channan

Ada

1	c rice	1	red chili
1/2	c yellow split pea	2	onions, chopped
1/4	c urad dal		Salt to taste
1/4	c gram dal		Oil
2	green chilies		

Soak rice for 3 hours. Soak dals separately for 1 hour. In a blender, blend the green chilies, red chili, and salt with a little water. Remove. Blend rice coarsely. Add dals to rice in blender, and grind them (not smooth). Pour mixture in a container; add onions. Heat oil in a frying pan. Pour some batter in the pan, and make a small hole in the center. Pour 2 tbsp oil around and at center of pancake. Cook on low heat till edges brown; turn and cook the other side. Serve hot. This can be eaten as it is, or served with pickles or honey according to taste.

Geetha Prasad

Chagoni

1 1/2	c water
3/4	tsp salt
1/8	tsp chili powder
1	pinch asafoetida (optional)
2	tbsp mung dal
2	tbsp sesame seeds
1	c rice flour
1	c oil

Boil water. Add salt, chili powder, asafoetida, and mung dal. Boil 3 more minutes. Add sesame seeds. Reduce heat. Immediately add dry rice flour, stirring constantly. Make sure that no lumps or balls form. Cover pan and leave on hot range for 5 minutes. Take out and cool rice dough. Apply oil on palms of the hand and make lemon-size balls of dough. On a smooth board, roll each ball into a thin rod and shape into small rings. Heat oil; drop rings in hot oil and deep-fry until brown. Cool and keep in a tight container. They stay crisp for 15 days or longer.

Ramani Seshu

Laddoo (Sweet Rice Balls)

1	c rice
1	c skinless mongo
1	c butter
1	c cheese, shredded
1/2	c confectioners sugar
4	pc cardamoms, ground
1	c melon seeds

Soak rice and mongo for 2 hours. Drain water and grind grains coarsely. Melt butter; pour grain mixture on it. Cook on low heat until light brown. Add cheese and cook till the butter separates. Add sugar, cardamom, and melon seeds. Remove from fire and shape into small balls.

Meena Channan

Rice Pappardam

4   c new rice
1   c sago
2   tsp salt
2   tsp baking powder

4   c water
1   tsp carom seeds
1   tsp cumin seeds

Clean and wash rice. Spread it in the hot sun until very dry. When dry, grind with sago into powder. Add salt and baking powder. Add mixture to boiling water over high heat. Stir vigorously until it forms a thick paste. Add carom and cumin seeds. Remove from fire. Make small balls of the mixture, and roll each ball into a tortilla. Spread polyethylene in the sun and put tortillas on it to dry. Dry them very well. (Dried tortillas can be stored in an airtight container for a long time.) Deep-fry tortillas in oil, and serve with any kind of sauce.

Meena Murarika

Dhokla with Tomato Chutney

3   c rice
1   c yellow split peas
1   tsp baking soda
1   c yoghurt
1   tsp turmeric powder
2   c water
1/2 c oil
50 grams mustard seeds
25 grams cumin seeds
2   stems curry leaves
    Salt to taste
2   green chilies, chopped

Grind rice and split peas together very well. Add baking soda. Soak ground mixture in yoghurt overnight.

Beat mixture while adding water and turmeric powder. Pour batter in a baking dish and bake in a double boiler. From time to time, check for doneness with a toothpick.

When done, remove from pan and cut into pieces. Set aside.

Heat oil in a pan; add the last five ingredients. After a minute, add the baked mixture that had been cut into pieces. Stir and mix slowly. Serve with tomato chutney.

Tomato chutney

4   ripe fresh tomatoes
50 grams coriander leaves
20 grams green chilies
1   tsp cumin seeds
1   tsp sugar

Grind all in a blender. Add salt according to taste.

Asha Tikku

Indonesia

In Indonesia, no meal is complete without rice. Rice is served as a main dish, a side dish, or as an ingredient in snacks or desserts. Rice is usually cooked or steamed plain and eaten with meat, vegetables, and fruits. In some regions, it is topped with thin strips of omelet. Many desserts or snack preparations, viz., pancakes, waffles, are made with rice flour.

Many Indonesians consume unpolished and red rice, which is more nutritious than polished rice. Sticky rice is used for making snacks, e.g., rice lumpia, rice cake wrapped in banana leaves.

Some traditional dishes are Nasi Goreng and Nasi Kuning, which are made for festive occasions such as weddings or communal feasts. Indonesian specialties include Ketuput Liontong, which is rice rolled and steamed in coconut leaves, and Nasi Goreng, or fried rice sprinkled with saffron or turmeric. For Nasi Kuning, a yellow rice for special occasions, rice is steamed or boiled in coconut milk with saffron. Another specialty is Nasi Tumpeng, a cone of white rice garnished with red, black, and yellow food.

Steamed Rice with Meat and Vegetables

1	c rice
1	c water
1 1/2	c coconut milk
1/2	tsp salt
2	carrots
2	onions
1	medium potato
1/4	c diced beef
	Pinch of chili powder
2	tsp soy sauce
1	tbsp vegetable oil
1	tsp ketchup

Clean and wash rice, and cook with salt, water, and coconut milk. Set aside. Peel carrots and potatoes; cut into small cubes. Heat oil in a saucepan; sauté all vegetables; add meat, then remaining ingredients with 1/2 cup water. Cover and cook on low heat for 5 minutes. Put one layer of cooked rice in a saucepan, spread over it a layer of cooked meat and vegetables. Use all rice and vegetables by spreading alternately. Cover and steam in a steamer or oven for 30-40 minutes. Cool before serving.

NOTE: Steaming can also be done using banana leaves. Spread mixture alternately on banana leaf; roll, fold over ends, and seal. Steam packet in a rice steamer.

Ikke Sunari

Rice with Prawns

4   cloves garlic
4   onions
6   chilies
2   blachan
1/4 c oil
1   lb prawn
1   lb cooked rice
    Salt to taste

Pound garlic, onions, chilies, and belacham coarsely. Heat oil, and sauté prawns and pounded ingredients. Add rice and salt and sauté for 5 minutes. Remove from fire and serve hot.

Faiza Pervaez
(Pakistan)

Rice Cake with Coconut Cream

1/2	lb sticky rice	1	oz brown sugar
2 1/2	c coconut milk		Pinch of salt
2	eggs		

Clean, wash, and soak rice in cold water for 1 hour. Drain. Put rice in a steamer and steam for 5 minutes. Put steamed rice in a saucepan and add 1 cup coconut milk and salt. Again steam for 10 minutes.

Prepare coconut cream by beating eggs and sugar until thick and fluffy. Add remaining coconut milk and salt. Cook mixture in a steamer for 10-15 minutes. The mixture should be like thick cream. Transfer the rice mixture to a serving dish and top with thick coconut cream. Cut like cake and serve warm or cold.

Ikke Sunari

Japan

The word for "meal" in Japan is "rice." For the Japanese, a meal lacking rice in any of its forms is unimaginable. Rice is so closely bonded to Japanese culture that it has a place in the country's history: during feudal times, chiefs were ranked according to their rice yield. In fact, in some areas, people were paid in rice.

In general, people consume rice during the three meals of the day. In recent times, however, this pattern has been altered because people have found substitutes for rice.

Two kinds of rice are used: glutinous and nonglutinous. Nonglutinous rice is used in daily meals and glutinous rice is used for special rituals.

Rice and pickles are the basic constituents of the traditional Japanese diet; ironically, that is considered the poor man's dish. The main dishes using rice are chicken rice, red rice, and chestnut rice, served with tempura, sukiyaki, or misutak with pickles. The most popular dish with rice, both in and out of Japan, is sushi.

The Japanese also prepare special dishes on festive occasions such as New Year's day and weddings. The most important New Year's food is mochi, which is glutinous rice that is steamed, pounded in a mortar, and formed into various shapes. These are usually flat and round cakes, kept for days and prepared for serving by toasting over a fire.

Many preparations made with rice can be classified into various categories: rice dumplings wrapped in banana leaves, a diamond-shaped lo-genge rice cake, white wine (made by adding some yeast and alcohol and leaving the mixture for months) used during girls' festivals, and a special rice cake, stuffed with sweet bean paste and wrapped in oak leaves. The latter is prepared during children's day (boys' day). Red bean rice, a special Japanese sweet, is made of glutinous rice; it is oval-shaped and coated with sweet red bean paste. This is traditionally served during spring and autumn and oftentimes during birthdays.

The most popular drink is saké wine made from rice, which is used on special occasions such as weddings. During weddings, custom requires that the bride and groom take three sips of cold saké from each other's cup.

Another traditional and interesting dish is known as Pot Rice. This is the new version of Tea Rice, which originated several years ago with the Buddhist priests. Now Pot Rice is prepared with soy sauce and mirin or fish sauce, instead of tea. Some people add seafood, meat, vegetables, and mushrooms to Pot Rice.

Sushi Salad

8   c cooked rice (Jasmine or Calrose)
3/4 c rice vinegar (Komesu)
1   c chopped ham, chicken, or smoked fish
1/2 c chopped nuts
1/2 c water chestnuts
1   c chopped celery
1/2 tsp sugar or Ajinomoto

Mix all ingredients. Chill. Serve with seaweed decorations.

Marge Litsinger
(USA)

Chestnut Rice

2	c rice	1/2	tsp salt
15	chestnuts	1	tsp saké
1	tsp shoyu	2	c water

Wash rice. Remove shells and brown skin of chestnuts. Soak nuts in water for one hour.

Put rice and chestnuts in a pot; add the rest of the ingredients. Bring to a boil. When water starts boiling, reduce heat and simmer for 15 minutes. Turn off heat and leave rice covered for 10 minutes before serving.

Kari Otsuka

Oyako Chicken Rice

200-250	grams chicken breast
1/2	tsp soy sauce
1/2	tsp rice wine
1/2	c snow peas
1/4	c kangkong
1	tbsp oil
1	white onion, sliced
2	c cooked rice

For soup
1 1/2	c water
2	tbsp soy sauce
2	tbsp sugar
2	tsp rice wine
1	tbsp chicken stock
1	tsp fish powder
4	eggs, beaten

Prepare soup by boiling together all soup ingredients except eggs. Set aside.

Cut chicken into pieces. Season with soy sauce and rice wine. Steam vegetables until half-cooked, then set aside. Heat oil in a saucepan, and sauté onion and chicken. Add prepared soup and bring to a boil. Add vegetables and beaten eggs immediately. Turn off heat but keep cover on for 2-3 minutes.

Divide cooked rice into four portions and place each in a soup bowl. Pour cooked chicken soup mixture on top of rice. Serves 4.

NOTE: The rice bowl can be garnished with some seaweed or thinly sliced red preserved ginger.

Kari Otsuka

Red Rice

2   c sticky rice
1/2 c red beans
5   c water
1   tsp salt
1   tbsp black sesame seeds

Clean and wash rice; set aside. Boil red beans in water until done. Add more water if needed. Pour bean water on raw rice. Set aside for a while. Boil rice and beans together in the same water; add salt. Serve garnished with roasted sesame seeds.

NOTE: This preparation is used only for some festive occasions such as children's festivals and weddings.

Fumiko Wada

Gonoku Gohan (Rice with Vegetables)

3 1/2 oz chicken breast, diced
1   tsp minced fresh ginger
2   tbsp saké or dry sherry
2   tbsp soy sauce
1   tbsp sugar
1/2   block konnyaku, cut into strips
1   tsp soy sauce
3   c raw rice
3   c dashi (bonito soup)
3   dried shiitake mushrooms, soaked in warm water for 20 minutes, drained, and cut into thin strips
1   pc abura-age, blanched then cut into 1/5-inch strips
1   burdock root, peeled and cut in "sausagi" (bamboo leaf) style; soaked in cold water for 20 minutes, and drained
1/2   carrot, peeled, cut into 1- × 0.5-inch slices
1   tbsp minced parsley

Bring to a boil soy sauce, saké, ginger, and chicken. When cool, drain chicken, reserving liquid. Boil konnyaku strips; drain. Heat 1 tsp soy sauce in pan, add konnyaku, and stir to coat with soy sauce.

Wash rice 1 hour ahead of cooking. Drain in a colander, and cover with a damp dish towel.

To reserved liquid from chicken, add enough dashi to make 3 1/4 cups liquid. Mix rice, liquid, 1 tbsp soy sauce, and put with all other ingredients, except parsley, in a heavy pan. Stir from bottom of pan, then cover. Cook over high heat until it boils; then cook about 12 minutes on low heat. Turn off heat. Let stand for 15 minutes. With a wooden spatula or fork, fluff up rice. Stir in 1 tbsp minced parsley just before serving.

NOTE: As rice cooked with soy sauce tends to burn easily and takes a longer time to absorb water, the heat should be a little lower than when cooking plain rice. Cooking time will be longer than usual.

Ritsuko Ikeda

Sushi Roll

4 c glutinous rice
1/2 c vinegar
5 tbsp sugar
1/4 c kapyo (dried gourd)
1/4 c dried mushroom
4 tbsp soy sauce
4 c water
4 eggs
2 tsp sugar
1/8 tsp salt
1/4 c string beans, chopped
  Some red pickled ginger
8 pc dried seaweed sheets

Clean, wash, and soak rice in water for one hour, then cook the usual way. Prepare vinegar solution by mixing vinegar, salt, and 2 tbsp sugar. Wash dried kapyo and boil in enough water 20 minutes until slightly tender. Drain and set aside. Wash mushroom and soak in 1 1/4 cup water for 1 hour. Squeeze water out and save it. In a pan combine 1 cup mushroom reserved water, 3 tbsp sugar, and soy sauce. Bring to a boil. Add kapyo and mushroom, and cook until the water dries. In a bowl, beat eggs, 2 tsp sugar, and salt. Cook in a greased frying pan. Cut into 1/3-inch-wide strips and set aside. Boil string beans for 2 minutes; slice red ginger into thin strips (boiled carrots or boiled shrimps can be substituted).

Spread the rice on seaweed sheets. Place a mixture of kapyo, mushrooms, egg strips, string beans, and red ginger in center of the rice layer. Moisten the edges of the seaweed and roll it closing tightly. Slice the rolled seaweed sheets with a sharp and wet knife.

Mitsuko Hibino

Korea

In Korea, the day-to-day meal consists of a bowl of steamed rice, taken with fish, soup, and kimchi. A one-meal rice dish known as Bap is popular. There are a variety of Baps, i.e., rice steamed with kimchi, soybean, bean sprout, fresh oysters, or clam in soup stock.

Bibimbap is rice mixed with assorted vegetables, stir-fried beef, and shredded omelet.

Yakbap is glutinous rice steamed with chestnut, dates, gintego nuts, and raisins, then mixed with honey and cinnamon, soybean and sesame oil, and again steamed. Yakbap is served on festive occasions such as birthdays, New Year, and other holidays.

During the harvest season, rice tea is offered to the ancestors with a prayer. During a wedding ceremony, newlyweds are seated in the middle of a long table loaded with a variety of rice cakes. Immediately, after the birth of a child, the mother is given two meals of rice and seaweed soup. On the 100th day of the newborn baby, a ceremony is held, and rice cakes and rice wine are offered to all the guests. The sharing of rice cakes among 100 people is a symbol of good luck and long life for the baby. When a child is 2 or 3 years old, he is dressed in a brand-new traditional outfit and seated in front of a table on which are found such objects such as a brush, ink, money, and rice. Koreans believe that if the child picks rice from the table, he will be a wealthy man.

Rice wine served on festive occasions is known as Bobju-wine. Sometimes medicinal wine is prepared with rice tea.

Stir-Fried Rice

2	oz lean beef	4	oz seasoned
	Salt and pepper		soybean sprouts
4	oz kimchee	1	tbsp green onion
1	tbsp sesame oil	1	tsp hot sauce
2	c cooked rice		(Kochu Jang)
			(optional)

Seasoning for sprouts
1   tsp sesame oil
1   tsp onion, minced
2   tsp ground sesame seeds
1/2 tsp crushed garlic
1/4 tsp salt

Marinate sprouts in seasoning sauce. Clean and wash beef; cut into strips and sprinkle with salt and pepper. Cut kimchee and set aside. Heat oil on a high flame, add beef; stir-fry until color changes. Add rice, stir; add kimchee and seasoned soybean sprouts. Cook and stir, sprinkle salt and pepper. Transfer to a serving dish, and garnish with chopped green onions. Serve with hot sauce.

Yeong Soo Kim

Rice with Bean Sprouts

2   c rice
1   can clams
200 grams bean sprouts
2   c liquid from clam and water
2   tsp saké
1   tsp soy sauce
1   tbsp green onion, finely chopped

Wash rice, drain very well. Drain clams but reserve liquid. Discard roots of bean sprouts. Wash sprouts and set aside.

Combine rice, sprouts, and liquid ingredients and boil on high heat for 5 minutes. Reduce heat and cook over very low fire until done. Stir in clams and simmer over low heat for 5 minutes. Cover and let stand for 5 minutes. Garnish with chopped onions.

Sue Ahn

Yaksik (Sweet Rice Cake)

5   c glutinous rice
15   chestnuts
     Pine nuts, pineapple, a few dates
300 grams brown sugar
1   tsp caramel sauce
1/4 c soy sauce
1   tbsp sesame oil
1/2 tsp ground cinnamon
4   c water

Soak glutinous rice in water for 4-6 hours. Peel chestnuts and cut into 2-3 pieces. Pit dates, and cut into small pieces. Wash glutinous rice and put in a rice cooker. Add all other ingredients, mix well, and cook.

Yeong Soo Kim

Malaysia

Diversity is a dominant characteristic of the population of Malaysia. The people come from three major ethnic groups, viz., Malays, Chinese, and Indians. With this multiracial composition, Malaysian cuisine combines the best of eastern and western cuisine in Asia.

The most popular Malaysian dishes are spicy, fragrant, and always served with rice. The traditional Malaysian dish known as Nasi dagang is made of unpolished glutinous rice mixed with coconut milk and other ingredients. It is eaten any time of the day and also on special occasions such as birthdays and family get-togethers. It is normally accompanied by a side dish such as Kerutup ayam, chicken curry, or solok lada (steamed stuff chilies), solok ikams (fried fish balls).

The most novel and popular rice dish is Banana Leaf Rice. A heap of fluffy rice and a choice of meats, vegetables, pickles, and crisps are served on banana leaf.

Rice preparations for festive occasions include Nieu koay, a cake made with very sweet sticky rice and offered to the deities on Chinese New Year and on Audul Pithra's, and served on get-togethers. Other delicacies are Long tong and Ketupat, rice wrapped in palm leaves.

Salmon Rice

1   small onion, chopped
1   chili (optional)
1   egg
3/4 c milk
2   tbsp butter
1/2 c cooked salmon
1/2 c cooked rice
1/4 c cooked green peas
     Salt and pepper

Chop onion and chili. Beat egg and add milk; set aside. Heat butter; add onion, and stir-fry until it becomes transparent; add chili. Turn off heat and add salmon, cooked rice, and beaten egg. Mix thoroughly. Add peas, salt, and pepper. Pour the mixture into a buttered dish and bake in a moderate oven for one hour or until cooked.

Avtar K. Singh

Tomato Rice

2   c rice
1   clove garlic
     A piece of fresh ginger
2   onions
2   tbsp ghee or butter
3/4 c tomato soup
2 1/4 c water
     Salt to taste

Clean, wash, and drain rice; set aside. Slice garlic and ginger. Chop one onion and slice the other. Heat butter in a pan; add garlic, ginger, and chopped onion.

Sauté till golden brown. Add rice and sauté, stirring constantly. Add tomato soup and water. Cover pan and cook on low heat until rice is done; add salt.

NOTE: Sauté sliced onion until golden brown and use it as garnish on top of rice.

Patti Heong

Fried Rice Malaysian Style

1/4 c oil
5   red chilies
2   onions, sliced
2   cloves garlic
     Few curry leaves
     Salt to taste
1/2 lb rice, cooked

Heat oil; sauté chilies, onions, garlic, but do not brown. Remove and grind coarsely. In the same oil, add curry leaves, salt, and rice. Mix thoroughly and cook a minute longer. Serve hot.

Siew-Fing Wong

Ketupat Pulut (Glutinous Rice Wrapped in Banana Leaf)

3   coconuts, grated (for 3 1/2 cups thick coconut milk)
1 1/2 tsp salt
1   kg glutinous rice, washed and drained
10   pc banana leaves, each 18 × 23 cm, singed

Put coconut milk and salt in a large saucepan and bring to a slow boil over low heat. Add glutinous rice and stir for 10-15 minutes until almost dry.

Cover saucepan and cook over low heat for 20 minutes until rice is half-cooked. Cool.

Put 3-4 tbsp cooked rice in the center of each banana leaf piece. Make a long roll, about 4 cm in diameter. Twist the two ends and tie securely with strong string or triple-strength nylon threads. Secure roll by tying the string around the center as well.

Steam rolls in a steamer for 2 hours over low heat. Cool, discard banana leaves and cut rolls into 2 1/2-cm-thick slices.

Ipin Mew

Nasi Himpit (Rice Cake)

2 1/2 c rice
5 1/2 c water
1/4   tsp salt
3   screw pine pandan leaves, knotted

Wash rice, then add water. Stir in salt and add screw pine leaves. Cook until rice is done. Mash rice with a wooden spoon while still hot and moist. Transfer to a 25- × 15-cm rectangular dish. Cover dish and place a heavy object on top to compress rice. Leave for 6 hours or overnight in the refrigerator. Cut into 2 1/2-cm cubes and serve with Rendang Tok.

Ipin Mew

Myanmar

Rice is the staple food in Myanmar. The Myanma people eat rice at breakfast, lunch, and dinner. Breakfast usually consists of glutinous rice mixed with coconut, sesame seeds, and jaggery or sugar. For lunch and dinner, boiled rice is eaten with fish, beef, mutton, chicken, or pork curry. Fried rice is also very popular. Rice is fried in groundnut oil with ground chilies, onions, tomatoes, and garlic and is eaten with vegetables. A rice and vegetable soup, which is hot and sweet, is a delicacy. The favorite rice dish in Myanmar is Mohinga, or rice noodles served with a rich gravy of fish, eggs, shredded tender banana stalks, and onions. Chopped green coriander leaves and leeks are sprinkled as garnish. Rice cooked in coconut milk is another delicacy.

The people prepare special dishes with rice and rice flour during festive occasions. During the harvest festival, a dish is made from rice harvested at milk stage. The rice is pounded and dried. Hot water is added to this flour until a soft dough is formed. Sugar is added to this dough before it is served. During wedding ceremonies, rice is colored yellow and sprinkled on the newlyweds as well as on their friends and relatives to wish the couple and everybody success in the future.

Fried Rice Burmese Style

4   c cooked rice
3   pc garlic, crushed
2   pc onions, sliced thinly
1   c cooked beef liver strips
1/2 c cooked, boneless chicken slices
1   c sliced cabbage
2   eggs, cooked omelet style
    Soy sauce
    Salt and pepper

Season cooked rice with soy sauce and refrigerate for 1 hour. Sauté garlic and onion in corn oil. Add beef liver, then chicken. Sprinkle with soy sauce, salt, and pepper. Add cabbage, then rice. Stir and cook over high heat. Garnish with omelet strips. Serve with sliced cucumber, chopped onions, chopped tomatoes, and coriander. Sprinkle with fish sauce and lemon juice before serving.

Lily Khin Win

Coconut Rice

3   c Basmati rice
5   c coconut milk
    Green peas
5-6 pc peeled pearl onions
1   onion, sliced and sautéed

Place all ingredients in a rice cooker. Mix thoroughly before switching cooker on. When rice is done, sprinkle it with crisp sautéed onions.

Winwin Aung

Sticky Rice with Coconut Milk and Ripe Mangoes

2   c glutinous rice
3   c freshly squeezed coconut milk (first extraction)
1   c sugar
2-3 pc jackfruit
6   ripe mangoes
    Toasted sesame seeds (optional)

Soak glutinous rice in coconut milk for 10-15 minutes. Add jackfruit and sugar. Cook the mixture in a rice cooker. Serve with ripe mangoes and toasted sesame seeds.

Winwin Aung

Nepal

Rice is more than a food crop in Nepal. It is the oldest of all food grains, the holiest of all crops, and the first in usefulness in the life of the Nepalese. It is considered holy because it grows in water and has grains covered with husk. It is a most useful crop because the entire biomass has numerous uses known since the dawn of history.

The rice grain is a most prestigious food item. It is consumed during both happy and sad occasions. There are many rice-based food dishes in Nepal; they are made from long-grain and short-grain varieties as well as from rice flour. Some of the most common are listed here.

Bhat	For normal staple diet (side dish).
Pilaf	Rice with spices (side dish).
Khichuri	Rice cooked with mungo.
Khatle	Roasted rice with oil (snack).
Chivara	Rice flakes with spices (snack).
Sel Rotti	Bread prepared for religious and cultural festivals.
Malpa	Rice pancake as sweet snack or dessert, and served on festive occasions.
Kheer	Rice pudding (dessert).
Dhakni	Sweet rice delicacy used for special get-togethers (dessert).
Turma	Sticky rice mixed with butter and oil. It is also used for religious festivals, death rituals. This dish is popular among the Tamang and Gurang Buddhist ethnic groups.
Kesar	Sweet rice pudding with saffron, popular among Brahmans and chattis, used mainly during weddings and Teenj (women's festivals).

Certain beverages are also made from rice.

The bhati jar (clay pot) is fermented juice that is a popular drink among hardworking mountain folks.

Nigar is also a fermented rice wine, but it is slightly sweet.

Rice is important not only as a grain in Nepal. It also has a prominent place in the sociocultural, religious, and economic life of the people. The rice grain symbolizes such sentiments as devotion, affection, generosity, and respect.

- Rice grains are offered to the holy priest, guru, or preacher as a token of respect.
- The edible rice grains are offered as bhiksha (holy gift) to the visiting Sadhu, saints, yogis, and monks (holy men).
- Rice is given to beggars of the social welfare group as an expression of humanitarian generosity.
- Rice grains mixed with yoghurt is used by elders as tika (holy mark) on the forehead of youngsters to symbolize blessedness during religious festivals.
- Rice grains are used as offering to the holy fire (Hoomes) during worship and at weddings.

- A food basket full of rice grains is given to Brahmins during cultural festivals, or on the birth of a baby, or even on death anniversaries.
- Rice grain is also used for the Durga Pcoja festival. Rice grains are germinated on a large leaf, and its young yellow sprouts are offered to the younger ones by elders as a blessing from the goddess Durga. Rice straw is used as animal fodder, cooking fuel, fence material, for making ropes and baskets, and for growing mushrooms.

Sel Rotti (Rice Bread)

1   kg rice
2   kg unsalted butter
4   c fresh milk
6   cardamoms
2   sticks cinnamon
4   peppercorns
200 grams sugar
      Cooking oil

Grind rice coarsely; add butter and mix thoroughly. Add fresh milk gradually, stirring constantly; add rest of the spices and sugar. Keep on stirring until the mixture is like a dough. Take 2 tbsp dough; flatten and shape like a pancake. Drop in hot oil and cook for a minute. Drain on paper towel. Serve hot.

Sushila Pradhan

Kanom Tueoy Foo (Rice Cupcake)

1 1/2 c rice flour
1/2 c sugar
3/4 c jasmine water
1 1/2 tsp yeast

Mix rice flour, sugar, and jasmine water (jasmine water should be added a little at a time during mixing). Add yeast to the mixture. Heat small cups in a steamer (or use muffin pans). Spoon mixture into the cups; cover and steam for 25-30 minutes. Remove cupcake from each cup and cool for 2-3 minutes before arranging for serving.

Amara Parejarearn

Kanom Chan (Layer Cake)

3-4 c pandan leaves, cut into small pieces
1 c rice flour
1 c bean flour
300 grams sugar
1/4 kg coconut milk
1 tsp jasmine juice
4 c water
1-3 drops of red food coloring

Pound pandan leaves and extract green juice. Mix all ingredients except food coloring. Divide mixture into 3 portions: add red food coloring to the first and green pandan extract to the second. Leave the third portion as is. Pour mixture into containers (either one large or several small ones), alternating the colors (i.e., one color per layer). Put filled containers in a steamer and steam for 30 minutes or until done.

Amara Parejarearn

Anarasa (Fried Rice Patties)

3 c rice flour
1 c sugar
1/4 c water
1/4 c yoghurt
1 tbsp sesame seed
1/2 c oil

Soak rice flour overnight, then steam in muslin cloth. Add sugar and some water to dissolve sugar. Cover with wet cloth for 1-2 hours. Form pingpong-size balls of the mixture; press and flatten the balls. More water or yoghurt can be added while forming the balls. Spread a few sesame seeds on one side of each ball. Flatten into patties and drop in hot oil for frying. The side with sesame seeds should remain on top.

Parbati Pakharel

Dhakni

2 c rice
4 c water (for soaking rice)
2 tbsp butter
1/2 c sugar
3 c milk
1/4 c roasted cashews (optional)
1 tbsp raisins (optional)

Soak rice in water overnight. Drain and set aside. Heat butter in a pan; add rice and sauté for a minute. As soon as it dries, add sugar and stir for a while. Add milk; bring to a boil. Cover and cook until it dries. Remove from heat and transfer to a platter. Garnish with cashews and raisins.

Sushila Pradhan

Pakistan

Although wheat is the number one staple food of Pakistan, occasionally, rice is also eaten by Pakistanis. Pakistanis generally prefer aromatic rice, commonly known as Basmati rice. This rice variety is also the country's major export commodity. In Punjab, Northwest Frontier Province, and Baluchistan, rice is eaten mostly as pullaw, or cooked with various kinds of meat: chicken, beef, and mutton. In Sindh Province, however, people eat plain boiled rice.

On festive occasions, rice is cooked as a main dish (Biryani), side dish (vegetable pullaw), and as dessert (kheer or rice pudding and zardah or yellow sweet rice with saffron).

Rice with Chicken

2   c rice (preferably Basmati)
3/4   kg chicken
10   cloves garlic, minced
5   c water
1/4   c corn oil
1/2   tsp cumin seeds
1/4   c chopped onions
1   tsp coriander powder
1   tsp curry powder
2   tsp salt
2   cinnamon sticks
2   pods of black cardamoms
5   cloves

Clean, wash, and soak rice for 20 minutes. Clean chicken and cut into medium-size pieces. Mix garlic with 2 cups water and set aside. Heat oil; sauté cumin seeds and onions until they are dark brown. Add 1/4 cup garlic water and stir. When the water dries, add chicken and all other spices, stirring constantly. Add some garlic water and fry chicken with spices. Keep on adding garlic water until chicken is almost done.

Drain rice and add to chicken; stir in 3 cups water. Cover pan and cook on low heat until rice is done. Serve hot with yoghurt or hot pickles or salad. Serves 6.

Nusrat Khan

Beef Pullaw

1/2 kg long-grain rice (preferably Basmati)
1/2 kg meat (beef or goat's meat)
3-4 c water
1   tsp salt
2   cloves garlic, crushed
1/2 tbsp ginger, grated
3   large onions, sliced
1   tsp coriander powder
1/2 c cooking oil
1/4 tbsp chili powder
1   tsp curry powder

Clean, wash, and soak rice in water for 30 minutes. Wash meat, add water, salt, garlic, ginger, one sliced onion, and coriander powder. Bring to a boil and cook on medium heat till meat is soft. Heat oil in a pan; sauté 2 sliced onions on medium heat till they turn brown. Add chili powder and curry powder. Sprinkle a few drops of water to avoid burning. Add boiled meat and fry until it browns; add meat broth. As soon as the mixture starts boiling, add presoaked rice and cook on low heat until rice is done. If broth is not enough, add some hot water. Serve hot.

NOTE: This can be served with chutney, pickles, or yoghurt.

Suriya Akbar

Zardah

4   c Basmati rice
8   c water
1   c oil, butter, or ghee
6   cardamoms
6   cloves
2   c sugar
1/4 c water or milk
     Red food color
1/2 c dry nuts, chopped

Clean, wash, and soak rice for 10 minutes. Boil 8 cups water, drain rice, and add to boiling water. Remove from fire when half-done. Drain rice and set aside. Heat oil in a heavy pan. Add cardamoms, cloves, sugar, water or milk, and food color. Stir and add nuts. Stir again. When sugar becomes syrupy, add boiled rice. Cover and cook on low heat until done.

NOTE: If using sticky rice, rinse boiled rice with cold water to remove stickiness.

Suriya Akbar

Philippines

Rice is the natural staple and substance of the Philippine diet. It is served in fluffy, steamy mounds on the humblest tin plate or the finest porcelain dish. Rice is served at each meal. At breakfast, the previous night's leftover rice is fried, flavored with garlic. Filipinos serve many dishes using rice: main dish, side dish, snacks, desserts, cakes, etc. Numerous cakes and desserts are made with sticky rice.

Steamed rice is usually eaten with chicken, beef, pork, and shrimps. Among the most popular rice dishes are bringe, tamales, paella, bibingka, and bilo-bilo. Rice cakes are considered a symbol of prosperity and good fortune. One kind of rice pancake has slices of native cheese and salted eggs as topping. Puto is another native rice cake eaten with grated coconut.

Biko (or sinukmani) is made of glutinous rice boiled in coconut milk and topped with a mixture of brown sugar and thick coconut milk.

The Philippines observes many rituals, most of them connected with rice. During the *Pahiyas* Festival that Filipinos in Lukban, Laguna, celebrate in May, houses and shops are decorated with rice wafers. *Chewis* is a rice ritual in which certain practices are done to ensure good harvest. The *Pagdidiwata* is a thanksgiving festival held in the house of a *babaylan* (spiritual medium). It consists mainly of the sharing of rice wine with the spirits.

In the Mountain Province where rice is grown on terraces, the local Ifugao tribes observe many rituals associated with rice. For the harvest ceremony, they cook colored rice. They make the rice wine *Tapuy*, which is used for purifying the sacrificial animal. Rice grains are arranged near the animal's body and prayers are said. Rice thus plays a significant role in Filipino life and culture.

✱ ✱ ✱

Arroz Valenciana

1	big chorizo de bilbao, sliced
1	tbsp chorizo de bilbao fat
1	clove garlic
1	onion
1	medium red pepper
1/2	c chicken liver
1/2	c chicken gizzard, sliced
1	c chicken breast, diced
1	c lean pork, diced
1/2	c tomato sauce
1/2	c soy sauce
1	c sweet peas
1	c raisins
4-5	saba banana, fried
2	c glutinous rice
2	tsp monosodium glutamate
	Salt and pepper to taste

Sauté garlic, chorizo, onion, and red pepper. Add meats and sauté until dry. Remove chicken liver, slice and set aside. Add tomato sauce and soy sauce, and simmer until meats are tender. Meanwhile cook glutinous rice in 2 cups water. Line bottom of pan to avoid burning.

When meats are done, add sweet peas, raisins, MSG, pepper, and salt. Simmer for 3 minutes. Add cooked rice. Stir to mix well. Garnish with fried saba bananas and chicken liver.

Lina Lopez

Paella

20-25 pc mussels
1   c squid, sliced (or 5 pc medium squid)
2   pc crabs
1/2   c medium-size shrimps
1/2   kg chicken breast, leg, gizzard, and liver
3   tbsp chorizo fat
2   tbsp oil
1/4   kg pork cut into 1-inch cubes
1/2   c ham cut into 1-inch squares
1   pc chorizo de bilbao, sliced
1   clove garlic, crushed
1   onion, chopped fine
1   c tomato sauce
3 1/2 c chicken broth
2   c rice, washed
1   pc red pepper, in strips
10   pc string beans
1   tsp soy sauce or patis
2   tsp salt
2   tsp monosodium glutamate
1/4   c sweet peas
2   hard-boiled eggs
1/2   c parsley

Steam mussels. Set aside 1 cup broth. Remove ink of squid. Slice and boil. Set aside. Boil crabs and shrimps together; set aside. Boil bony parts of chicken; set broth aside. Heat fat and oil in skillet. Fry chicken, pork, ham, and chorizo. Cook until half-done. Remove from skillet. Sauté garlic, onion, and tomato sauce. Add chicken broth and rice. Mix well. When rice is half-done, add red pepper, string beans, mussels, squid, and other meats. Season with soy sauce, salt, and MSG. Cover tightly and cook without stirring until broth is absorbed. During last 5 minutes of cooking, put shrimps, crabs, and peas on top. Garnish with sliced eggs, strips of pepper, and parsley.

Lina Lopez

Bringe (Rice with Coconut Milk)

2   tbsp chorizo de bilbao fat
2   cloves garlic, minced
1   onion, sliced
1   kg chicken, cut into serving pieces
1   pc chorizo de bilbao, sliced
      Salt to taste
1   tsp pepper
2   tbsp patis
3   tbsp turmeric juice
3 1/2 c coconut milk from 1 coconut
1/2   c glutinous rice, washed
1 1/4 c rice, washed
1   bay leaf
      Banana leaves
2   pc red pepper, cut into strips
1   hard-cooked egg, in wedges

Sauté garlic and onions in fat. Add chicken pieces and chorizo. Season with patis. Simmer 5 minutes. Add turmeric juice and coconut milk and simmer 5 minutes more. Blend in washed rices. Stir to prevent burning at bottom. Add bay leaf. Cook 2 minutes more. Transfer 1/2 of mixture to skillet. Cover both pans with banana leaves and continue cooking in oven at 350 °F. Serve on a platter, garnished with egg wedges and pimiento strips.

Bing Salacup

Tamales

Dough

2 coconut, grated
2 c rice flour
3 tbsp lard or cooking oil

1 tsp salt
1 tsp monosodium glutamate

Filling

3 tbsp lard or cooking oil
3 cloves garlic, crushed
1 onion, minced
1 c cooked pork, cubed
1 c cooked chicken, cut into small pieces
1 c ham, cubed

1 c chopped peanuts
1 tsp salt
1 tsp monosodium glutamate
2 tsp black pepper
3 hard-cooked eggs, sliced into strips

Wrapping

Banana leaves wilted over fire
String for tying

Extract pure coconut milk. Set aside. Add water to pulp and make a second extraction. Put rice flour in a big pan and pour 3 cups diluted coconut milk, salt, and MSG and cook over slow fire, stirring constantly to prevent lumping. When mixture starts to thicken, add pure coconut milk, and continue stirring until dough is done. Remove from fire. Add 3 tbsp lard or cooking oil, then set dough aside.

In a skillet, heat 3 tbsp lard or cooking oil. Brown garlic and onions. Add pork, chicken, ham, peanuts, salt, MSG, and pepper. Cook for a few minutes and then remove from fire.

Place 1 tbsp cooked dough on one piece of banana leaf. Flatten the dough and spread over it 1 tbsp of filling. Top with egg strip and then fold dough over filling. Fold banana leaf over dough and tie securely, but not tightly, with string. Place tamales in steamer and steam for 30 minutes.

Bing Salacup

Easy Cheezy Pie

2 c hot cooked rice
1/2 c grated cheddar cheese
1/4 tsp salt
1/4 tsp ground black pepper
1/2 c sour cream
1/4 c bacon bits

Combine rice, cheese, and seasonings in saucepan. Cook until cheese melts, stirring frequently. Top each serving with 2 tbsp sour cream and 1 tbsp bacon bits.

Alit Mackill

Pancit Bihon (Rice Noodles)

1   kg rice noodles
1/2   c cooking oil
1   tsp garlic, crushed
2   small onions, cut into strips
1/2   kg pork, cut into cubes
1   whole chicken breast,
      cut into small pieces
1/2   kg shrimps, shelled and cut into small
      pieces
1/2   c dark soy sauce
      Shrimp juice from the heads and shells of
      shrimps
2   small carrots, cut into thin strips
2   c chicharo (Chinese peas)
2   c cabbage, cut into strips

1/2   c Chinese celery
1/2   c green onions, cut into small pieces

Soak rice noodles in water; set aside. Heat oil, then brown garlic and onions. Add pork, chicken, and shrimps. Add soy sauce, then shrimp juice. Simmer for a while. Add carrots, Chinese sweet peas, and cabbage. Drain rice noodles and add. Add green onions and Chinese celery last. Sprinkle with black ground pepper.

Lucy Bonman

Baked Rice Custard

3   eggs, well beaten
1/2   c sugar
1/4   tsp salt
2   c milk, scalded
1   c cooked rice
1/4   c raisins
1   tsp vanilla
1/4   tsp cinnamon
1   tbsp butter

Combine eggs, sugar, and salt. Stir in hot milk slowly. Add cooked rice, raisins, and vanilla. Pour into buttered 6-cup baking dish. Set in pan of hot water. Sprinkle with cinnamon and dot with butter. Bake at 325 °F for 60-70 minutes. Makes 6 servings.

Alit Mackill

Tropical Rice Pudding

1   c uncooked rice
2   c water
2   c milk
1   tsp salt
1   tbsp butter or margarine
2   eggs, separated
1   c half-and-half
     (cream and milk)
1/2 c sugar
2   tsp vanilla extract
1   can (16 oz) crushed pineapple, drained
1/2 c flaked coconut, toasted

Combine rice, water, milk, salt, and butter in a 3-quart saucepan. Bring to boil; cover and simmer about 30 minutes, stirring occasionally. Beat egg yolks; add half-and-half. Stir into rice mixture. Add 1/4 cup sugar and vanilla. Cook for about 3 minutes. Cool. Beat egg whites with remaining sugar until stiff but not dry. Fold into pudding. Spoon onto serving dish. Spread pineapple on top. Sprinkle with coconut. Serve chilled. Makes 6-8 servings.

Alit Mackill

Glutinous Rice Pudding

1 1/2 c glutinous rice
1 1/2 c thick coconut milk (first extraction)
3   c thin coconut milk (second extraction)
1/4   kg brown sugar cake (panocha)
1   tsp anise seeds

Wash rice, then cook in thin coconut milk. Set aside. Cook sugar-coconut sauce by melting sugar cake in thick coconut milk; add anise seed. Add cornstarch to thicken.

Spread cooked rice in pan lined with aluminum foil or banana leaves. Spread sugar-coconut sauce on top. Place in oven and bake for 15 minutes. Then broil 5 minutes to brown topping.

Vilma Garrity

Rice Cheese Cake

3   eggs
1 1/2 c sugar
1 1/2 c cottage cheese
1/2   c milk
2   tsp grated lemon peel (or orange peel)
5   c cooked rice

Beat together eggs and sugar about a minute. Mash cheese slightly and mix with milk and lemon peel; add to egg mixture. Beat or process in blender till smooth. Stir in rice. Pour into a buttered 9-inch square baking dish. Bake at 350 °F for 1 hour. Serve warm.

NOTE: Leftover cake may be covered with foil and reheated at 250 °F about 30 minutes to restore its original fresh moist texture and delicious flavor.

Lucy Bonman

Rice Flour Muffins

2   c sifted rice flour
2   tsp baking powder
1/2   tsp salt
1/2   tsp baking soda
2   tbsp sugar
2   eggs, beaten
1   c buttermilk
1/4   c water
1/4   c butter or margarine, melted

Mix and sift dry ingredients. Combine eggs, milk, water, and butter and stir into dry ingredients. Fill greased muffin tins three-fourths full and bake at 425 °F for 20 minutes. Makes 12 muffins.

Alit Mackill

Rice Flour Brownies

2   squares unsweetened chocolate (2 oz)
1/3 c shortening
2/3 c sifted rice flour
1/2 tsp baking powder
1/2 tsp salt
2   eggs
1   c sugar
1   tsp vanilla extract

Melt chocolate and shortening together over hot water; cool. Sift flour with baking powder and salt twice. Beat eggs until light. Add sugar, vanilla, then chocolate mixture, and blend. Add flour and mix well. Pour batter into a greased 8- × 8- × 2-inch pan. Bake at 350 °F for 30-35 minutes (325 °F if using glass baking dish). Do not overcook. Cool slightly. Cut into squares. Makes 16 brownies.

Alit Mackill

Palitaw

3   c sticky rice flour (malagkit)
1 1/2 c water
1   small grated coconut
1   c sugar
1/4   c sesame seeds, toasted and powdered

Combine rice flour and water. Blend thoroughly. With floured hands, shape dough into egg-size ovals. Flatten with thumb. Drop palitaw oval in 2 cups boiling water. Scoop out with skimmer as soon as they float. Roll in grated coconut. Serve at once with sugar mixed with toasted sesame seeds. Good for six persons.

Alit Mackill

Ginataan Palarosdos or Bilo-bilo

2 c glutinous rice flour and water
2 big coconuts, grated
1 c cubed ubi or gabi
1 c cubed sweet potato
1 c sliced saba banana
1-1 1/2 c refined sugar
1 c sliced jackfruit
1/4 c rice flour dissolved in 1/2 c water

Mix flour and water, form into small balls. then set aside. Extract pure coconut milk by using coconut water. Set aside. Make second extraction by adding 2 cups water to pulp. To second extraction, add sugar, ubi, sweet potato, and banana. Let boil until cooked. Drain fruits. Let coconut milk boil again. When boiling add rice balls and jackfruit. Balls will come up to the surface when cooked. Add rice flour dissolved in water to thicken. Add pure coconut milk and let boil for 1 minute.

Bing Salacup

Bibingka

250 grams glutinous rice
1 egg
25 grams goat's milk cheese
1/2 liter thin coconut milk
1/4 tsp salt
100 grams sugar
100 ml thick coconut milk
1/4 tsp anise seed powder

Soak rice in cold water for 6 hours. Grind rice into a fine powder. Beat egg. Cut cheese into thin slices. Pour thin coconut milk into a saucepan and bring to a boil. Then add rice, egg, salt, and continue to boil. Lower the heat, add sugar and stir to blend thoroughly. Line a cake tin with banana leaves and place the rice mixture on top. Add sliced cheese and thick coconut milk; sprinkle anise seed powder on top. Cover. On the lid, spread live charcoal and cook bibingka for 15-20 minutes.

Cora De Jesus

Sri Lanka

Sri Lanka has more than 15 types of rice. Each type has grains of a distinct size (short to long), shape (round, pearl), taste, and color (white and burgundy). Many dishes are prepared from rice and rice flour. The most common way of cooking rice is by boiling. Cooked rice may be garnished with cashew, raisins, and hard-boiled eggs.

Rice dishes are served for breakfast and as soups, main meals, side dishes, snacks, cakes, and desserts. During special occasions, rice is cooked in coconut milk and delicately flavored with spices. Turmeric is often added to color the grains a bright yellow. A very popular and spicy dish known as Lampries curry is cooked with meat, and the rice is cooked in meat stock. Other rice dishes are *Appa* (homemade noodles) made of rice flour, and *iddiappam* (string noodles) made of rice vermicelli. A salted rice dish, *Karibath* with coconut milk, is prepared on the first day of every month and eaten with different curries. This dish is also prepared on festive occasions.

Mutton Rice Soup

4	oz rice
1	lb mutton
4	c water
3	large onions
15	peppercorns
4	cloves
	Salt to taste

Soak rice overnight; wash, then drain. Clean, wash, and cut mutton into small pieces. Boil water, add mutton. When the water boils again, add rice, onions, peppercorns, and cloves. Again bring to a boil, then simmer slowly for 2 hours till meat and rice are very well cooked. Add salt and serve hot.

Olga Ponnamperuma

Ghee Rice (Buttered Rice)

2   c Basmati rice or other long-grain rice
1   c ghee or butter
1   large onion, finely sliced
4   cloves
6   cardamom pods, crushed
1   3-inch piece cinnamon stick
3 1/2 c hot beef, chicken, or mutton stock;
     or water and stock cubes
2 1/2 tsp salt

Wash rice well and drain at least 30 minutes. Heat ghee in a saucepan and sauté onion until golden; add spices and rice. Sauté, stirring with perforated metal spoon for 5 minutes over moderate heat. Add hot stock and salt and bring to a boil. Reduce heat to very low, cover pan tightly, and cook 15-20 minutes without lifting lid. At end of cooking time, uncover and allow steam to escape; let it stand for 5 minutes. Gently fluff up rice with fork, removing whole spices. When transferring rice to a serving dish, use perforated metal spoon to avoid crushing rice grains. Serve hot, accompanied by curries of meat and vegetables, pickles, and sambols.

Olga Ponnamperuma

Kokis

2   c rice flour   2   eggs
1   tbsp sugar (optional)   Salt to taste
2   c coconut milk   Oil for frying

Put flour, sugar, and salt in a bowl; add about half of the coconut milk to make a smooth paste. Beat eggs and gradually add to the batter with the rest of the milk. Beat together until smooth. The batter should be thicker than pancake batter. Have ready a deep pan of boiling oil. Dip 3/4 of a kokis mold in batter, taking care not to let the batter run over the mold. Plunge the mold into the hot oil and fry for a few minutes. Then slip the kokis out of the mold by shaking it a bit. Fry the kokis a minute longer to cook the inside. Drain on paper. They will keep crisp in an airtight tin.

NOTE: Kokis is a special mold in the form of a flower.

Olga Ponnamperuma

Vevara

1   egg yolk
6-10 oz coconut milk
1/2   lb roasted rice flour
1   tsp salt
1/4 c sugar
4   oz sugar syrup
      Water

Beat egg yolk very well; mix with coconut milk and beat again. Add rice flour to it. Knead mixture into a smooth dough. Form different shapes like cookies and deep-fry.

Boil sugar and water until sugar syrup is thick. Dip fried vevara in sugar syrup; drain and allow to dry.

NOTE: Vevaras can be stored in an airtight can for one day and can be deep-fried a second time before dropping into the sugar syrup.

Olga Ponnamperuma

Rice Cake with Rice Frosting

2   c brown sugar
1   c water
1/2   tsp salt
3   c grated coconut
4   c rice flour (not sticky)
1   tsp vanilla
      Anise seed powder

Frosting
1 1/2 c rice flour
1   c coconut milk
1/2   tsp salt

Boil sugar, water, and salt until sugar dissolves (about 5 minutes). Add coconut, mix well. After 2-3 minutes, add rice flour and flavoring. Cook until the mixture hardens. Spread in a very thin layer on a buttered dish or wax paper. Let cool for half an hour. Cut into small pieces (different shapes, if desired). Mix rice flour, coconut milk, and salt to form a thick paste-like frosting. Coat each piece with this paste and deep-fry.

Tilaka Senanayake

Thailand

Rice is the staple food of Thailand. The Thai people eat rice three times a day. Rice preference varies from region to region. Glutinous rice is preferred in the northern and northeastern parts of the country, while long-grain, nonglutinous, fluffy, and white rices are preferred in the other parts. High-quality rice (long, slender grains with high percentage of head rice) is normally sold in the market.

Rice is eaten in many forms: boiled or fried with vegetables, seafood, or meat. Noodles made from rice flour are a delicacy in Thailand and are the preferred staple for lunch.

Rice is used in main dishes as well as side dishes and snacks, cakes, and desserts. In Thailand, the most popular dishes made with rice are garlic rice, saffron rice, colored rice (cooked in coconut milk), fried rice (cooked with a variety of meats and sprinkled with tomato ketchup or fish paste).

Many sweets are made of rice: rice balls, rice cakes, rice pudding with coconut milk, etc. Thais also make the rice wine Lao Rong.

Chicken Rice Soup

1/2 c rice
2   c water
1/4 c chicken meat, cubed or
1/4 c ground pork
1   tbsp fish sauce
1   egg
1   tsp chopped ginger
1   tsp chopped green onions
1/2 tsp chopped coriander leaves

Clean and wash rice, and boil in 2 cups water. Cook for half an hour or until done. Remove from pan and mash. Set aside.

Boil chicken bones in 1 cup water for 5 minutes. Discard bones. Add rice to chicken broth. Cook for 2 minutes, then add chicken or pork. Season with fish sauce. Break egg in a serving bowl. Pour rice soup on top of egg. Sprinkle with ginger, green onions, and chopped coriander leaves. Serve hot.

Cheli Banta
(Philippines)

Pineapple Fried Rice

1/2 c oil
1/4 c bread
1 1/2 tbsp dried shrimps
1/4 c pork, diced
1 tbsp onions, diced
1/2 tsp Maggi sauce
2 c cooked rice
1/4 c diced pineapple
1 red pepper
1 tsp chopped coriander leaves

Heat oil, sauté bread and dried shrimps until golden brown. Remove from pan and drain on paper towels. In the remaining oil, sauté pork and onions. Stir-fry a minute, add Maggi sauce, stir again. Add cooked rice and pineapple, stirring all the time. Garnish with dried shrimps and fried bread and top with chopped coriander leaves. Serve hot.

Savitri Sood
(India)

Rice Balls

1 c glutinous rice
1/2 c coconut milk
1/2 c sugar
1/2 tsp salt
Food color

Clean, wash rice, and soak in hot water for 10 minutes. Steam rice for 10 minutes or until done. In a pan boil coconut milk, sugar, and salt. Cook over low heat for a while. Add rice, stirring constantly. Cook until dry. Divide rice into 3 portions. Add different food color to each portion. Make small balls and serve.

NOTE: These rice balls also can be rolled in desiccated coconut.

Visaka Panditya

Vietnam

Rice is a staple food of the Vietnamese people. The Vietnamese usually have three meals a day. The family dinner has three dishes, each of which goes with rice. To guests they serve soup or salad first, rice last. Rice is taken with soup, fried shrimps, fish, vegetables, and bean sprouts.

Rural workers take rice with clear broth in the morning and evening meals. The urban workers' home meal consists of rice with salted fish cooked in fish sauce and a small amount of meat.

The Vietnamese serve ordinary rice for meals. Sticky rice is a special kind of glutinous rice. It can be served alone for breakfast or it can go with some grilled or baked meat dishes. Sticky rice may be cooked with coconut milk or with assorted sautéed meats. The Vietnamese serve a variety of rice dishes and use a lot of rice flour to make rice cake, rice noodles, and other delicacies.

Alcohol is also made from rice. The Vietnamese sticky rice wine is very similar to the Japanese *saké*. The "moonshine" rice wine is a very strong and tasty rice wine that is popular in the countryside. The Vietnamese rice wine Ba-Xi De, which is often served with meals during feasts, is made of fermented glutinous rice.

Com Chien (Fried Rice)

1/4 c oil
1   green onion, chopped
1   red onion
1   c cooked rice
1/4 c ham, chopped
1   carrot, sliced
1   egg, beaten
1/2 c green peas, cooked
1   tbsp soy sauce
    Salt and pepper to taste
1   tsp chopped parsley

Heat oil until it starts sizzling; add both kinds of onions and sauté for a minute. Add cooked rice, ham, and carrot; cook over medium heat, stirring constantly, until rice turns light brown. Add egg, peas, soy sauce, salt, and pepper. Stir mixture for about 5 minutes. Serve hot, garnished with parsley.

Tham Aurin

Sticky Rice and Meat

1   c sticky cooked rice
1   tbsp chopped onion
1/4 c fried chicken (or any kind of meat)
1/4 tsp salt
1/4 tsp sugar
1   tbsp oil

Heat oil, sauté onion until brown. Add meat, salt, and sugar, and cook 5 minutes. Combine sautéed meat and cooked rice. Serve for breakfast or lunch.

Tham Aurin

Fried Sticky Rice

1   c sticky cooked rice
1/2 c oil

Shape cooked rice into balls; flatten each into a cake. Heat pan, add oil, fry cake until golden brown. Drain on paper towels. Serve hot with charcoal-broiled chicken.

Tham Aurin

Middle East

Most Middle Eastern cuisines have certain similarities. The chief starch staple is wheat, followed by rice. Rice, whole wheat, and cracked wheat are boiled or steamed, but rice is also cooked into a pilaf. Sautéed rice grain with vegetables, fruits, and nuts is popular. Rice is also used as a stuffing in many Middle East preparations.

In Iran, wheat bread is the main staple. Nevertheless, in certain areas along the Caspian Sea coast, Iranians eat rice at every meal. In wheat areas, rice is eaten as a side dish. Iranians prefer long-grain rice, which is cooked without washing. In the rural areas, people eat a bowl of rice with a glass of sweetened tea in the morning. In cities, the well-to-do eat rice with grilled meat called *chelo kebab* and a thick soup made with yoghurt and vegetables.

There are two basic types of rice dishes in Iran: *chelo* and *polo*. The basic method of cooking the two is identical, but the difference lies in their serving. Chelo is plain boiled rice topped with butter and various sauces and meats. Polo resembles a pilaf; it is salty boiled rice served with yoghurt and meat. Another version of polo is a sweet rice called *Shaker polo* or sugar pilaf, which is served on festive occasions. Another popular dish served on festive occasions is *Alo-balo-polo*, colored rice with saffron, chicken, and cherries.

Although rice is not grown in Iraq, it is relished with meats. The Iraqis love short- and coarse-grain rice, cooked in many ways. Plain boiled rice is usually served in a large platter topped with a special paper-thin bread made of wheat. This bread is moistened by sprinkling water on it. The whole family gathers around the meal and eat the rice and bread with their hands.

A special rice dish in Iraq is known as yaprakh: rice is cooked with tomatoes, seasoned with salt and spices, and then stuffed in bell pepper, onions, or tomatoes, and wrapped in grape leaves. Rice is also stuffing for chicken or turkey. Sweet rice is cooked with nuts as a dessert.

Egypt has the highest rice production among the Middle East countries. Egyptian farmers usually eat rice once or twice a day, but their main rice meal is eaten at noon. City people also have a liking for rice, but they eat rice only two or three times a week. What is interesting in Egyptian cooking is that they always sauté rice in butter before they cook it for any rice dish.

Some popular rice dishes of Egypt are Orze Shara or rice cooked with vermicelli, Mahshy or baked eggplant stuffed with rice, Orze Madses, or Orze Moumer. Orze Madses is cooked with meat and Orze Moumer is cooked in two ways: as baked sweet rice or as sweet rice cooked on slow fire.

Egyptian rice production consists solely of japonica rice. The Egyptians like short-grain and fluffy rice; they do not relish sticky rice.

Iran

Rice with Potato Crust and Saffron

1	c rice	1/2	tsp warm water
4	c water	2	small potatoes
1/4	tsp saffron	1/4	c melted butter

Clean, wash, and soak rice for 30 minutes. Cook in a pan with 4 cups water. Boil on high heat for 5 minutes. Reduce heat, stir rice, and leave on low heat again for 5 minutes, then drain in a sieve.

Mix saffron and warm water; set aside. Peel potatoes and cut into thick round slices.

Pour saffron in a pan, add 2 tbsp melted butter and potatoes, and mix very well. Spread sliced potatoes in the bottom of the pan and spoon all rice over. Sprinkle with remaining butter. Cover pan with aluminum foil and leave on very low fire until done. Transfer rice to a platter so that sliced potatoes are on top of rice.

Tohri Sigari

Kesh-Mesh Polo

1/2	kg chicken	1	onion, sliced
1/4	c butter	1/4	c raisins
1/4	tsp salt	1/4	tsp turmeric powder
2	c raw rice	1/4	tsp cinnamon

Clean, wash, and roast chicken. Remove chicken meat from bones. Cook rice with salt and 4 tsp butter until done. Drain rice grain under cold water. Heat butter and sauté onion; add raisins, turmeric, and cinnamon.

Melt remaining butter in a large pot. Spread 1-inch layer of rice in the bottom; cover with a thin layer of raisins. Arrange chicken pieces over raisins. Cover chicken with a layer of rice and another layer of raisins. Cover with a lid. Simmer until done. The bottom layer of rice will be crunchy Serve hot.

K. Drukshan

Kashani Polo

1 c long-grain rice
1 tsp salt

2 oz butter
3 carrots, sliced

Saffron liquid
  Pinch of saffron
1 tbsp sugar
2 tbsp boiling water

1 onion, sliced
1 tbsp whole
    coriander
1 potato
  Saffron liquid

Soak rice overnight with salt; drain and cook in water until almost done. Drain rice again and rinse with cold water. Heat butter and sauté carrots until light brown.

Remove from saucepan. Add onion to the same butter and sauté for a while; add coriander. Mix carrots, onions, and coriander with rice. Butter a large heavy-bottom pot and cover bottom of pot with potato slices. Spread rice mixture over potatoes. Mix ingredients of saffron liquid and pour over rice. Turn down heat as low as possible and steam for half an hour until rice and potatoes are brown. Turn rice onto a platter and arrange browned potatoes around it.

K. Drukshan

Iraq

Chalabis Red Magloube

1   c rice
1   c water
1/4 c oil
1   eggplant, sliced
1   onion, sliced
1   piece lamb shank

1/2 c tomato sauce or
    paste
    Salt to taste
1   cinnamon stick
2   cardamoms, whole

Clean, wash, and soak rice in water. Drain after 30 minutes. Sprinkle salt on sliced eggplant. Heat half of oil; sauté sliced eggplant until light brown. Remove from pan and place on paper towel. Sauté sliced onion until tender. Set aside. In another pan, heat remaining oil, saute

lamb shank. Stir for a minute. Add tomato sauce, water, salt, cinnamon, and cardamoms. Simmer for 30 more minutes. Add rice and simmer for 30 more minutes.

Arrange a layer of eggplant in a wide teflon frying pan; top with a layer of onions. Place lamb shank on top of onions. Pour rice mixture on top of meat. Simmer for 30 minutes. Turn onto a platter, with rice layer down. Serve hot.

Nusrat Khan
(Pakistan)

Yaprakh (Iraqi Rice)

3	large tomatoes
1/2	kg small round eggplants
8	sweet peppers
1 1/2	kg large onions
1/4	c oil
4	c glutinous rice
1/2	c tomato paste
1	head celery leaves, chopped
2	tsp white cumin seeds
1/2	kg ground beef
1/2	c ghee or butter
	Salt to taste
1/4	tsp chili powder
50	pechay leaves

Wash all vegetables. Slice round the top of tomatoes and set aside; scoop out all pulp and put in a bowl. Do the same with eggplant and sweet pepper. Reserve tops as cover.

Sprinkle some water inside tomatoes and eggplants. Peel onions and cut lengthwise on one side (not at center). Press each onion between the palms of hands to separate layers. The smaller inner layers can be chopped.

Heat 1/2 of oil; sauté eggplant pulp and chopped onion until slightly tender, but not brown. Wash rice and add to onion and eggplant mixture. Add tomato paste, vegetable pulp, chopped onion, chopped celery, and cumin seeds. In another skillet, heat remaining oil; add beef and fry till cooked. Add beef mixture to rice mixture. Add ghee or butter, salt, and chili powder. Mix very well. Fill onions, eggplants, tomatoes, and sweet peppers with mixture and cover them with vegetable tops tightly; set aside.

Spread some pechay leaves in a large and wide pan. Arrange first layer of stuffed onions, individually wrapped in pechay leaves tightly. Arrange tomato layer on top of onions; repeat, using sweet pepper and eggplant. Cover vegetables with a very heavy plate and place another heavy weight on top of the plate. Pour 3 cups water into the pan and cook on medium heat for 30-40 minutes. Leave on very low heat for some time until done.

Nusrat Khan
(Pakistan)

Lebanon

Lamb Rice Soup

1/4 c butter
3   onions
4   oz rice
     Salt to taste
1   lb lamb, finely chopped
4   c water
1/4 c soft cheese
3   eggs, beaten
1/4 c whipped cream

Melt half of butter, add and sauté onions until they are transparent. Sauté rice with salt and cook until tender. Remove from heat and set aside. Heat remaining butter in a saucepan. Add lamb and cook until done. Add rice and water. Let boil; add cheese and eggs when soup is boiling. Serve with cream.

Katia Sayegh

Mujaddarah

1/4 c olive oil
4   onions, chopped
2   c lentils
1   c water
1   c rice
     Salt to taste

heat until well done. Before serving, heat remaining sauteed onions and pour over cooked lentil and rice. Serve with hot pickles.

Katia Sayegh

Heat oil. Sauté chopped onions until light brown. Set aside. Cook lentils in boiling water for 10 minutes; add rice, half of sautéed onions, and salt. Cook on low

Egypt

Orze Shara (Rice with Vermicelli)

1/4 c vermicelli
1   tbsp butter or
1   tbsp cooking oil
1   c rice
2   c water
     Salt to taste

Cut vermicelli into small pieces. Melt butter or heat oil; add vermicelli and sauté until brown. Add rice, stir for a minute; add salt and water and leave on slow fire until done.

Atiat Balal

Mahshy (Stuffed Eggplant with Rice)

1   kg eggplant
1/4 tsp salt
2   tbsp butter or oil
1   onion, chopped
1   kg tomatoes, chopped
     Parsley
1/2 c short-grain rice
     Salt and pepper to taste
1   c chicken broth or beef broth

Wash and core eggplant. Prick with fork, and sprinkle with salt; set aside. Heat butter or oil, sauté onion, add tomatoes and parsley, and sauté for a while. Add rice; stir and mix well. Remove from fire; set aside for 10 minutes. Fill eggplants with rice mixture and place in a deep baking tray or casserole. Pour meat broth over, cover with foil, and bake at 250 °F until rice is done.

NOTE: Any kind of meat can be added to the rice mixture.

Megda Reda

Orze Madses (Egyptian Salty Rice)

2   c rice
1/2 kg beef
3   c fresh milk
     Salt to taste

Clean and wash rice and soak for 2 hours.
Clean and wash meat and cut into cubes.

Combine rice, meat, and milk and pour
into a flat casserole. Add salt. Bake at
250 °F for 30-35 minutes.

Samie Serafy

Orze Moumer (Sweet Rice)

2 c rice   1/4 kg sugar
3 c milk   1/4 c raisins

Clean, wash, and soak rice for 2 hours.
Combine all ingredients. Pour into a
casserole and bake at 250 °F for 30-45
minutes.

Samie Serafy

Orze Be Laban (Sweet Rice)

2 c rice   1/3 kg sugar
3 c milk   1/4 c raisins
1 c water

Clean and wash rice very well and soak
for 2 hours. Combine rice and milk and
boil for 15 minutes. Add water and let boil
for 10 more minutes. As soon as rice is
cooked, add sugar and cook on low heat
for 15 more minutes. Put in a bowl, and
sprinkle raisins on top before serving.

Samie Serafy

Africa

Generally speaking, rice is a secondary staple food on the African continent. Cassava, yams, corn, and millets are the major staple food in most African countries. Only a few countries—Liberia, Sierra Leone, Guinea, Ivory Coast, parts of Nigeria, Ghana, and Madagascar—have rice as a major staple food. Egyptians consume much rice; however, their dishes are discussed in the section on the Middle East, because their food habits are similar to those of the people of that region.

There are only a few rice dishes in Africa. Most of the people eat plain boiled rice with soup, meat, fish, or seafood. In Sierra Leone, rice is cooked with meat and coconut. In Liberia, Jollof Rice (fried rice with tomatoes, vegetables, and meat) is very popular. These countries also have cakes, muffins, and bread from rice flour. Some tribes in Liberia and Sierra Leone prefer red rice to white rice because they consider red rice more nutritious.

Nigeria

Coconut Rice with Meat

1   lb chicken
1/4 tsp salt
     Dash of black pepper
1/2 c oil
2   c water
2   coconuts, grated
2   c rice
2   onions, chopped
1/2 c tomato paste
1/4 tsp hot pepper (optional)

Clean, wash, and cut chicken into small pieces; marinate in salt and pepper for 15 minutes. Heat oil; fry chicken until brown then simmer in water until tender. Remove meat from broth. Combine broth and coconut; boil for 5 minutes. Wash rice and add to liquid mixture. Continue cooking.

Heat 1 tbsp oil. Add chopped onion, sauté for a minute. Add tomato paste, simmer for 5 minutes, then add chicken. Stir and leave on low fire. When rice is almost done, add chicken mixture. Simmer for 10 minutes. Serve hot.

Delia Abifarin

Liberia

Jollof Rice

1 lb chicken
1 lb stewing beef
1/2 lb smoked ham or bacon
1/4 c flour
1 medium onion, chopped
1/2 c cooking oil
1 small can tomato paste
2 c rice
1 pkg frozen mixed vegetables
3 c water
Salt and pepper to taste

Cut up chicken, beef, ham, and bacon. Season with salt and pepper. Coat with flour and fry.

Heat oil in a pan, sauté onion; add ham, beef, bacon and tomato paste. Stir well, cover and simmer with 1 cup water for 1 hour. Add remaining water, salt, and pepper. Bring to a boil. Add chicken and rice and simmer until rice is done. Add vegetables 5 minutes before removing chicken-rice mixture from fire.

Rhoda Tubman

Rice Bread

1 c rice meal
1 tsp baking powder
1/8 tsp soda
1/4 c sugar
1/4 tsp nutmeg
1/4 tsp salt
3/4 c mashed plantain
3/4 c milk or water
1/4 c vegetable oil or margarine

Mix all dry ingredients; set aside. Combine mashed plantain and liquids; add to dry ingredients and mix well. Bake in greased 8- × 12-inch baking dish or pan at 350 °F for about 1 hour.

NOTE: Cream of wheat may be substituted for rice meal, and bananas may be substituted for plantain.

Rhoda Tubman

Rice Meal Muffins

2   c rice meal
2   c ground or mashed plantain
4   tsp baking powder
1/4 tsp soda
1/2 tsp lime juice
1/4 c sugar
1/2 tsp salt
1/4 c water
2   tbsp cooking oil

Sift rice meal; mix with all other
ingredients and blend thoroughly by hand.
Pour mixture into greased muffin tins.
Bake at 400 °F for 1 hour or until nicely
browned.

NOTE: Rice meal preparation:
Wash and soak 1 1/2 pints rice in
water for 30 minutes. Drain and
dry well. Grind rice into powder.
Sift before using.

Indu Virmani
(India)

North and South America

Although rice is not a staple food of North America, rice consumption is on the increase among many regional and ethnic groups because this cereal is an important ingredient in their cuisine. Rice is a star in the "healthy food" show. Seven of the 51 states in the USA grow rice. These states are Arkansas, California, Louisiana, Mississippi, Missouri, Texas, and Florida. New rice novelty and convenience products are appearing on supermarket shelves almost daily.

In the U.S., short-grain rice is grown extensively in California. In Louisiana, rice is served with a sauce or gravy, or simply buttered and sprinkled with toasted sesame seeds. Housewives also make orange rice that goes with simple fish or barbecue. Many dishes are prepared with rice: rice salad, main dish, side dish, breads, cakes, and desserts. Examples are seafood rice salad, green and chili rice, Texas hash, baked raisins pulao, and baked beans and rice. Chicken Jambalaya is a native pilaf and is served with a simple green salad and fresh bread or rolls.

In many southern homes, Hopping John is served on New Year's Day with a topping of homemade chutney, or accompanied by corn bread, pecan pie, and either red or white wine.

The staple foods of Latin America are maize, potatoes, and wheat, but rice is a supplementary food in Mexico, Peru, and Brazil.

Mexicans eat rice only two or three times a week; their main staple foods are maize and beans. However, they relish a highly seasoned soup made of rice noodles or macaroni and cut-up pieces of tortillas. They eat rice, not as a companion dish, but as a dish by itself. They have a variety of colored rice—red, green, yellow, or white. They eat cooked or fried rice with or without meat. Mexicans also have special preparations for festive occasions such as red rice, which is served with the special dish *mole*, made with chicken. In rural areas, tamales is served during wedding ceremonies. This dish is made with rice flour, meats, peanuts, and coconut milk and is steamed, wrapped in banana leaf. Several sweet preparations are made with rice and rice flour: rice pudding and rice cakes.

In Peru rice has been adopted as a staple food, but in rural areas people have not yet developed a taste for rice. Peruvian preference is for long-grain, nonsticky rice usually prepared with garlic, salt, and oil. Rice dishes strongly resemble Spanish dishes adapted to the Peruvian taste; examples are the famous *Paella* (seafood rice) and *Arroz con pato* (rice with duck).

Brazilian cuisine is a fascinating mixture of Portuguese, primitive Indian, and West African influences. Although Brazil's main crops are cassava (manioc), corn, and sweet potatoes, rice is also one of the staple foods.

Brazilians like soft, nonsticky, and aromatic rice. They cook rice in various ways. In one special method, dried rice grains are fried with onions and chopped tomatoes, and then cooked in salted water on low fire. Cooked rice is also baked with meat, various sauces, and cheese. A popular dish in Brazil is rice with manioc and beans. Throughout the most populated regions of Brazil, rice and black beans are cooked with farinha de mandioca or manioc meal. Many desserts are prepared with rice and coconut milk.

✳ ✳ ✳

Brazil

Arroz com Feijao (Rice with Beans)

Rice

2   c rice
    Pinch of salt
1   tbsp butter

Put butter and salt in a cooking pan; sauté rice, then add water. Let boil until rice is cooked.

Beans

1   c beans (black or red)
4   tsp oil
2   cloves garlic
1   onion, sliced
1   laurel leaf
    Pepper

Wash beans; leave in 2 cups water overnight. The following day, boil until beans are soft.

In a frying pan, heat oil. Sauté garlic and onion until brown or transparent. Add 1 tsp of cooked beans, and mash. Add salt and pepper, cook a little longer, then add to the bean pot. Cook with laurel leaf until soup becomes creamy. Serve hot with rice.

Neiares Singh

Arroz con Leche (Sweet Rice)

1   kg rice
1   c coconut milk
3   egg yolks
2   tsp butter
1/4   c sugar

Boil rice with coconut milk. When done, add egg yolks and butter. Cook for a while. Meantime, prepare caramel sugar and set aside. Remove boiled rice from fire and spread on a platter. Pour caramel sugar over it.

Neiares Singh

Mexico

Mexican Rice

3 tbsp oil
2 c rice
3 cloves garlic, minced
1 onion, chopped
5 tomatoes, sliced
1 tsp salt
1 bouillon cube
2 c water
1 c cubed boiled carrots
1 c cubed boiled potatoes
1 c c green peas, cooked

Wash rice well. Heat oil in a pan; add rice, stirring from time to time until grains are brown. Set aside. Sauté garlic, onion, and tomatoes. Add bouillon cube and 2 cups water; season with salt. Add mixture to rice, along with carrots, potatoes, and peas. Mix well. Cook on low heat for 15-20 minutes.

Licha Quintero

Ecuadorian Rice

1/2 kg chicken
1 c water
20 ml soy sauce
100 grams butter
2 red peppers, diced
2 green peppers, diced
3 onions, chopped
1/2 kg rice
10 olives
50 grams roasted pili nuts
6 prunes
1 tbsp raisins
Salt and pepper to taste

Boil chicken in water with salt. When done, remove from broth and cut into serving pieces. Cook rice in chicken broth; add soy sauce for color.

Heat butter; add onions, peppers, and chicken; sauté for a while. Stir in cooked rice. Add olives, roasted nuts, prunes, and raisins.

Licha Quintero

Orchata

2 c uncooked rice
2 pieces cinnamon bark
1 1/2 c sugar
2 cans evaporated milk
4 liters water

Soak rice in water for 3 hours. Put in a blender and add cinnamon. Blend till smooth. Transfer to a big bowl; add milk and sugar. Serve with ice.

Lily Cinco

Peru

Caramelized Rice

3	c water
10	grams anise seeds
6	cloves
	Cinnamon stick
1	c rice
1	lb chancaca (brown sugar loaf)
2	tbsp raisins
2 1/2	tsp chopped nuts
	Salt
1/2	tsp ground cinnamon

Boil water with anise seeds, cinnamon, and cloves. When boiling, add rice. Simmer until done. In another saucepan, boil the sugar loaf in enough water to cover. When the liquid thickens, add cooked rice, salt, nuts, and raisins; mix well. Put in a dish and sprinkle with ground cinnamon. Serve cold.

Cecilia Chujoy

USA

Curried Rice Salad

3	c cold cooked rice (NOT long-grain)
1	c chopped celery
1	tsp instant minced onion
1	tsp curry powder
1/2	tsp dry mustard
3/4	tsp salt
	Dash of pepper
3/4	c mayonnaise
	Juice of 1/2 lemon, strained
1	c finely chopped fresh pineapple (or drained, diced, canned)
	Chopped toasted cashew nuts
	Lettuce

Toss together lightly all ingredients except nuts and lettuce. Serve on crisp lettuce leaves. Sprinkle with cashew nuts.

Sunny Chandler

Kalo-Lau-Aiia (Hawaiian Rice Spinach Salad)

3	c cooked rice (mixed rice with wild rice is best)
1	c chopped tomatoes
1	c chopped cooked spinach
1/2	c chopped onions
1/2	c vinaigrette dressing
	Tabasco and sesame oil to taste
	Grated coconut

Mix all ingredients and refrigerate for 1-24 hours. Sprinkle with grated coconut before serving.

Marge Litsinger

Mandarin Rice Salad

3	c cold cooked rice
1	can (16 oz) mandarin orange segments, drained
1 1/2	c diced green pepper
3/4	c sour cream
1	tbsp lemon juice
1	tsp salt
1	tsp pepper

Blend all ingredients thoroughly. Chill. Serve on salad greens and sprinkle with sliced almonds, if desired. Makes 6 servings.

Virginia Bockhop

Seafood Rice Salad

1	pack (8 oz) frozen cooked shrimps
1	can (6 to 7 oz) tuna, drained
2	c cooked rice
1/2	c each finely chopped onions and sweet pickles
1 1/2	c thinly sliced celery
1/4	c sliced pimientos
3	hard-cooked eggs, chopped
1	tbsp lemon juice
1	c mayonnaise

Combine all ingredients and toss lightly. Season to taste. Chill. Serve on salad greens. Garnish with tomato wedges, if desired. Makes 6 servings.

Alit Mackill

Green Rice

3	c cooked rice
2	eggs, well beaten
1/4	c butter
1/4	c sharp cheese, grated
1/2	tbsp chopped onion
1/3	c parsley, minced
2/3	c spinach, minced
1/4	tsp salt

Combine all ingredients; transfer to a greased and floured 2-quart casserole (8-inch). Bake at 325 °F (moderate oven) for about 45 minutes. Serve hot with meat or meat sauce, creamed chicken, fish, or vegetables. Serves 8.

Ruth Cowan

Chili Rice

1	c chopped onion	1/8	tsp pepper
1/4	c margarine	3/4	c green chilies, chopped
4	c hot cooked rice		
2	c sour cream	2	c cheddar cheese, grated
1	c cottage cheese		
1	bay leaf, crumbled		Pinch of chopped parsley
1/2	tsp salt		

Cook onion in margarine until soft, but not brown; mix with rice, sour cream, cottage cheese, bay leaf, salt, and pepper.

Drain. In a large buttered casserole, spread 1/3 rice mixture, 1/3 chili, and 1/3 cheddar cheese. Repeat twice. Bake uncovered for 25 minutes at 325 °F. Garnish with parsley. Serves 10-12.

Gennie Bostian and
LaRue Pollard

Texas Hash

1 1/2	lb lean ground beef
2	c chopped onions
2	c chopped green pepper
1-2	tbsp chili powder
1	tbsp salt
1/2	tsp pepper
1/2	tsp garlic powder
2	c (16 oz) canned tomato
3	c cooked rice

Sauté beef, onions, green pepper, and seasonings until meat is no longer pink and vegetables are tender. Stir frequently to crumble meat. Add tomato and rice. Spoon into a buttered 2-quart casserole. Bake at 350 °F for 25 minutes or until thoroughly heated. Makes 6 to 8 servings.

Marlene Smith
(Recipe of the Rice
Council of America)

Chicken Jambalaya

1	bouillon cube
1	c white wine
1/2	tsp basil
1/2	tsp thyme
1	small bay leaf
1/2	c chopped onions
1/4	c chopped green
1	c raw rice
1/2	c lean ham, cubed
1	c canned tomatoes or tomato sauce
3	chicken breasts, split and skinned
1/4	c chopped parsley pepper

Preheat oven to 350 °F. In a saucepan, bring to a boil the bouillon, wine, herbs (basil, thyme, bay leaf), onion, and pepper. Place rice, ham, tomatoes, and chicken in a large casserole and pour herb sauce over all. Cover tightly and bake for 25-30 minutes. Add parsley; turn heat off and allow casserole to remain in the oven for 10-15 minutes. Enough for 6 servings, with 350 calories per serving.

Judy Buresh

Fried Rice

1/4 c chopped onions
2 tbsp chopped green pepper
2 tbsp salad oil
2 c cooked rice
1 can (5 oz) water chestnuts, drained and thinly sliced
1 can (3 oz) sliced mushrooms, drained
2 tbsp soy sauce
3 eggs, beaten

In large skillet, cook and stir onion and green pepper in oil until onion is tender. Stir in rice, water chestnuts, mushrooms, and soy sauce. Cook over low heat for 10 minutes, stirring frequently. Stir in eggs; cook and stir 2 to 3 minutes longer. Makes 4 to 5 servings (about 1/2 cup each).

Billie Cooper

Baked Raisin Pilau

1/4 c butter or margarine
1 small onion, sliced
1/4 c slivered almonds (preferably blanched)
1/4 c golden raisins
1 c uncooked long-grain rice (aromatic type especially good)
2 c hot, canned, clear chicken broth, diluted if condensed

In saucepan, melt butter or margarine and sauté onion, almonds, and raisins until onion slices are golden. Add rice, mix well. Add hot chicken broth. Place mixture in greased 6-cup casserole. Cover. Bake at 375 °F for 25-30 minutes, or until all liquid is absorbed.

Sunny Chandler
(a Good Housekeeping recipe)

Creamy Rice and Cheese Bake

2 eggs, beaten
1 c half-and-half (cream and milk)
3 c cooked rice
1/2 tsp salt
1/2 tsp onion powder
1/2 tsp powdered mustard
1/2 tsp ground black pepper
  Dash of ground red pepper
1 c Swiss or cheddar cheese
2 tbsp chopped parsley

Combine all ingredients; mix well. Turn into a buttered 8- × 8- × 2-inch baking dish. Bake at 350 °F for 20 minutes or until firm near center. Do not overcook.

Rice Council of America

Mini Rice Quiches

3	c cooked rice
1 1/2	c grated Swiss cheese
4	eggs
1/2	c real bacon bits
1	can (4 oz) diced green chilies
1/4	c each diced pimientos and snipped parsley
1	c half-and-half
3/4	tsp each salt and ground cumin
1/8	tsp hot pepper sauce

Combine rice, 1 cup cheese, and 2 eggs, slightly beaten. Press 1 tbsp of the mixture in bottoms of 48 buttered miniature muffin cups. Bake at 400 °F for 15 minutes, or until lightly browned. Combine bacon, chilies, pimientos, parsley, and remaining cheese. Spoon evenly over rice layer. Blend half-and-half, seasonings, and remaining eggs. Spoon evenly into each cup. Return to oven; bake 15 minutes, or until set. Makes 48 appetizers.

Rice Council of America

Broccoli Frittata

2 1/2	tbsp finely chopped onions
2	tsp butter or margarine
1	package (10 oz) frozen chopped broccoli, cooked and drained
1/2	small clove garlic, crushed (optional)
1	c cooked rice
2 1/2	tbsp grated parmesan cheese
2	eggs, slightly beaten
1/4	c milk
1/2	tsp salt
	Dash of ground black pepper
1/2	c grated mozzarella cheese

Sauté onion in butter until tender but not brown. Add broccoli, garlic, rice, and parmesan cheese; mix well. Combine eggs, milk, and seasonings. Stir into rice mixture. Turn into a well-buttered shallow 1-quart casserole. Top with mozzarella cheese. Bake at 350 °F for 20 to 25 minutes or until set. Makes 2 servings.

Rice Council of America

Baked Red Beans and Rice

1	lb dried red kidney beans (2 1/2 cups)
4	c water
1	c chopped ham
2	tsp tabasco sauce
1	large onion, chopped
2	stalks celery with leaves, chopped
1	tsp salt

Soak beans overnight in water. Pour into a large heavy pan or dutch oven. Add remaining ingredients. Simmer for 3 hours or until beans are tender. Add water when necessary. Water should barely cover beans at the end of cooking time. Remove 1 cup of beans at the end of cooking time and mash to a paste. Add back to the mixture and stir until liquid is thickened. Serve over rice.

Judy Buresh

Europe

Traditionally European cooking makes much use of wheat and potatoes, which are baked or boiled and eaten with a variety of meats and vegetables. Europeans started eating rice through cultural adaptation to their colonies in Asia. The preference is for long-grain, aromatic rice. Rice is used in a number of dishes, such as kedgeree (rice cooked with fish haddock and spices), which is part of breakfast. Traditional rice pudding and rice cakes are eaten, especially during winter. Because of the Asian cultural influence, raw rice grains are also used during weddings in U.K., where rice grains are showered on the newly wedded couple as a symbol of blessings.

Germans are basically wheat and potato eaters. Although rice is not a staple food in Germany, Germans have rice in some of their meals and desserts. They prefer long-grain rice with white meats such as chicken and turkey. Their traditional rice dessert is rice pudding, which they prepare for special occasions.

* * *

Germany

Rice Trautamanndorf (Sweet Rice)

100 grams rice
3/4 liter milk
100 grams sugar
1/2 vanilla stick
    Pinch of salt
2 tsp gelatin
125 grams mixed fruits (tinned)
1/4 c whipped cream
    Cointreau or maraschino

Boil rice in milk slowly; add sugar, vanilla, and pinch of salt. Dissolve gelatin in another pan; add to rice mixture. Allow to cool. Mix fruit with Cointreau and arrange over rice mixture. Pour whipped cream on top of fruits.

Annemarie Lampe

Reisauflauf (Rice Pudding)

125	grams rice	40	grams sugar
1/2	liter milk	2	eggs, separated
20	grams margarine		Some butter
	Rind from 1/2 lemon		

Put rice, milk, margarine, and chopped lemon rind in a pot and boil slowly about 20 minutes. Remove from heat. Add sugar. Let cool a little, then add 2 egg yolks. Beat egg whites until very stiff, then carefully fold into the rice.

Transfer the mixture to a well-buttered ovenproof bowl. Put some butter flakes on top. Bake at 200-225 °F for 45 minutes. Serve with fruit sauce and fruit slices.

Marie L. Kürschner

United Kingdom

Kedgeree

2	hard-boiled eggs
1	tbsp parsley
4	c water
1	tsp salt
2	c long-grain rice
1/2	lb smoked haddock
1	oz butter
2	tsp curry powder

Boil eggs and rub through a sieve. Chop parsley fine and set aside. Boil water, add salt. Pour rice in boiling water slowly; let boil uncovered for 15 minutes. Meanwhile, boil haddock in another pan on high flame for 10 minutes. Remove from fire; remove bones from fish and flake meat.

Drain rice and set aside. Heat butter in a saucepan; add curry powder and rice; stir. Add smoked haddock to rice and cook for 5 minutes; add 1/2 of hard-boiled eggs. Remove from fire and place on a platter. Garnish with remaining eggs and parsley.

Wendy Woodhead

Tomato Rice with Meatballs

2   c cheddar cheese
1   egg
1/2   lb beef, minced
1   tbsp cooking oil
4   oz rice
1   small onion, chopped
1   c tomato soup
1/2   pint water
1/2   tsp salt
     Dash of pepper
1/4   tsp mustard
1/4   tsp mixed dried herbs

Grate cheese and beat egg. Add to meat and mix well. Shape mixture into balls, adding dry flour if needed. Heat oil and fry balls until brown. Put rice and balls in a casserole. Sauté onion and cook for 2 minutes; add tomato soup, water, salt, pepper, and herbs. Bring to a boil, stirring constantly. Pour this mixture into the casserole. Cover and bake 350 °F for 40 minutes. Stir before serving.

Isabel Wy

Rice Cake

4   oz butter or margarine
4   oz sugar
2   eggs
1   tbsp water
1/2   tsp vanilla essence
3   oz rice flour
1   oz self-rising flour
1/4   tsp salt

Cream butter or margarine and sugar together in a bowl until light and fluffy. Beat eggs, water, and vanilla essence together and gradually add to creamed mixture, beating after each addition. Fold in rice flour, self-rising flour, and salt. Spread mixture in a 7-inch sandwich tin. Bake in 375 °F oven for 30 minutes. Serve cold.

Kate Kirk

Australia

In the past, Australians ate very little rice. But because of the country's increasingly cosmopolitan population, with a large Asian component, rice is now more commonly part of the everyday diet.

Traditionally, Australians used to eat rice in English dishes such as rice pudding and fish kedgeree. The practice is a carryover from colonial days. The next major rice influence came from Chinese cuisine, which became popular earlier this century: fried or boiled rice to accompany other foods. Since then, rice has crept into the diet on a more regular basis: as a potato substitute, often for salads, and now in other Asian dishes.

Australians prefer long-grain rice, and although Australian rice is a japonica type and is slightly sticky, the usual way of cooking it leaves the grains separate and not soft. In recent years brown rice has become popular. Supermarkets regularly sell Australian rice, but specialty and health food stores sell Basmati, Thai, and other rices.

✳ ✳ ✳

Golden Glow Rice Salad

1/4 c peas
1/4 c corn kernels
1/4 c carrots, diced
1/4 c cauliflower, sliced
2   c cooked rice
1/2 c diced cheddar cheese
1/2 c mayonnaise
     Salt and pepper to taste

Clean, wash, and boil all vegetables. Cool. Combine rice, vegetables, and cheese. Season with salt and pepper. Add mayonnaise and toss gently. Serve with grilled meat.

NOTE: Frozen or tinned vegetables can be used.

Joy Smith

Gold Coast Luncheon Salad

1/2 c diced pineapple
1   tbsp mint
2   c cooked rice
1/2 lb luncheon sausage, diced
1/2 c mayonnaise
     Salt and pepper to taste

Combine pineapple and mint and toss very well until pineapple is coated with mint. Add rice and sausages with salt and pepper. Add mayonnaise and toss gently. Serve as luncheon dish or as an accompaniment to meat.

Marlene Quick

Curried Nut Rice

1   c rice
1   tbsp butter
1/4 c almond slivers
4   shallots or spring onions
1/2 tsp curry powder
     Salt and pepper to taste

Cook rice in boiling salted water for 10 to 12 minutes or until tender; drain. Melt butter in pan, sauté almonds, finely chopped shallots, curry powder, salt, and pepper until golden brown. Add hot boiled rice; and toss gently to mix.

Joy Smith

Orange Minted Rice

2   c long-grain rice
1/4 c butter
2   tbsp finely chopped celery
2   onions, finely chopped
     Salt and pepper to taste
1/4 c finely shredded orange rind
3/4 c orange juice
1/2 c water
2   tbsp finely chopped mint

Cook rice in boiling water until tender. Heat butter in pan, sauté celery and onions; add salt, pepper, and orange rind. Add orange juice, water, and mint; bring to a boil and cook until vegetables are done and liquid has evaporated. Remove from heat, then stir in cooked rice. Cover and let stand for 5 minutes before serving.

Alice Flinn

Rice and Shine

1/4 c raw rice
1/4 c condensed milk
     Pinch of salt
     Water

Grease a heavy-bottomed saucepan well with butter. Add enough water to condensed milk to make 1 pint. Blend very well. Place rice, milk, and salt in a saucepan; leave on very low heat. Cook for 1 hour or until rice is tender. Stir from time to time to prevent rice from sticking to the pan.

NOTE: During winter, this recipe may be served hot as a rice porridge for breakfast. Sprinkle with brown sugar or dot with butter. During summer, this preparation can be stored in a refrigerator and then served with coarsely grated apples and a few sultanas. It is especially good for children.

Joy Smith

Beverages and Appetizers

Passion Julius

1 200-ml pkg passion fruit frozen
    concentrate
1/2 c skim milk powder
1 1/3 c milk
4 tbsp confectioners' sugar (icing
    sugar)
12-18 ice cubes

Blend all ingredients in a blender until
mixture is "slushy."

Rae Bourquein
USA

Keoke Coffee

Pour 3/4 ounce Kahlua and 3/4 ounce
dark creme de cocoa into a coffee cup. Fill
with coffee. Float with brandy. Top with
whipped cream.

Marlene Smith
USA

Orange Shake

1 c orange juice   1/2 tsp vanilla
1/3 c nonfat dry milk   1/2 c ice cubes
1-2 tbsp sugar

Place all ingredients in a blender. Cover,
blend until ice is crushed. Makes 2 cups
(239 calories).

Judy Buresh
USA

Chocolate Shake

1/2 c nonfat dry milk
1/4 c water
3 tbsp chocolate-flavored syrup
1 c ice cubes

Place all ingredients in a blender. Cover,
blend until ice is crushed. Makes 1 1/2
cups (260 calories).

Judy Buresh
USA

Mulled Wine

1 1/3	c sugar
2/3	c water
15	whole cloves
4	cinnamon sticks
1	tsp nutmeg
	Peel of lemon and orange
2	c orange juice
2	bottles dry red wine (750 ml each)
1	orange

Boil sugar, water, cloves, cinnamon, nutmeg, and peels for 5 minutes. Put orange juice and wine in a large pot. Add sugar mixture to the pot, stirring it. Heat. Decorate with clove-studded orange sections. Serve warm.

Judy Buresh
USA

Jal-Jeera (Spicy Hot)

100	grams tamarind
8-10	sprigs of fresh green mint
	Sugar and salt to taste
1/2	tsp ground cumin powder
1/4	tsp red chili powder

Soak tamarind in 6 glasses of water for 30 minutes; strain. Add sugar and salt. Grind mint finely with other ingredients and add to tamarind water. Chill before serving.

Usha Ladha
India

Green Mango Juice

4	green mangoes
8	c water
	Black pepper or chili powder as per taste (optional)
1	tsp cumin powder
	Salt to taste
4	tbsp sugar

Roast or boil the mangoes. Peel and remove pulp. Combine pulp with water and sugar, mix well. Add salt and cumin powder. For those who like it spiced, chili powder or black pepper can be added according to taste. Chill before serving.

Usha Ladha
India

Sweet or Salted Yoghurt Drink

1   c fresh yoghurt
1   c cold water
2   tbsp sugar
2   drops of rose extract or
1/4 tsp vanilla

Blend all ingredients well. Put 2 ice cubes in a glass and pour in blended yoghurt.

NOTE: For those who like it salted, instead of sugar and extract, use 1/2 tsp cumin powder and salt to taste.

Usha Ladha
India

Mango Shake

2   medium-size ripe mangoes
2   c fresh milk
1/3 c sugar
10 ice cubes
1/3 c sugar

Wash and peel mangoes. Remove seed and put pulp in a blender; add milk. Blend at high speed. Add ice cubes and sugar, blend again at high speed. Pour into glasses and garnish with cherry or sprig of mint.

Indu Virmani
India

Kahewa (Green Tea)

6   almonds
6   cardamoms
1   stick cinnamon,
    2-inch-long
6   c water
2   tsp crushed green tea leaves
6   tsp sugar

Grind almonds, cardamoms, and cinnamon stick into coarse powder and set aside. Boil water; add tea leaves and sugar. Let boil for 5 minutes. Add ground powder; let boil another minute. Serve hot.

NOTE: This special green tea is very popular in Kashmir.

Shashi Raina
India

Chicken Kebabs

1 tbsp ground garlic
1 tsp corn oil
1/2 kg minced chicken
1 egg
2 medium-size onions, finely chopped
1 tsp grated ginger
1 green chili (optional)
1/4 tsp chili powder
1 tbsp calamansi juice
1/4 c bread crumbs
1 tbsp roasted cumin seeds
1/2 tbsp coriander powder
1 small bunch of fresh coriander
Salt to taste

Fry garlic in oil until brown. Cool. In a bowl, mix minced meat, egg, fried garlic, and the rest of the ingredients. Shape like cocktail sausages and cook in shallow oil in a frying pan. Serve with mint chutney.

Savi Singh
India

Baked Clams

1 can (8 oz) minced clams
8 oz cream cheese
1/2 c mayonnaise
1/4 tsp celery seed
Salt to taste

Beat together all ingredients until well blended. Bake, uncovered, about 30 minutes. Serve with crackers or sturdy potato chips.

Ilse Zandstra
Canada

Fish Pakora (Fish Fritters)

1/2   kg fish (lapu-lapu or tanigue or any big fish)
1/2   tsp paprika
1/4   tsp carom seed powder (if available)
1/2   tsp chili powder
      Pinch of salt
1/2   tsp coriander powder
1/4   c pea flour
8   cloves garlic, minced
1/2   c water
      Oil for deep-frying

Wash and clean fish. Remove skin and cut fish into bite size pieces. Mix all spices with pea flour and add garlic with water to make a paste. Coat fish with paste and keep in the refrigerator 4-6 hours. Deep-fry fish in hot oil, 2 or 3 pieces at a time. Be sure oil is smoky hot. As soon as you drop the fish, reduce heat; fry pieces until done. Sprinkle cumin powder and calamansi juice on top for flavor. Serve with mango or mint chutney.

Indu Virmani
India

Quiche Lorraine Appetizer

      Baked pastry shell
14   strips bacon (the leanest you can find)
1 1/4 c shredded swiss cheese
4   eggs
1 1/4 c whipping cream
1/2   c milk
      Ground nutmeg

Cook bacon until crisp. Cool, then crumble. Evenly distribute bacon and cheese over bottom of baked pastry shell.

Beat eggs lightly. Add cream and milk combined, and beat to blend well. Pour egg mixture over cheese and bacon. Sprinkle a little nutmeg. Bake uncovered in a 325 °F oven for 25 minutes or until filling is set. (If air accumulates, prick with fork.) Cut in small squares. Serve hot or at room temperature.

Baked pastry shell
1 1/2 c unsifted   9   tbsp butter
     all-purpose flour   or margarine
1/8   tsp salt   1   egg, beaten

Combine flour and salt in a bowl. Cut butter in small pieces and add to flour mixture. With pastry blender, cut/blend until mixture is the size of small peas. Add beaten egg and blend well with fork. Form dough into a ball, then roll out on a well-floured surface (or between 2 sheets of wax paper) to fit a 10- × 15-inch shallow baking pan. Trim off excess dough. Prick bottom with fork. Bake uncovered at 425 °F for 12-15 minutes. Cool.

Baby Duff (Philippines)
France

Baked Mussels

1 kg fresh mussels
1-2 tbsp pounded garlic
1 c butter
2 tsp chopped parsley
1/2 c grated cheese

Clean mussels well. Steam in a little water. When they are about to open, remove from heat. Remove meat from shells and discard half the shells. Arrange shells on tray or cookie sheets. Place one mussel on each shell. Mix butter, garlic, parsley, and cheese. Place a small amount on each mussel and broil at 340 °F until golden brown (5 to 10 minutes).

Lucy Bonman
Philippines

Tarte à l'Oignons (Onion Pie)

15 big onions (yellow, red, or white)
Oil for frying
1 c raisins
Pimiento (optional)
Basil or parsley
1 c fresh cream (or Nestlé cream)
2 whole eggs
Salt to taste
Black pepper
Baked pie crust

Pie crust
500 grams flour
25 grams salt
375 grams unsalted butter
3 eggs, beaten
Little water

Mix flour and salt; cut in the butter until the mixture is the size of small peas. Add eggs and water and blend well. Roll out to fit a 9-inch pie pan. Bake at 425°F for 12-15 minutes.

Cut onions into big slices and cook 1 or 2 minutes in oil very slowly. (Onions need to be tender but never roasted or transparent.) Add raisins and pimiento; set aside. Prepare sauce with the rest of the ingredients and mix with onion. Pour filling into prebaked pie crust and bake at 350 °F about 30 minutes or until filling is brown. Serve immediately.

Françoise Prot
France

Dendeng (Dried Spiced Meat)

1	kg round or topside steak
5	tbsp peanut oil
2	cloves garlic, crushed
1/2	tsp finely grated ginger
2	tsp ground coriander
1	tsp ground cumin
1/2	tsp dried shrimp paste
1 1/2	tsp salt
1	tsp sambal ulek
6	tbsp dark soy sauce
2	tbsp tamarind liquid (or lemon juice)
3	tsp palm sugar (light brown sugar)

Cut meat into small strips. Heat oil and fry garlic, ginger, coriander, cumin, and shrimp paste. Then add salt, sambal ulek, soy sauce, and tamarind liquid. Add meat and stir-fry. Reduce heat, cover pan and let cook over very low heat for 30-35 minutes. Stir occasionally. When liquid has almost evaporated, add palm sugar and stir to dissolve. Turn meat till liquid has gone. Place meat on an oven tray. Place in the oven to dry at 125 °C (250 °F) for 30 minutes. Turn meat, then cook for another 30 minutes.

Alice Flinn (Australia)
Indonesia

Chicken Liver Paté

4	oz butter
1/2	onion, finely chopped
1	clove garlic, crushed
250	grams chicken livers
2	tsp whiskey
1	tsp French mustard
	Dash of nutmeg
	Salt and pepper

Melt 1 oz of butter and cook onion and garlic until soft. Add chicken livers and cook until done. Put this mixture and remaining ingredients into a blender and blend until smooth. Put in a container and cover top with plastic wrap to keep air out and prevent discoloration. Cool. (This freezes well.)

Alice Flinn
Australia

Vadas (Farina Balls)

1 1/4 c farina (suji)
1   c water
1   medium yellow onion,
       finely chopped
1 or 2 green chilies, drained and chopped
1 1/2 tbsp chopped coriander leaves
1/2   c cashew nuts, chopped
4   tbsp plain yoghurt
3/4   tsp freshly minced ginger root
1/2   tsp salt
       Vegetable oil for frying

Bring water to a boil. Place farina in a bowl and add water, stirring to make a dough. Add onion, chilies, salt, coriander leaves, cashew nuts, yoghurt, and ginger root and mix well. Take 2 tbsp of dough mixture and make a thick, round patty.

Cut with a doughnut cutter or use fingers to make a hole in center of patty. Repeat with remaining dough. Heat vegetable oil to 375 °F. Fry about 3 to 4 vadas at a time for 8 to 10 minutes, turning as necessary, until light brown. Drain on paper towel. Serve hot with chutney.

Kumari Pingali
India

Low-calorie Samosas

1/2   tsp cumin seeds
600   grams potatoes, peeled, cut into cubes
20   grams cooked green peas
1   tsp ground cumin powder
1/2   tsp turmeric powder
3/4   tsp red pepper (cayenne pepper)
3/4   tsp garam masala
8   spring roll wrappers
4   tsp coriander oil
       Salt to taste

Heat 5 tbsp oil in a heavy pot over medium heat. Add cumin seeds. When seeds start to crackle, add potatoes, green peas, spices (except garam masala), and salt to taste. Put lid on and reduce heat.

After 5 minutes, add 2 tsp water. After another 10 minutes, add garam masala; mix well, and turn off heat. When filling cools, divide it among wrappers and roll like spring rolls. Heat oven to 400 °F. With finger, brush each roll with 1/2 tsp oil and place on ungreased cookie sheet. Bake about 10 to 15 minutes or until golden brown. Makes 8 samosas. Serve with ketchup.

Yokiko Vaughan (Japan)
UK

Samosa

Filling

6	medium-size potatoes
2	tsp oil
1	large onion, finely chopped
	A little piece of ginger
1 1/2	tsp coriander powder
1/2	tsp chili powder
1/2	tsp garam masala
1	large carrot, finely chopped and steamed
1	c cooked green peas
	Salt to taste

Dough

2	c plain flour
1/2	c shortening
1/2	tsp salt

Boil and peel potatoes; cut into small cubes. Heat oil. Fry onion and ginger till light brown. Add spices, fry for 2 more minutes, then add potatoes, peas, and carrots, together with salt. Mix well, cooking on low flame. Remove from heat and cool.

Mix shortening, salt, and flour well. With a little water make a dough, as hard as that for pie. Knead till smooth. Make about 1-inch balls of the dough. Roll into circles 4 inches in diameter, cut each into two. Using the thumb and forefingers, Make a triangle with each half; fill one with a little potato filling, cover with the other triangle, and close by pressing the edges. For smooth closure, moisten edges with a little water. Deep-fry triangles over low flame till slightly brown. If you intend to freeze them, fry until half-done, then cool thoroughly before freezing.

Usha Ladha
India

Nimki

1   c all-purpose flour
      Salt to taste
      Pinch of caraway seeds
      Pinch of black cumin seeds
      Pinch of white cumin seeds
1/4 tsp sambhar spice (optional)
1   tsp ground roasted cumin
1/4 tsp crushed red chilies
1   tbsp butter, melted
5   tbsp water
      Vegetable oil for deep-frying

Sift flour before measuring. Combine flour, salt, caraway seeds, black and white cumin seeds, sambhar spice, roasted cumin, and chilies. Add butter and enough water to make a soft dough. Knead dough for about 10 minutes, until satiny and smooth. Divide into 20 equal portions. Roll each between the palms of hands to form a ball. On a lightly floured board, roll out each ball into a very thin circle, about 3 inches in diameter.

With a knife make 4 or 5 parallel cuts in the pastry, approximately 1/2 inch apart, just to the edge but without cutting through the edge of the circle.

Heat vegetable oil to 375 °F. Fry nimkis until golden brown. Then drain on paper towel.

NOTE: Finished pastries may be frozen. Before serving, heat frozen nimkis in a preheated 350 °F oven for about 7 minutes, or until they are warm and crisp.

Kumari Pingali
India

Potato Bondas (Fried Potato Balls)

Filling
1/2 kg potatoes
4   large onions, finely chopped
4   green chilies, chopped
1/4 tsp red chili powder
1/4 tsp fresh ginger, chopped
2   tsp lime juice
2   tsp oil
       Salt to taste

Batter
3/4 c besan (chickpea flour)
1   tsp rice flour
1/4 tsp baking powder
1/4 tsp red chili powder
       Salt to taste
Oil for deep-frying
       Pinch of baking soda

Boil and peel potatoes; set aside. Fry onions in 2 tbsp oil until soft. Add green chilies, chili powder, and ginger; cook 4-5 minutes. Mash potato slightly and add to the onion mix. Add salt and lime juice.

Mix well. Remove from fire after 3 minutes. Cool. Make lemon-size balls; set aside.

Mixing all batter ingredients except oil; add enough water to make a light batter as for pancake. Heat oil over high flame. Dip potato balls in batter, 2 at a time, then deep-fry 3 or 4 at a time. Reduce flame to medium. Turn ball when one side becomes slightly hard and yellowish brown. Remove when evenly cooked. Serve hot with tomato sauce, mint chutney, or ketchup.

NOTE: If pea flour is not available, soak 1/4 cup yellow split pea and 1/2 tsp rice for 1-2 hours. Grind to make a smooth paste. Use for pea flour.

Geetha Prasad
India

Spicy Lentil Balls

1   c split peas
2   green chilies, chopped
1/4 chili powder
3   large onions
1   tsp grated ginger
       Oil for deep-frying
       Salt to taste

Soak split peas for 1-2 hours. Wash well and drain completely. Blend coarsely. Add rest of the ingredients. Mix well and make patties 1/2 inch in diameter and 1/2 inch thick. Fry patties in hot oil, a few at a time. Reduce the flame to medium. Fry till evenly brown. Serve with tomato sauce.

Geetha Prasad
India

Cornflakes Chivra

2	c cornflakes
3/4	c peanuts
10-15	curry leaves
	Handful of raisins
	Handful of cashew nuts
2-3	green chilies
	Oil for deep-frying
	Salt to taste
1/2	tsp sugar
1	tsp red chili powder

Heat oil in frying pan. Deep-fry cornflakes, then set aside. Deep-fry peanuts, cashew nuts, raisins, curry leaves, and chilies. Add all to cornflakes; add salt, sugar, and chili powder according to taste.

Smita Gadgil
India

Chivra (Spicy Pinipig Mix)

3	c pinipig
1/2	c peanuts
1/3	c cashew nuts
1/4	c raisins
1/4	c dry coconut slices (optional)
1/2	tsp chili powder or
1/2	tsp garam masala (optional)
	Salt to taste
	Oil for frying

Deep-fry pinipig in hot oil; scoop up immediately with a large sieve. Drain on paper towel to remove excess oil. Toast nuts, raisins, and coconut in 2 tbsp oil until brown. Mix pinipig, spices, and salt thoroughly. Cool completely, then store in airtight jar.

Usha Ladha
India

Rough Buns

2	c flour
1	c sugar
2	tsp baking powder
1 1/2	tsp nutmeg
1/2	tsp salt
3	tbsp butter
1	medium egg
1/2	c milk
1	c water
	Oil for deep-frying

Sift flour into a mixing bowl. Add sugar, baking powder, nutmeg, salt, and butter. Set aside. Beat egg; add milk and water. Pour mixture onto the dough and blend thoroughly. Knead for 5 minutes. Put 1 tbsp of dough separately, 5-6 at a time, in hot oil and deep-fry until light brown. Repeat until all dough is used. Serve hot.

Djakoto
Ghana

Upuma

1	c cream of wheat or farina
3	tbsp oil
1	tsp mustard seeds
1 1/2	c black gram dal (optional)
	Curry leaves
1	tsp chopped ginger
2	green chilies
2	large onions, chopped
1	tbsp chopped coriander leaves
1 1/2	c water
	Juice of 2 lemons
	Salt to taste
2	tbsp cashew nuts
1	tbsp butter

Roast cream of wheat until light brown, set aside. Heat oil in a frying pan (a wok is better). Add mustard seeds, dal, and curry leaves; fry until mustard seeds crackle. Add ginger, chilies, onions, coriander leaves, and water. Cook about 5 minutes or until water boils. Gradually add cream of wheat, stirring constantly. Cook about 20 minutes. Add more water if mixture is too dry. Cover with a lid and cook gently a few more minutes. Add lemon juice and salt. Fry cashew nuts separately in butter, then sprinkle on top.

NOTE: This can be served with coconut, chutney, or any kind of pickles.

Vijji De Datta
India

Vegetable Pakora (Fritters)

1	c chickpea flour
1/2	tsp red chili powder
1/2	tsp garam masala (curry powder)
1/4	tsp baking soda
1	tbsp chopped coriander leaves, if available
	Oil for deep-frying
	Onion and potato rings (most commonly used) and/or
	Eggplant slices (2 inches long) and/or
	Whole small onions and/or
	Cauliflower, cut into thick slices and/or
	Spinach leaves whole, and/or
	White pumpkin cut into thin slices, and/or
	Raw banana slices, etc.

Mix the first 4 ingredients and make a batter. Dip all vegetables in the batter and deep-fry. Serve with mango chutney.

NOTE: If chickpea flour is not available, 1 cup mongo soaked for 4-5 hours and ground into a paste serves the purpose well. It tastes equally good.

Usha Ladha
India

Cha Gio (Vietnamese Lumpia)

2   c fresh lean pork, ground
1   c fresh shrimps, chopped
1/4 c chopped onions
2   eggs, slightly beaten
    Vietnamese lumpia wrapper or any lumpia
    wrapper
1   tbsp finely chopped kinchay
1   c sotanghon
1   tsp salt
1/4 c dried wood ears
1/2 tsp black pepper
    Vegetable oil for frying

Soak wood ears until expanded, then cut into halves. Thoroughly mix all ingredients except wrappers. Place 3 tsp of mixture in each wrapper, then roll into a cylinder. Seal by moistening edge with water. In preheated oil in a frying pan, fry lumpia on both sides until brown.

Tham Aurin
Vietnam

Beef Tapa (Sun-dried Coriander Beef)

1 1/2 kg beef
5   cloves garlic
2   tbsp coriander seeds, lightly toasted
3   tbsp peppercorn
4   tbsp sugar
1   tbsp salt
3   tbsp fish sauce (patis)
3   tbsp soy sauce

Cut beef into thin slices. Crush garlic, coriander seeds, and peppercorn together. Mix with beef. Combine sugar, salt, fish sauce, and soy sauce. Add to beef.

Marinate beef at least 5 hours or overnight in the refrigerator.

Stretch marinated beef on a drying basket or cake rack. Put out in hot sun for 2 hours. Turn and dry other side for another 2 hours. If it is not well dried, keep it longer under the sun. Fry dried beef slices in hot oil until crisp.

Visaka Panditya
Thailand

Pork Toast

6-7 peppercorns
3 cloves garlic
200 grams minced pork
1 egg
Oil for deep-frying
1 tsp sugar
2 tbsp fish sauce (patis)
1 stalk green onion, chopped
5-8 slices stale bread

Crush peppercorn and garlic together. Add to minced pork. Add egg, sugar, fish sauce, and green onion to the pork mixture. Trim crust off bread slices and cut bread into desired shapes. Spread pork mixture on top of bread. With pork side down first, deep-fry in hot oil until brown on both sides. Drain on paper towel. Serve hot with chili sauce or cucumber sauce.

Visaka Panditya
Thailand

Cheese Straw

1 c flour
1 1/2 tsp baking powder
1/2 tsp salt
2 tbsp butter
1/2 c sharp cheddar cheese, shredded
1/3 c cold water

Sift together flour, baking powder, and salt. Cut in butter with a pastry blender or fork until mixture is crumbly. Add cheese; toss until well blended. Sprinkle water over mixture; mix lightly with a fork just until pastry holds together and leaves sides of bowl clean. Roll out on a floured surface to a 12- × 10-inch rectangle. Cut in half lengthwise; then cut each half crosswise into 1/2-inch strips. Lift strips one at a time; twist and place 1 inch apart on ungreased cookie sheets. Bake in a preheated oven (425 °F) for 10 minutes or until lightly golden. Cool on wire racks.

Judy Buresh
USA

Soups and Salads

Egg Soup

3	eggs
3	pc tomatoes
5	c hot water
2	tbsp cornstarch, dissolved in 2 tbsp water
	Pinch of salt
	Pepper to taste
	Dash of vetsin

Beat eggs and set aside. Chop tomatoes and set aside. Heat pan and pour water into it. Boil for 5 minutes. Add tomatoes and boil for 5 minutes. Add starch and water solution, stirring constantly. Boil for 3 minutes. Add eggs, stir. Season with salt, pepper, and vetsin. Serve hot.

Liu Zhen No
China

Pumpkin Soup

4	stalks celery, chopped
1/2	kg pumpkin cubes
1-2	potatoes, diced
1	tbsp soy sauce
1	large onion, chopped
	Parsley
	Stock cubes or vegemeat
	Pinch of basil and oregano
	Clove garlic, crushed
	Salt to taste
125	grams cream

Mix everything except cream and parsley and cook about 20 minutes. Blend or leave chunky according to taste. Add cream. Sprinkle with parsley.

Marlene Quick
Australia

Erwtensoep (Dutch Pea Soup)

2	c split green peas
3	qt cold water
1	c bacon
1	lb potatoes, sliced
4	tsp salt
1/2	c celery, diced
1	bunch leeks, cut up
2	big carrots, diced
2	onions, diced
4	frankfurters or German sausage

Soak peas in cold water for 12 hours. Boil gently for at least 2 hours (unless quick-cooking peas are used). Add bacon, potatoes, salt, celery with leaves, carrot, leeks, and onions. Cook until everything is done and soup is smooth and thick. Add frankfurters in last 10 minutes of cooking.

NOTE: The soup tastes even better when served one day after it is cooked. That is why it is made in big quantities.

Kathy HilleRisLambers
The Netherlands

Cream of Spinach Soup

2   tbsp butter
1   tsp cumin seeds
1   onion, finely chopped
4   c chopped spinach, boiled in 2 c water
    and blended
2   c water
3   c milk
    Salt and pepper to taste
1   c fried bread cubes
1/2 c cream

Heat butter in a pan and sauté cumin seeds. When slightly brown, add chopped onions and sauté, but do not brown. Add spinach and water, and simmer for 2 minutes. Add milk and bring to a boil. Add salt and pepper; cook till done. Serve topped with bread squares and cream.

Romy Talewar
India

Hot Sour Soup

6   oz chicken, sliced against the grain into
    very thin 1-inch strips
2   tsp cornstarch
2   tsp soy sauce
1   tsp hot sauce
1/2 tsp sugar
4   c chicken broth
6   black mushrooms, soaked in warm water,
    and cut into thin strips (stems discarded)
2   tsp white pepper
3   tbsp vinegar
1/2 tsp salt
1   tbsp cornstarch, dissolved in 3 tbsp water
1   egg, beaten
1   tsp sesame oil
2   tbsp chopped green onions

Mix meat with cornstarch, soy sauce, hot sauce, and sugar; set aside to marinate. In a large pot, combine chicken broth and mushroom strips. Bring to a boil over high heat. Add meat, and while stirring, bring to a second boil. Add pepper, vinegar, and salt. Boil about 1 1/2 minutes. Add dissolved cornstarch and stir until slightly thickened. Very slowly pour in beaten egg, stirring constantly. Add sesame oil, stir well, and serve immediately. Garnish each serving with green onion.

Nancy Chang
Taiwan, China

Mushroom Vegetable Soup

1   tbsp butter
3   onions, sliced mushrooms, sliced
7   cloves garlic, coarsely ground
2   segments capsicum, cut into thin strips
500 ml water
100 grams
2   tomatoes, skinned and chopped
     Salt and pepper to taste
75   grams grated cheese
1   tbsp coriander leaves, chopped

Heat butter; add onions and garlic, and sauté; do not brown. Add capsicum and sauté. Add water and bring to a boil. Add tomatoes and mushrooms; cook until tender. Add salt and pepper to taste. Serve topped with coriander leaves and cheese.

Romy Talewar
India

Tom Yum

1/2 kg shrimps (fish or meat can be used)
6   c water
3   stalks lemongrass or tanglad (leaves only)
6   thin slices of white ginger
1/2 tsp salt
1   onion, chopped
1   pc tomato, chopped
1/2 c calamansi juice
1   c fresh button mushrooms, halved
4   tbsp patis (fish sauce)
4-8 pc chili, lightly crushed
1/8 c wansuy, chopped

Wash and trim shrimps. Devein but keep the shell intact. Set aside. Make a broth by boiling water and adding lemongrass, white ginger, salt, onion, tomato, and calamansi juice. Cover and simmer 15-20 minutes. Add shrimps and simmer until they turn pink. Add mushroom and season with patis. Before serving, put chili at the bottom of a bowl, depending on desired degree of hotness. Fill bowl with soup. Decorate with wansuy. Yield: 6 servings.

Cheli Banta (Philippines)
Thailand

Tomato Soup

1   kg ripe tomatoes, cut into large pieces
250 grams carrots, peeled and cut into large
     pieces
2   c chicken stock
1   c milk
2   c water (if needed to thin the soup later)
1/2 c cream
1/2 c fried bread cubes
1/4 c grated cheese
     Salt and pepper to taste

Steam tomatoes and carrots in chicken stock in a pressure cooker for 3 minutes. Cool, then blend vegetables. Heat milk and add blended vegetables; add water if necessary. Add salt and pepper. Boil for 2 minutes. Serve hot with grated cheese, bread cubes, and cream.

Mohinder K. Singh
India

Burmese Sweet Soup

1/2 kg chicken
1   tsp salt
1   small head cauliflower
4   cabbage leaves
5   green beans
2   tomatoes
3   onions
2   pods garlic
1/2 c bean sprouts
1/2 c vegetable oil
3   c water
1   tsp Knorr seasoning
2   pints boiling water
1   tsp MSG
     Salt to taste
2   eggs, unbeaten
     Pepper to taste

Cut chicken into small pieces and season with 1 tsp salt. Slice vegetables except bean sprouts into medium-size pieces. Cook chicken in oil with 3 cups water. When tender, add vegetables and Knorr seasoning. Cook 10 minutes. When vegetables are half-tender, add 2 pints boiling water and MSG, salt to taste, eggs, and pepper to taste.

Lily Khin Win
Myanmar

Bean Soup

30 grams cooking oil
2 kg beans
  Pinch of salt
3 c coconut milk (optional)
20 grams onions
10 grams curry powder

Wash beans, then cook until tender. Sauté onions with curry powder; add salt and coconut milk. When mixture boils, add beans; stir and cook until done. Serve with rice, ugali, or boiled sweet potatoes.

Eva Kanyeka
Tanzania

German Pea Soup

3 slices streaky bacon, diced
1 large onion, sliced
1 large carrot, sliced
75 grams celery, sliced
1 ham bone, soaked overnight
400 grams peas, soaked overnight
1 tbsp salt
  Some pepper
1/2 tbsp dried thyme
2 bay leaves
1.5 liters hot water
1 kg potatoes, peeled and soaked in water

In large saucepan, fry bacon in its own fat until lightly brown. Drain. Sauté sliced vegetables in same fat, until onion is tender. Return bacon to the pan and add ham bone, peas, seasonings, herbs, and water. Cover and bring to a boil. Reduce heat and simmer for about 1 hour or until peas are tender. Remove bay leaves. While soup is simmering, cut potatoes into cubes and boil in salted water until tender. Remove ham bone; cut off any meat and add to soup. Lastly, add boiled potatoes.

NOTE: You can add smoked sausages, one for each person, if you like. Instead of peas you can use lentils or beans.

Uschi Neue
Germany

Gingered Carrot Soup

4	tbsp butter
1	c chopped onion
2	tsp grated fresh ginger
1	clove garlic
4	c chopped carrots
1	medium potato, chopped
4	c water
1 1/2	tbsp brown sugar or honey
1/4	c lemon juice
1/2	tsp salt
1	jalapeno pepper, seeded and minced (optional)

Sauté onions in butter in a large pot. When translucent, add ginger and a split clove of garlic and stir well. Add carrots, potatoes, and water. Cover and cook until tender, about 20 minutes. Puree the mixture in a blender or food processor. Add lemon juice, honey, and salt. Garnish with minced hot pepper or a sprig of parsley. Serves 4-6.

Judy Buresh
USA

Bean Curd and Meatball Soup

1	tbsp cooking oil
3	cloves garlic, minced
4	c stock
3	pc soft bean curd, cut into cubes
1 1/2	tsp salt
1/2	tsp MSG
	Dash of pepper
1	stalk spring onions, chopped
1	stalk coriander leaves, chopped

For meatball

1	c minced meat
1	tsp light soy sauce
2	tsp sugar
1	tsp MSG
2	tsp tapioca flour
	Salt to taste

Mix all ingredients for meatball and form small marble-size balls. Set aside. Heat oil in a pan; sauté garlic until slightly brown. Put meatballs in stock, and bring to a boil; add bean curd, salt, MSG, and pepper. Simmer for another 10 minutes. Garnish with spring onion and coriander leaves. Serve hot.

Harmit Wasan
Singapore

Curry and Oat Soup

1/2	c lentils
1/4	c oil
2	tsp cumin seeds
2	cloves garlic, chopped
2	c onion, chopped
2	tbsp tomato paste
2	tbsp curry powder
6	c stock
1 1/2	tsp or more red pepper (cayenne pepper)
2	tsp salt
1	c carrots, diced
1	c green pepper, chopped
2/3	c oatmeal (not instant type)
50	grams yoghurt

Wash and soak lentils in water. Heat oil and add cumin seeds. When seeds start to crackle, add garlic and onion; sauté over medium heat for 10 minutes or until onion is transparent and light brown. Add tomato paste; mix well. Add curry powder, red pepper, salt, carrots, and drained lentils. Sauté for 2 minutes. Add stock and bring to a boil. Then lower the heat, and simmer, covered, for 40 minutes. Add green pepper and oatmeal; simmer for 10 more minutes. Top each portion with 2 tbsp yoghurt. Serves 8.

Yokiko Vaughan (Japan)
UK

Cream of Zucchini Soup

1	onion, chopped
1/4	c butter
3	c chicken stock
6	medium zucchinis, sliced
1/4	c white wine
	Celery leaves
	Parsley
	Dash of thyme
1 1/2	c light cream
	Salt and pepper to taste

Sauté onions in butter until soft and golden. Add stock, zucchini, a few celery leaves, parsley, and thyme. Simmer until zucchini is soft. Purée in a blender. Add wine, cream, salt, and pepper to taste.

Caren Hill
USA

Cuttlefish Salad

1   cuttlefish
2   large onions
3   stalks green onions
2   sprigs fresh coriander

Dressing
2   cloves garlic, minced
2   pc stems of fresh coriander
5-6 chilies or
1   tsp chili powder
2   tbsp lime juice or calamansi juice
2   tbsp fish sauce (patis)

Clean cuttlefish and cut into 2- × 1/2-inch pieces. Slice onions lengthwise. Cut green onion into 1-inch pieces. Cook cuttlefish in boiling water for a few minutes. Drain well; set aside. Prepare dressing in a bowl; add cuttlefish, and white and green onions. Arrange on serving plate (lined with lettuce, if desired). Decorate with fresh coriander leaves.

NOTE: This can be served together with other dishes or as a main course.

Visaka Panditya
Thailand

Cranberry Salad

2   3-oz packages raspberry gelatin
1   tsp salt
2   c hot water
1   c cold water
3   tsp lemon juice
1/2 c chopped nuts
2   c whole berries
     Cranberry sauce
1   c canned crushed pineapple, drained

Dissolve gelatin and salt in hot water. Add cold water, and lemon juice, and chill. When slightly thickened, add the rest of the ingredients. Spoon into a mold or bowl and chill until firm. 12 servings.

Judy Buresh
USA

Causa Salad

4   tsp lemon juice
1   onion, finely chopped
      Salt and pepper to taste
1   tsp chili
1 1/2 kg potatoes
1   tsp oil
10   black olives
3   hard-boiled eggs, chopped
1/2   kg fresh cheese, cubed

Mix lemon juice with onion, salt, pepper, and chili. Boil potatoes, peel and mash very well. Add marinated onion mixture; beat with fork to make a smooth paste.

Gradually add oil (adjust seasoning, if necessary). Place mixture in a mold. Garnish with olives, chopped hard-boiled eggs, or cubed cheese.

Cecilia Chujoy
Peru

Goi-Ga (Chicken and Cabbage Salad)

1   lb chicken
1   lb white cabbage
1   green pepper

Sweet and sour sauce
4   tbsp vinegar
4   tbsp sugar
2   tbsp shredded onion
12   peppercorns
1   tsp garlic

Boil chicken until tender. Remove bones and shred meat, cabbage, and green pepper. Mix. Prepare sweet and sour sauce: combine vinegar and sugar; stir until sugar has melted. Add peppercorn, garlic, and onion. Pour mixture over meat, cabbage, and green pepper. Mix thoroughly until well blended. Serve immediately.

Tham Aurin
Vietnam

Buco-Pineapple Salad

10   buco (young coconut) grated
1   big can pineapple tidbits
1   small can nata de coco
1/2   small can Nestlé cream
1   small can condensed milk (optional)

Combine all ingredients; chill for 5 to 7 hours before serving.

Cheli Banta
Philippines

Green Mango Salad

2   green mangoes
1/2   c vegetable oil
6   onions, sliced
3   cloves garlic, minced
4   tbsp dry prawns
2   tbsp patis (fish sauce)
1   tsp MSG

Peel mangoes; cut into thin slices; soak in salted water. Heat oil; sauté onion and garlic until brown and crisp. Remove from oil and keep in an airtight bottle. Pound dry prawns and set aside. Drain mangoes and mix with the rest of the ingredients including pounded prawns. Top with fried onions.

Lily Khin Win
Myanmar

Cebiche

2   lb white fish
3   fresh chilies
3   medium onions, sliced
2   tbsp ground chili
      Juice of 10 small lemons
      Juice of 2 oranges (optional)
      Salt and pepper to taste
1   head lettuce
2   large cooked corn ears
2   lb cooked sweet potatoes

Clean fish; cut into cubes. Chop chili after removing seed. Put fish in a large colander and pour boiling water over the pieces. Shake fish well and put in another bowl; add onion, chili, fresh chilies, lemon juice, orange juice, salt, and pepper. Cover tightly and marinate 3 hours until fish is cooked (white but not transparent). Serve with lettuce leaves, corn ears, and sweet potatoes.

Cecilia Chujoy
Peru

Tabouli

1   c parsley
2   small onions
1/4 c olive oil
1   c tomatoes, chopped
1/4 c fresh mint, chopped
1/2 c cracked wheat (fine wheat germ)
    Salt and pepper to taste
1/2 c lemon juice

Wash parsley very well; chop fine. Put in a colander and squeeze out excess water. Spread out to dry further on paper towel.

Cut onions and tomatoes. Mix with parsley. Soak cracked wheat in water for 3 minutes, then squeeze to remove excess water. Add salt, pepper, chopped mint, olive oil, and lemon juice. Mix all very well.

NOTE: Tabouli should be sour enough to give a lemon flavor.

Katia Sayegh
Lebanon

Sweet and Sour Fruit Salad

3   c fruit cocktail (preferably fresh fruit)
1   c sweet potato, boiled and cubed
1/2 c potato, boiled and cubed
1/2 c calamansi juice
1   tsp cumin powder
    Salt to taste
    Pinch of pepper
    Pinch of paprika
1/4 c tamarind juice
2   tbsp brown sugar
1/2 tsp chili powder

Mix fruit cocktail with sweet potatoes and potatoes. Add the rest of the spices, calamansi juice, tamarind juice or pulp, and brown sugar. Mix and toss well before serving.

Indu Virmani
India

Carrot-Raisin Salad

2	c shredded raw carrots
1/2	c raisins
1/4	c mayonnaise
1/4	c low-fat yoghurt
2	tbsp lemon juice
1/8	tsp salt

Combine raisins and carrots. Mix together mayonnaise, yoghurt, lemon juice, and salt. Pour over salad and mix. Serves 6.

Judy Buresh
USA

Greek Salad

5	large tomatoes
1	medium onion
4	long green peppers
4	cucumbers
1/4	c fresh parsley
1/3	c black olives
1/4	c cheddar cheese

Dressing

1/4	c olive oil
1/4	c vinegar
1	tsp salt
5	drops tabasco sauce
1/2	tsp mustard sauce

Cut tomatoes into wedges; slice onions thinly. Cut pepper into rings; slice cucumber. Mix all ingredients and refrigerate. Mix all dressing ingredients; put in an airtight jar and refrigerate. Before serving, shake dressing well and add to salad.

Vivi Moridis
Greece

Potato Yoghurt Salad

2	small potatoes
1	c yoghurt
1/2	c cold water or fresh milk
1/4	tsp roasted cumin powder
	Pinch of paprika
	Salt and pepper to taste
1	tsp chopped fresh coriander leaves
1	tsp fresh mint leaves or sprig of mint

Boil potatoes; peel and cut into cubes. Beat yoghurt; add water or milk and mix well. Add potatoes, then the rest of the spices. Garnish with fresh coriander leaves or mint leaves.

Indu Virmani
India

Cucumber Yoghurt Salad

3/4 c shredded cucumber
1/4 c shredded carrots
1 c yoghurt
1/2 c fresh milk or cold water
1 green chili (optional)
1/2 tsp roasted cumin powder
1/4 tsp paprika
Salt and pepper to taste

Beat yoghurt with beater or fork; add cold milk or water. Combine cucumbers, carrots, and yoghurt. Add rest of the spices. Pour dressing over the vegetables. Garnish with fresh coriander or mint leaves.

Indu Virmani
India

Sushi Salad

2 1/2 c medium-grain rice
6 tbsp vinegar (preferably Japanese rice vinegar)
3 tbsp oil
1 tbsp sugar
1 tsp salt
1 tbsp fresh ginger, grated
4 c lettuce, shredded
1/2 c parsley, chopped
1 can water-packed tuna, drained
1 c shrimps, cooked and shelled
2/3 c black olives, sliced
1 c radish, sliced
2 c tomatoes, quartered

Cook rice in 4 cups water. Prepare dressing by mixing vinegar, oil, sugar, salt, and ginger. While rice is still hot, mix with 3/4 of the dressing. Cool rice. Toss lettuce with remaining dressing. To rice, add tuna, shrimp, lettuce, black olives, radish, and half the parsley. Mix gently. Place in a serving bowl and top with tomatoes and remaining parsley. Serves 6.

Michiko Hibino
Japan

Gado Gado (Indonesian Salad)

1	lb kangkong (Chinese spinach or kale)		
1	lb long beans		
1	lb cabbage		
1	lb bamboo shoots		
2	cucumbers		
3	bean curds		
3	potatoes		
3	hard-boiled eggs		
24	small red onions		
1	lb krupuk		

Sauce

20 dried chilies (or 20 fresh red chilies)
5   green chilies
5   small onions
4   cloves garlic
2   tsp shrimp paste (optional)
3   oz brown sugar
3   c coconut milk
1/4 c tamarind or lime juice
2   lb peanuts, toasted and ground

Boil kangkong about 2 minutes. Cut long beans into pieces and boil until tender. Slice cabbage and boil until tender. Scald bamboo shoots and rinse. Peel and slice cucumbers. Fry and slice bean curd. Boil and slice potatoes. Slice hard-boiled eggs. Fry sliced onions until light brown. Fry krupuk.

Grind chilies, onions, and garlic with shrimp paste. Sauté spices in 2 tbsp oil, then add sugar, coconut milk, and tamarind or lime juice to taste. Bring to a boil, then add ground peanuts. Arrange vegetables on a platter or bowl and pour sauce over them. Add krupuk and fried onions as garnish.

Lucy Tappan (USA)
Indonesia

Vegetables

Cauliflower Medley

1 medium-size cauliflower
25 grams butter
4 shallots or a bunch of
   spring onions
1/2 c mayonnaise
2 tbsp crunchy peanut butter
1 tbsp lemon juice
1/4 c cream
1 hard-boiled egg
2-3 tbsp chopped parsley
3/4 c soft fresh bread crumbs
75 grams grated cheddar cheese

Wash and separate cauliflower into florets. Cook in lightly salted water until tender and firm. Drain well. Melt butter, sauté chopped onions or shallots for 1 minute.

Place cauliflower in buttered shallow ovenproof dish. Sprinkle spring onion or shallots over cauliflower

Combine mayonnaise, peanut butter, lemon juice, and cream. Spread over cauliflower, then sprinkle grated hard-boiled egg over it. Combine bread crumbs, grated cheese, and parsley and sprinkle over the layer of egg and cauliflower. Dot with butter. Bake at 180 °C (350 °F) for 15 minutes or grill until cheese is puffed and golden.

Marlene Quick
Australia

Cauliflower with Potatoes

1 kg cauliflower
1/4 kg potatoes
1/2 c corn oil for frying
1/4 c corn oil for cooking
3 medium-size chopped onions
1/2 tsp cumin seeds
1/2 tsp minced garlic
1 tsp grated ginger
1/4 tsp turmeric powder
1 tsp coriander powder
1 tsp curry powder
4 medium tomatoes, chopped
1/2 tsp salt
   Fresh coriander leaves

Wash cauliflower well. Cut into small pieces. Peel potatoes, slice lengthwise into 4 pieces, and wash. Fry cauliflower and potatoes separately till half-cooked.

Heat oil in a wok on high flame. Add cumin seeds and chopped onions. Cook for a few minutes. Add garlic and ginger, cook for 5 minutes on low heat. Add 2 tbsp water and cook a few minutes more. Add turmeric powder, coriander powder, curry powder, tomatoes, and salt. Cook for 5 minutes. Add cauliflower and potatoes and stir for a few minutes. Add 2 tbsp more water and cover. Cook on low flame till done. Sprinkle fresh coriander leaves on top and serve with any kind of bread like chapatin or panis. Serves 4 to 5.

Indu Virmani
India

Cauliflower Curry

1 tbsp corn oil
1/4 tsp cumin seeds
5 small pieces of ginger
1 tbsp butter
1 medium-size cauliflower, separated into florets
2 medium-size potatoes, quartered
1/4 tsp turmeric powder
Salt to taste
1/2 c chopped tomatoes
1 tsp coriander powder
Pinch of red chili powder
Pinch of crushed black pepper
Coriander leaves

Heat oil in a saucepan; add cumin seeds and sauté till they turn black. Add ginger pieces and brown them. Add butter. Add cauliflower and potatoes and cook, covered, on high heat for 5 minutes. Add turmeric powder and reduce flame. Cook for a few minutes in covered pan. Add salt, tomatoes, and rest of dry spices. Cook until done. Garnish with chopped fresh coriander leaves.

Savi Singh
India

Kisanvu (Cassava Leaves)

1 kg tender cassava leaves
30 grams cooking oil
20 grams onions
10 grams curry powder (optional)
1 c coconut milk or peanut butter
Pinch of salt

Pound cassava leaves in a mortar until very fine. Boil water, then add salt and pounded cassava leaves, stirring constantly until done. Set aside. Sauté onions and curry powder. Add coconut milk or peanut butter. When mixture is boiling, add cooked cassava leaves; stir for sometime, then remove from fire. Serve with rice or ugali.

Eva Kanyeka
Tanzania

Mchicha (Spinach or Amaranthus)

1   kg spinach
3   tbsp oil
20 grams onions
30 grams tomatoes
1   tsp salt
10 grams curry powder
30 grams peanut butter or
1   c coconut milk

Wash spinach, then cut into small pieces. Sauté onion, tomatoes, salt, and curry powder. Add spinach. When cooked, add peanut butter or coconut milk. Cook stirring so that mixture will not stick to the cooking pot. Serve with rice or ugali. Serves 4.

Eva Kanyeka
Tanzania

Cabbage Rolls

2   tbsp oil
2   medium onions, diced
1   small green pepper, diced
1/2 c tomato paste
1/4 tsp oregano
1/2 c water
2   bay leaves
1   tsp salt
6   large cabbage leaves
6   vegelinks (sausages)
250 grams cheddar cheese, cut in strips

Sauté onions and green pepper in oil till lightly browned. Add tomato paste, oregano, and water; mix thoroughly.

Season to taste (place bay leaves in sauce, remove when serving). Wash cabbage leaves, cook in salted water 5 minutes after boiling starts, or until leaves are limp; drain. Split vegelink lengthwise, but not all the way through. Fill with cheese strips. Roll a cabbage leaf around each vegelink. Place rolls in greased casserole and pour tomato sauce over. Bake in moderate oven at 180 °C (350 °F) for 30 minutes. Serves 6.

Marlene Quick
Australia

Turnip Curry

3   tbsp cooking oil
    Pinch of fennel seeds
1/2 kg turnips, sliced
1/2 tsp turmeric powder
    Salt to taste
1/2 tsp ground cumin seeds
3/4 c evaporated milk
1/4 tsp crushed red chili
2   tbsp chopped coriander leaves

Heat oil in a pan. Add fennel seeds and turnips. Sauté, stirring, for 4 minutes over medium heat. Add salt, turmeric powder, and cumin powder. Cover and cook over low heat until turnips soften. Drain excess oil from sauce. Add evaporated milk and cook over medium heat for a while. Remove from stove, garnish with chili and coriander leaves. Serve with rice or bread. Serves 4 to 6.

Kumari Pingali
India

Spinach Squares

2   packages (10 oz each) frozen chopped
    spinach
3   tbsp butter
1   small onion, chopped
1/2 c sliced mushrooms
4   eggs
1   can condensed cream of mushroom soup
    Pepper, dry basil, oregano to taste
1/4 c fine dry bread crumbs
1/4 c grated gruyere cheese (parmesan)

Squeeze out as much moisture from spinach as possible. Set aside. Melt butter in frying pan; add onion and mushrooms, and cook, stirring, until soft. In a large bowl, beat eggs lightly. Stir in onion-mushroom mixture, bread crumbs, soup, 2 tbsp cheese, pepper, basil, oregano, and spinach. Grease a 9-inch square baking pan. Pour mixture into the pan; sprinkle with remaining cheese. Bake in 325 °F oven for about 35 minutes or until golden brown.

NOTE: These tasty squares can be offered hot or cold, as a side dish, appetizer, or first course.

Heidi Graf
Switzerland

Spicy Fried Kangkong

400 grams kangkong
3 tbsp cooking oil
3 fresh red chilies
3 candlenuts
8 shallots
1 tsp shrimp paste
60 grams dried shrimps, pounded coarsely
Salt to taste

Break off kangkong leaves; cut tender parts of the stalks into 3-inch-long pieces. Discard woody parts. Pound together chilies, candlenuts, shallots, and shrimp paste. Heat oil in the frying pan and fry pounded spices until fragrant. Add dried shrimps and cook another minute. Add kangkong and sauté until just done. Add a little water, if necessary, and salt to taste. Cook for a while. Remove from fire, and serve.

Siew-Fing Wong
Malaysia

Fried Okra with Sauce

3 tbsp oil
1/2 kg okra, cut lengthwise into 4 pieces
1/4 tsp turmeric powder
Salt to taste
4 big onions, sliced
3 cloves garlic, crushed
5 tomatoes, chopped
2 tbsp water
1 tsp coriander powder
1 tsp curry powder
1/4 c cooking oil

Heat oil in frying pan. Add okra, turmeric powder, and salt. Sauté all on medium heat until okra is golden brown. Remove from fire and drain oil from okra. In another pan heat oil, and sauté onions till golden brown. Add garlic and tomatoes. Cook for a few minutes; add 2 tbsp water and spices. Cook sauce very well. Add okra, cover pan, and cook on low heat for 20 minutes. Serve with any kind of bread, Serves 4 to 5.

Indu Virmani
India

Zucchini with Oyster Sauce

3   tbsp vegetable oil
1/2 kg zucchini, unpeeled
1   c chicken broth
1   tsp cornstarch
3   tsp oyster sauce
2   stalks of green onion cut in 2-inch lengths

Heat oil in a wok; add zucchini. Stir for a minute. Mix chicken broth with cornstarch and add to zucchini; cook, stirring well.

Add oyster sauce and green onion. Mix all very well. Remove from fire and serve.

Nancy Chang (Taiwan)
China

Tomato Omelet

5   green chilies
1/2- inch piece ginger
5-6 pc garlic
     Coriander leaves
2   c besan (yellow split pea flour)
2   big tomatoes, chopped fine
1   onion, chopped
1   tsp cumin powder
.1   tsp coriander seed powder
     Salt to taste
     A pinch of baking powder
     Oil for shallow frying

Make a paste of chilies, ginger, garlic, and coriander leaves in a grinder. To the besan, add paste, onions, tomatoes, cumin powder, coriander powder, salt, and baking powder. Add 3/4 to 1 cup water. Set aside batter for 10 minutes. Heat 3 tsp oil in a frying pan. When sufficiently hot, pour 1/4 cup batter at a time. Fry both sides. Serve hot.

Smita Gadgil
India

Roasted Potatoes

3   baking potatoes, sliced 3/8-inch thick
1/4 c butter or margarine, melted
1   clove garlic, minced
1/2 tsp salt
1/2 tsp ground pepper
1/4 tsp thyme

Preheat oven to 450 °F. Arrange potato slices in a jelly roll pan. In a bowl, combine all other ingredients and drizzle over potatoes. Bake 25 minutes. Makes 4 servings.

Marlene Smith
USA

Hvancaina (Potatoes)

8   potatoes (yellow is better), cooked
8   lettuce leaves
1/2 lb fresh cheese (white cheese)
2   chilies (seeds removed)
1/2 c evaporated milk
1/2 tsp ground paprika
    Pinch of salt and pepper
1   c oil
2   ears of corn, sliced and boiled
8   black olives
2   onions, sliced
2   tbsp lemon juice

Peel potatoes and cut in halves. Arrange on lettuce leaves in a dish. Liquefy the fresh cheese and chili. Add milk, paprika, salt, and pepper. Form a smooth paste.

Heat oil in a skillet and add paste, stirring constantly. Lower heat when all is well mixed. Pour sauce over potato. Garnish with corn slices and olives. Serve cold with onion sauce, prepared by slicing onions and seasoning with lemon juice, salt, pepper, and chili. Makes 8 servings.

Cecilia Chujoy
Peru

Oven French Fries

4   medium potatoes
1   tbsp oil

Preheat oven to 475 °F. Peel potatoes and cut into long strips about 1/2 inch wide. Dry strips thoroughly. Toss in a bowl with oil as if making a salad. When thoroughly coated with oil, spread strips in a single layer on a cookie sheet and bake for 35 minutes. Turn strips periodically to brown on all sides. If you want to make strips more crispy, brown potatoes under a broiler for a minute or two. Sprinkle with salt before serving. Serves 6.

Judy Buresh
USA

Tomato with Spring Onions

2   c yoghurt
1   tbsp oil
1/2   tsp mustard seeds
       Few curry leaves
1/4-   inch pc ginger, chopped
1   green chili, chopped
1   medium onion, cut into round slices
1/2   green onions with leaves, chopped
1   c tomatoes, chopped
       Salt to taste
1   tbsp coriander leaves, chopped

Mix yoghurt with salt and beat till smooth. Heat oil in a frying pan; add mustard seeds, curry leaves, ginger, and green chili. Add onions and sauté for 2-3 minutes. Add tomatoes and sauté for 1 more minute. Remove from fire and add yoghurt. Turn into a serving bowl and garnish with coriander leaves.

Usha Ladha
India

Broccoli-Carrot Casserole

1 kg fresh broccoli
1/4 c butter
   Salt and pepper to taste
1 can baby carrots
1 can cream of mushroom
   soup
1 c sour cream
1 onion, minced
1/2 c grated cheese
1/2 c crushed crackers

Cut broccoli into bite-size pieces; boil in salted water then drain. Add butter, salt, and pepper. Place in a greased casserole together with carrots. Mix mushroom soup, sour cream, and minced onion. Pour mixture over broccoli and carrots. Bake at 325 °F, uncovered, until bubbly—about 30 minutes. Top with grated cheese and crackers. Return to oven until cheese melts.

Harmit Wasan
Singapore

Mushrooms with Sauce

150 grams mushroom
45 grams butter
1 tbsp lemon juice
1/2 liter strained beef broth (or broth made
   from beef cubes)
35 grams flour
   Pepper
2 tbsp dry white wine (optional)
1 egg yolk
2 tbsp cream

Clean mushrooms; slice and sauté in 10 grams butter and lemon juice for about 5 minutes. Add broth and boil for 5 more minutes. Use 15 grams butter and flour to make a thick sauce: on moderate heat melt butter, stir in flour, add broth little by little while stirring constantly. Strain when all broth is added and sauce boils. Add pepper, wine, and salt, if desired. Mix some of hot sauce with egg yolk, then add to sauce. Add cream and mushrooms.

NOTE: Can be served with light boiled meat, eggs, mashed potatoes, rice, spaghetti, or white beans.

Cobie Penning de Vries
The Netherlands

Hotspot (Mixture of Carrots, Onions, and Potatoes)

1 1/2	kg thick carrots
1/2	kg white onions
2	kg potatoes
	Pinch of nutmeg
80	grams butter
1	c boiled milk
1/2	tsp salt
	Pinch of pepper

Cut carrots into small pieces, slice onions, peel potatoes. Put all in a large casserole. Add water to cover 3/4 of the vegetables.

Boil everything until tender (about 25 minutes). Mash all vegetables together. Add the rest of the ingredients. Serve with beef stew ("hachee"), fried chicken, or fish fillet.

Cobie Penning de Vries
The Netherlands

Eggplant Casserole

1	kg eggplants, thinly sliced (sprinkle little salt while cutting)
2	cloves minced garlic
1	chopped onion
1	small can tomato sauce
1	tsp oregano
1	tsp thyme
2	c water
1/2	c grated cheese (quick melt)
	Salt and black pepper to taste
	Oil
	Flour
1	tbsp tamarind sauce (optional)

Dip eggplants in flour and salt, then fry lightly. In same frying pan, sauté onions and garlic till golden brown. Add tomato sauce, oregano, thyme, and black pepper. Add water and simmer for 30 minutes. Place eggplant in layers in a casserole. Cover each layer with sauce and cheese. Top with tamarind sauce. Cover casserole with foil and bake at 350 °F for 20-30 minutes.

Indu Virmani (India)
USA

Sweet and Sour Eggplant

1/2 kg eggplants
1/2 c oil for frying
1/2 tsp chili powder
1 tbsp water
1/4 tsp cumin seeds

2 cloves
1/4 tsp curry powder
1 tsp tamarind pulp
1/2 c water

Slice eggplants into 1-inch-long pieces. Heat oil, fry slices until deep brown. Remove from pan and set aside. Pour 1 tbsp oil in a pan; add chili powder, sprinkle 1 tbsp water, and leave pan on low flame for 5 minutes. Add cumin seeds and cloves, stir for a while; add curry powder and tamarind pulp, stir again. Add 1/2 cup water and let boil; add fried eggplants and cook till water evaporates completely. Serve hot with bread or rice.

Shashi Raina
India

Eggplant-Mushroom Casserole

1 kg eggplants
1/4 c onion cube
1/2 tsp chili powder (optional)
2 tsp ground ginger
1 1/2 tsp cumin powder
1-2 tsp paprika
1-2 tsp chili, chopped
2 tbsp oil
1/2 c cheddar cheese cubes
1/2-1 c sliced button mushroom
2 eggs
Bread crumbs
Butter

Boil eggplants. Peel and mash very well. Combine all ingredients except bread crumbs and butter. Put in a greased casserole. Top with buttered crumbs. Bake at 375 °F for 30 minutes or until top is golden brown.

Fauzi Bhuiyan
Bangladesh

Eggplant with Yoghurt

2 medium eggplants
3 tbsp oil or ghee
2 medium onions, finely chopped
3 cloves garlic, finely chopped
2 tsp finely grated fresh ginger
   Salt to taste
   Pepper to taste
1/2 tsp coriander powder
1/2 tsp ground turmeric powder
1/2 tsp chili powder
1/2 tsp garam masala (curry powder)
1 c yoghurt
2 tsp ground cumin powder

Roast eggplants 6 inches away from flame till skin is blackened and eggplants are soft. Cool and peel, then mash or chop into small pieces. Sauté onions, garlic, and pepper till onions are soft and golden.

Add coriander, cumin powder, turmeric, chili powder, and ginger; sauté, stirring, for 1 minute. Add salt and mashed eggplants. Stir and cook for a few minutes. Sprinkle garam masala, cover and cook for 5 more minutes. Beat yoghurt till smooth and add to eggplant before serving. Serve with rice and curries.

Durga Pathak
India

Eggplant Curry

1/2 kg eggplants
4-5 tomatoes
5 green chilies
5 big onions
1 tsp black pepper
2 tsp curry powder
2 tbsp calamansi juice
   Salt to taste
1 c thick coconut milk

Cut eggplants into 5- × 1-cm pieces, and deep-fry till light brown (about 10 minutes). Remove from oil. Cut tomatoes into 4-6 pieces, chilies into 2 pieces, and onions into round slices. Mix these spices with fried eggplants and add pepper, salt, calamansi juice, and curry powder. Place eggplant mixture in a pot, then add coconut milk. Cook curry 5-8 minutes until coconut milk is concentrated.

Tilaka Senanayake
Sri Lanka

Spicy Stuffed Eggplant

1 kg medium-size eggplants
3 tbsp butter or margarine
1 tbsp snipped parsley
1/3 c chopped onions
1 clove garlic, minced
3/4 c soft bread crumbs
1/4 c chopped olives
1/4 tsp chili powder
1/2 tbsp dried basil
2 tbsp lemon juice
3/4 c shredded cheese
2 tbsp cooking oil
4-6 tomatoes, sliced

Halve eggplants lengthwise. Scoop out and reserve pulp, leaving 1/4-inch-thick shells. Boil shells for 2 minutes or till tender, and drain. Chop uncooked pulp fine, and cook in butter with onion, garlic, and parsley till tender. Remove from flame and add all other ingredients except tomatoes. Stuff shells with this mixture, then arrange in a greased casserole. Cover and bake at 350 °F for 20 minutes. Top with tomato slices and brush with oil. Bake uncovered for 5-10 more minutes.

Durga Pathak
India

Sambal Buncis (Green Beans in Coconut Milk)

1 c chopped onions
1 clove garlic, minced
2 tsp grated lemon rind
1 tsp dried, ground chili
1 tomato, peeled and chopped
4 tbsp oil
1 lb green beans, French style
1 tsp salt
1 tsp sugar
1 bay leaf
1 c coconut milk

Pound or chop to a paste the onions, garlic, lemon rind, chilies, and tomato. Heat oil in a saucepan; sauté the mixture for 3 minutes, stirring almost constantly. Add the rest of the ingredients. Bring to a boil, cover loosely, and cook over low heat for 15 minutes. Cool.

Lucy Tappan (USA)
Indonesia

Rhamadan Vegetable Delight

1/4	kg ground French beans
1/4	kg ground carrots
1/4	kg grated potatoes
1/4	kg cabbage, chopped coarsely
1/4	kg cauliflower
1-2	tbsp vegetable oil
1	tbsp tomato paste
3-4	pc onion, sliced
1/2	kg beef tenderloin, cut into cubes
1/2	tsp black pepper
4-5	pc green bell pepper
1/4-1/2	c water
1	tsp salt

Sauté vegetables separately for 2-3 minutes. Sauté onions and tomato paste in vegetable oil; add beef and fry until beef is done. Add vegetables and simmer for 2-5 minutes. Add green and black pepper with a pinch of salt and some water. Simmer 5 more minutes. Serve hot with bread, brown rice, or any African maize dish.

Djokoto
Ghana

Vegetable Tempura

1	sweet potato	1	eggplant
1	small carrot		Corn oil for frying
12	Baguio beans	2	tbsp grated radish
4	small bell peppers	1	tbsp grated ginger

Batter

1	c flour
1	tsp baking powder
1	egg
6	tbsp water

Sauce

1/4	tsp monosodium glutamate
1/4	c hot water
4	tbsp Kikkoman soy sauce
4	tbsp Mirin or sherry
1/2	tsp sugar

Peel sweet potato, slice 1/4-inch thick, soak in water for 10 minutes, then drain well. Peel carrot, cut in half lengthwise, then in 1/4-inch slices lengthwise; make notches at 1/4-inch intervals leaving 1/2 inch uncut at the bottom. String Baguio beans and cut each into 3. Cut eggplant into 4 lengthwise; remove stem and seeds.

Prepare batter. Sift flour with baking powder; add beaten egg and water (more water can be added if batter is too thick). Mix well and refrigerate.

Prepare dipping sauce by mixing MSG and hot water. Then add all other sauce ingredients.

Heat corn oil to 180 °C (determine by adding a drop of the batter; if batter drops to the bottom of the pan and then immediately floats, the oil has reached the desired temperature).

Dip vegetables in batter and deep-fry until coating is golden yellow. Serve tempura with grated radish and ginger, and dipping sauce. Makes 4 servings.

Koko Watanabe
Japan

Split Peas with Zucchini

1	c split peas
1/4	tsp chili powder
1/4	tsp turmeric powder
1	tsp salt
1	medium-size zucchini, peeled and cut into 1-inch cubes
1 1/2	tbsp corn oil
1/4	tsp cumin seeds
1	tsp finely chopped ginger
1	big onion, finely chopped
1/2	c peeled and chopped tomatoes
1	tsp roasted cumin powder
	Fresh coriander leaves

In a saucepan bring 3 cups water to a boil. Wash split peas, add to boiling water with turmeric, chili powder, and salt. Reduce heat and partly cover the pan. When peas are half-done, add zucchini and tomatoes and continue cooking until peas are soft. Remove from fire.

In a pan, heat oil and sauté cumin seeds until brown. Add ginger and onion, and sauté until golden brown. Pour peas over fried onions and cover. Sprinkle roasted cumin powder on top. Garnish with fresh coriander leaves. Serve with piping hot rice or with chapati.

Savi Singh
India

Peas and Potato Curry

6	medium-size potatoes
2	medium-size onions
1	green chili
1/2-inch	pc ginger
4	tomatoes
3	tbsp oil
1/2	tsp cumin seeds
1/2	tsp chili powder
1/2	tsp turmeric powder
1/2	tsp garam masala
2	tsp coriander powder
1	c green peas
	Salt to taste
4-6	coriander leaves

Peel and cut potatoes into 4 pieces each. Chop onions, green chili, and ginger finely. Purée tomatoes in a blender. Heat oil and fry potatoes slightly, then set aside. Add cumin seeds, green chili, ginger, and onions to same oil and sauté till brown. Add all other spices and tomato purée. Simmer for 5-8 minutes. Add potatoes and peas with 1 1/2 cups water. Reduce heat when mixture starts boiling. Cook till done. Garnish with chopped coriander leaves.

Usha Ladha
India

Corn with Beans

1   kg corn kernels
1   kg beans or peanuts or cowpea
20 grams onions, chopped
10 grams curry powder
30 grams cooking oil
     Pinch of salt
     Water

Wash corn and beans, then add enough water to immerse grains. Cook until well done, then season with onions, curry powder, and salt. Add oil and cook for 10 minutes. Cool before serving.

Eva Kanyeka
Tanzania

Sabzi-Bhaji (Dry Mixed Vegetables)

3   large carrots
4   c green beans (French)
1/4 kg cauliflower
1/2 small cabbage
1/2 tsp black mustard seeds
8   curry leaves (optional)
2   cloves garlic, crushed
2   tsp finely grated fresh ginger
1   tsp turmeric powder
1/4 tsp chili powder
     Salt to taste

Scrape carrots and cut into thin slices. Cut beans diagonally and cauliflower into slices with some stem. Shred cabbage coarsely. Heat oil in a large pan and sauté mustard seeds and curry leaves for 2 minutes, stirring. Add garlic, ginger, turmeric, and chili powder and stir for a minute or two. Add carrots, beans, and cauliflower. Stir over medium heat till half-cooked. Add cabbage and continue to toss and cook for 5 minutes till vegetables are tender but crisp. Sprinkle with salt, mix well, cover and cook for 2 minutes. Serve immediately.

NOTE: Vegetables should not be overcooked.

Durga Pathak
India

Burmese Mixed Vegetables

1/2 kg chicken
4 onions
4 segments garlic
2 cauliflower heads
1 small cabbage
4 tomatoes
1 tsp ginger
1 c oil
1 tsp sugar
1 tbsp Knorr sauce
1 tsp monosodium glutamate
1 tp salt
1/2 c water

Boil chicken. Separate meat from bones, and cut into small pieces. Slice onions, garlic, cauliflower, cabbage, and tomatoes into medium-size pieces. Pound ginger. Heat oil, sauté onions, garlic, ginger, chicken, sugar, and Knorr sauce with 1/2 cup water; cover and cook for 5 minutes. Add cauliflower, cabbage, MSG, salt, and water, and cook covered for 5 minutes.

Lily Khin Win
Myanmar

Mixed Vegetables with Sauce

2 medium sayote, cubed
3 medium carrots, sliced
1 medium cauliflower, sliced
2 medium sweet pepper
1/2 pc fresh corn
1 big onion, sliced
1/4 kg chicharo (snow pea)
1 tbsp chopped parsley

Heat butter in a saucepan on low flame and sauté garlic until brown. Add cornstarch; stir till light brown. Add water, stirring constantly until mixture is smooth and bubbly. Add black pepper, chili powder, and salt.

Durga Pathak
India

Heat oil. Sauté vegetables separately, one at a time, until half-cooked. Put all in a serving bowl. Pour sauce over, and sprinkle with parsley.

Sauce
2 tbsp butter
2 segments garlic, chopped
2 tbsp cornstarch
1 c water
1 tsp black pepper
1/4 tsp chili powder
   Salt to taste

Homos (Chick-pea with Sesame Seeds)

2	c chick-pea
1/2	tsp soda
1	c sesame seed paste (tahini)
1/2	kg calamansi
8	pods garlic, minced
	Salt to taste

Soak chick-pea overnight. Boil with soda for 20 minutes. Put chick-pea in a blender and grind to a paste. Transfer to a bowl. Add sesame seed paste, calamansi juice, garlic, and salt. Stir and mix all very well.

Katia Sayegh
Lebanon

Chick-pea Curry

2	c chick-pea
1/2	tsp baking soda
1-inch	pc ginger, chopped
2	green chilies, finely chopped
2	whole cardamoms
2-3	cloves
4-6	whole black pepper
1-inch	cinnamon stick
	Salt to taste
4	tbsp oil
1	tsp cumin seeds
1	bay leaf
2	large onions, finely chopped
4	cloves garlic, crushed
1	tsp chili powder
1	tsp curry powder
1	tbsp coriander powder
1	tsp turmeric powder
6	tomatoes, puréed
1/4	c tamarind pulp
1 1/2	c water
	Coriander leaves

Soak chick-pea overnight with baking soda. Rinse well and boil, preferably in a pressure cooker, with chopped ginger, green chilies, cardamoms, cloves, black pepper, cinnamon, and salt. Remove from heat when soft.

Heat oil. Sauté cumin seeds, bay leaf, and onions. When light brown, add all spices and tomato purée. Simmer for 5 minutes. Add chick-pea, tamarind pulp, and water. Boil till well mixed and thick. Sprinkle with coriander leaves just before removing from fire.

Usha Ladha
India

O Qua Don Thit (Bitter Gourd With Pork)

5   big ampalaya
2   c fresh lean pork, ground
2   c fresh shrimps, chopped
1/4 c onion, finely chopped
2   whole eggs, slightly beaten
1/2 tsp black pepper
1   tbsp finely chopped kinchay
1   c sotanghon
1   tsp salt
1/4 c dried wood ears, presoaked
4   c water

Mix all ingredients thoroughly, except ampalaya and water. Cut ampalaya lengthwise into halves; remove seeds. Place 2-3 tbsp of pork mixture in each half. Tie halves together with a string to keep mixture inside. Boil in a covered saucepan until cooked.

Tham Aurin
Vietnam

Lentil Loaf

1   c cooked lentils or
1/2 c chopped walnuts
    (or any other nuts)
1   egg
1   13-oz can evaporated skimmed milk
1   small onion, chopped
1/4 tsp sage
1/2 tsp salt
1/4 c oil
1 1/2 c cornflakes or bread crumbs

Preheat oven to 350 °F. Mix all ingredients. Place in an oiled 9- × 5- × 3-inch loaf pan and bake for 45 minutes. Serve with plain brown gravy or cranberry sauce. Makes 6 servings, 300 calories per serving.

Judy Buresh
USA

Vegetables with Shrimps

Oil for frying
2 onions
2 cloves garlic
2 tsp ginger
1 lb fresh shrimps
2 red chilies
1 lb cabbage, chopped
2 carrots, peeled and cubed
2 lb cauliflower, separated into florets
1 lb green beans, cut into 1-inch pieces
2 eggplants, sliced into 2-inch pieces
2 tsp salt
2 bay leaves
4 c coconut milk

Sauté onions, garlic, ginger in a skillet. Add shrimps and stir for 2 minutes. Add the rest of the vegetables and salt. Cover and cook over low heat about 5 minutes. Add coconut milk and bay leaves and cook on low heat, uncovered. Stir constantly. Serve while vegetables are still crisp.

Faiza Pervaz (Pakistan)
Indonesia

Indonesian Cabbage

1	kg cabbage
2	tbsp oil
2	onions, chopped
2	cloves garlic, minced
3 1/2	c coconut milk
1/4	tsp shrimp paste
2	red chilies, crushed
	Salt to taste
1	lb fresh shrimp, shelled and chopped

Clean cabbage and cut coarsely. Heat oil; sauté onions and garlic until light brown. Add cabbage, sauté for a minute. Add coconut milk, shrimp paste, chili, and salt. Bring to a boil. Add shrimp and cook for a few minutes, stirring constantly.

Faiza Pervaz (Pakistan)
Indonesia

Dal (Lentil Pulse)

1/4	kg red lentils
1/2	tbsp oil or ghee
1	large onion, finely sliced
2	cloves garlic, finely chopped
1	tsp finely grated fresh ginger
1/2	tsp ground turmeric
3	c hot water
1	tsp curry powder
	Salt to taste

Wash lentils thoroughly, removing those that float. Drain well. Heat oil and sauté onion, garlic, and ginger until golden brown. Add turmeric and stir well. Add drained lentils and sauté for a minute or two. Add hot water and bring to a boil; reduce heat to simmer. Cover and cook for 15-20 minutes or until lentils are half-cooked. Add salt and curry powder; mix well and continue cooking until lentils are soft and consistency is similar to that of porridge. If there is too much liquid, take lid off the pan to hasten evaporation.

Serve plain or garnish with golden fried onions. Eat with plain rice or "chapati" (Indian bread) or as a light meal itself.

NOTE: Any type of lentil can be used for this, but red lentil or mongo is the quickest cooking type and does not need soaking. Other types should be soaked overnight before cooking.

Durga Pathak
India

Sambhar (Peas with Fresh Vegetables)

1	c tur dal
4	c water
2	tsp salt
1/4	tsp ground turmeric
2	tbsp vegetable oil
1	eggplant (about 1 pound), washed, but not peeled, and cut into 2-inch cubes
	Big pinch of salt
2-3	tbsp dried tamarind or 1/3-1/2 c lemon juice may be used
1	c boiling water
1/2	c vegetable oil
	Pinch of fenugreek seeds
	Pinch of black mustard seeds
1/4	lb green beans, cut into 2-inch pieces
1	green pepper, chopped
4-6	small white onions, peeled
6-8	radishes, halved
1-2	green or red chilies
1	bay leaf
1 1/4	tsp sambhar powder
1/4	c chopped coriander leaves
1	large tomato, seeded and roughly chopped
1/4	c fresh chopped coconut

Wash tur dal and soak for 15 minutes. Add salt, turmeric and 2 tbsp vegetable oil to soaking water. Boil 30 to 40 minutes or until dal is tender. Remove from heat. Place eggplant pieces in a bowl and sprinkle with salt; set aside for 30 to 40 minutes.

Place tamarind in another bowl, add boiling water, and set aside to soak for 15 minutes. Strain tamarind mixture through a strainer set over a bowl and keep the liquid, discarding tamarind pulp. (Or use lemon juice to taste.)

Drain eggplant pieces on paper towel. Heat vegetable oil in a large pan over moderate heat. Sauté fenugreek seeds and black mustard seeds until they crack open. Add green beans, green pepper, onions, radish, chili, and bay leaf; cook for 2 to 3 minutes, or until vegetables are light brown. Add eggplant pieces and continue cooking and stirring about 5 more minutes. Stir in sambhar powder, coriander leaves, tomato, and coconut and cook for another 2 minutes. Cover and cook gently until vegetables are tender but not mushy. Mix in tamarind liquid (or lemon juice) and boiled lentil mixture. Stir to blend well. Simmer uncovered for 10 to 15 minutes. Sprinkle with some more chopped coriander leaves. Serve with boiled rice or Indian bread.

Kumari Pingali
India

Baked Beans

1/2 kg dry kidney beans
2   medium-size onions
2-3 cloves garlic
1   c oil
3-4 medium ripe tomatoes, peeled
     Parsley
2   tsp salt
     Pepper

Soak beans in water overnight. Drain, cover with cold water, and boil for 1 hour. Sauté onions, garlic. Add drained beans, tomato, parsley, salt, and pepper. Cover and bake at 350 °F until beans are cooked.

Vivi Moridis
Greece

Bitter Gourd with Eggs

1/2 kg bitter gourd
1   tbsp oil
1/4 kg pork (optional)
3   cloves garlic
1   medium-size onion, chopped
4   tomatoes, chopped
1/2 c water
2   eggs
1   tsp salt
     Salt to taste

Clean bitter gourd, and slice in rounds. Soak in salted water for an hour; squeeze. Heat oil, add pork, stir-fry for a while.

Remove pork from oil. In the same pan saute garlic for a minute, then add onion and tomato. Stir for a minute, add bitter gourd. Cover and cook for 5 minutes. Add water; stir, then add eggs beaten with 1 tsp salt. Cook covered until bitter gourd is tender. Add salt to taste and remove from fire. Serve with rice.

Cora de Jesus
Philippines

Poultry
Meat
Seafood
Fish

Main Dishes

Fluffy Eggs

4	eggs, separated
4	pc buttered toast
4	baked tomato halves
	Parsley sprigs
	Salt

Beat egg whites with salt until stiff; pile onto toast. Make depression in the center. Carefully drop one yolk in the depression and draw egg white over top. Bake in moderate oven, (180 ºC or 350 ºF) till egg is set and top is lightly browned. Garnish with parsley and serve hot with baked tomatoes.

Marlene Quick
Australia

Khageena

5	tbsp oil
2-3	c finely sliced onion
1	green chili, finely chopped or
1/4	tsp chili powder
1/4	tsp coriander powder
6	big eggs
1/6	tsp turmeric powder
	Salt to taste
2	medium pieces garlic, crushed
4	small pieces ginger, crushed
	Few coarsely chopped coriander leaves (optional)

Heat oil in pan, then sauté onion on medium flame. Add green chili or chili powder, coriander powder, turmeric powder, and salt. Immediately pour some water into the pan to avoid burning the spices. Sauté spices for 3-5 minutes on low heat, adding a few drops of water often. Add ginger and garlic; sauté the same way. Break eggs, and place slowly on top or as sunny side up. Then stir slowly at separate places in the pan till the eggs are done. Remove from stove and garnish with coriander leaves. This can be served with any kind of bread.

Nusrat Khan (Pakistan)
Iraq

Tamago-Dofu

1 1/4 c dashi stock
2/3   tsp salt   )
1   tsp light soy sauce)   *Seasoning 1*
2   tsp mirin   )
4   eggs
1   c dashi stock
       A little salt   )
1   tsp mirin)   )   *Seasoning 2*
1   tsp light soy sauce)

Make the tamago-dofu: boil 1/4 c dashi stock, add seasoning 1, then let cool. Beat eggs well. Add 1 c dashi stock and the boiled dashi stock, then strain once. Pour into a container and steam over medium heat for 2-3 minutes, then over low heat for 15-20 minutes. Let cool.

Boil 1 c dashi stock; add seasoning 2, and let cool.

Cut tamago-dofu into four. Pour dashi soup on each piece, and serve.

Ritsuko Ikeda
Japan

Eggs Foo Yung

4   eggs, beaten
1/2   kg mungbean sprouts
1/2   c cooked and chopped shrimps or chicken breast
1   small onion, chopped
1/2   tsp salt
1/8   tsp pepper
1   tbsp Kikkoman soy sauce
2   tbsp salad oil
       Chinese sauce

Combine all ingredients except oil and Chinese sauce. Drop by spoonfuls into hot oil in griddle or frying pan. Spread gently to distribute sprouts evenly. Cook until set and brown around the edges. Turn and brown other side. Add oil as necessary. Place on hot platter and serve immediately with Chinese sauce.

Chinese sauce
Combine 3/4 cup chicken broth (or 3/4 cup hot water and 1 chicken bouillon cube), 1/2 tsp molasses, and 1/2 tsp soy sauce. Add 1 tbsp cornstarch dissolved in 1 tbsp cold water. Cook on low heat, stirring constantly until mixture boils. Makes about 3/4 cup sauce.

Baby Duff (Philippines)
China

Fried Chicken Slices with Lemon Sauce

3/4 lb chicken breast
2   tbsp oil for frying

Marinade
1/2 tbsp wine
1/2 c light soy sauce
1   egg yolk
1/2 tsp salt
1/8 tsp pepper
1   tbsp cornstarch
1   tbsp cold water

Chicken coating
6   tbsp cornstarch
3   tbsp flour

Seasoning sauce
3   tbsp fresh lemon
     juice
3   tbsp sugar
3   tbsp soup stock
1/2 tsp salt
2   tsp cornstarch
1   tsp sesame oil

Remove skin from chicken breast, then cut meat into thin slices. Marinate in next 7 ingredients (marinade) for about 10 minutes.

Mix ingredients for seasoning sauce in a small bowl.

Combine cornstarch and flour on a plate, and coat each chicken piece. Deep-fry chicken slices over low heat about 1/2 minute or until golden brown. Reheat oil until very hot, then fry chicken for 10 more seconds. Drain and put in a platter.

Heat 1 tbsp oil. Stir-fry seasoning sauce. When it boils and thickens, splash with 1 tbsp hot oil to make it shiny. Pour sauce on fried chicken slices. Serve hot.

Nancy Chang
China

Burmese Chicken Curry

1   kg chicken
15   big onions
2   tbsp chili powder
3   segments garlic
1   small pc ginger
3   tbsp fish sauce
2   tbsp monosodium glutamate
1 1/2 c vegetable oil

Cut the chicken into 12 pieces. Pound onions, garlic, ginger, and chili powder together. Mix fish sauce, MSG, and pounded ingredients and set aside for 15 minutes. Fry chicken in hot oil; add pounded ingredients, and cook covered for 5 minutes. Add 1 pint water and cook till chicken is tender.

Lily Khin Win
Myanmar

Chicken with Mushrooms, Celery, and Ham

500 grams celery
250 grams mushrooms
450 grams chicken breast fillet
2 chicken cubes for broth
Salt and pepper
1/2 liter water
75 grams butter or margarine
150 grams boiled ham
100 grams grated parmesan cheese

Clean celery, separate leaves from stems and cut stems into pieces. Clean mushrooms; cut the big ones into two. Rinse chicken breast fillet with water. Boil chicken cubes in water. Add celery; boil for 5 minutes. Add fillets, bring to boil again, then simmer on low heat for 10 minutes.

Fry mushrooms in 50 grams butter over low heat for 5 minutes. Sprinkle with salt and pepper.

Transfer celery to a greased casserole. Put chicken on top of celery, cover with ham slices, mushrooms (with frying butter), and parmesan cheese. Dot with the remaining butter. Put the casserole under a broiler for 10 minutes or until cheese is brown. Serve with mashed potato or rice.

Cobie Penning de Vries
The Netherlands

Chicken with Walnuts

1 1/2 lb chicken breast, skinned, split, and deboned
3 tbsp soy sauce
2 tsp cornstarch
1 tsp sugar
1 tsp grated ginger root
1/2 tsp salt
1/2 tsp crushed red pepper
2 tbsp oil
2 medium green peppers (cut into 3/4-inch pieces)
4 green onions (bias-sliced into 1-inch length)
1/2 c walnut halves

Cut chicken meat into 1-inch pieces. Set aside. In a small bowl blend soy sauce and cornstarch; stir in sugar, ginger root, salt, and red pepper.

Preheat a wok or large skillet over high heat; add cooking oil. Stir-fry green peppers and green onions in hot oil 2 minutes. Remove. Add walnuts to wok; stir-fry 1-2 minutes or until just golden. Remove (add more oil if necessary). Add half of the chicken to the wok, stir-fry 2 minutes. Remove. Stir-fry remaining chicken for 2 minutes. Return chicken to wok. Stir soy mixture; add to chicken. Cook, stirring until bubbly. Stir in vegetables and walnuts, cover and cook 1 minute. Makes 6 servings.

Judy Buresh
USA

Chicken Casserole with White Sauce

1/2 kg boneless chicken, in thin slices
1   tbsp salt
1/4 tsp black pepper, ground
1/2 tsp paprika
1   tsp poultry seasoning
1/2 tsp oregano
1   tsp curry powder
1/2 tbsp coriander powder
3   eggs, beaten
1   c bread crumbs

Marinate chicken in next 7 ingredients for 20-30 minutes. Dip chicken in eggs, then roll in bread crumbs. Fry lightly in a wide frying pan. Drain. Arrange chicken slices in a greased casserole. Pour white sauce over them. Bake, covered, at 350 °F for 30-40 minutes.

White sauce
3   tbsp butter
3   tbsp flour
3   c milk

Melt butter in a pan on slow fire. Add flour and stir till it absorbs the butter. Pour milk into the pan and let mixture boil till thick.

Gurdev Athwal (India)
USA

Curry Chicken Pie

Dough
150 grams sifted flour
75   grams cold butter
     Salt
3   tbsp water

Put all ingredients in a bowl. Use 2 knives to cut the butter into sifted flour until mixture is crumbly and flour and butter are completely mixed. Add water. Shape mixture into a ball, cover with foil, and store in the refrigerator for about an hour. Roll dough into a flat piece on a flour-dusted surface.

Filling
1   tbsp butter
2   pc chicken fillet (about 350 grams)
1   c water
50   grams butter
1   small onion, chopped
1/2 apple, diced
1   sweet red pepper
2   tsp curry powder
     (use a good brand)
8   small carrots, boiled
1   small can of green peas
2   hard-boiled eggs, quartered
1/2 c chicken broth
4   tbsp cream
1   tsp paprika powder
1   tsp fresh parsley
     Pinch of sugar
     Salt to taste
1   egg, beaten

Fry chicken fillets in 1 tbsp butter on low heat; after 2 minutes add water. Simmer on very low temperature for 8 minutes. Remove from fire and set aside. Take out chicken pieces, slice, and set aside. Fry onions, apple, and sweet pepper together with curry powder on low heat until golden brown. Transfer this mixture to a buttered oven dish with chicken, carrots, peas, and hard-boiled eggs. Mix chicken broth with lukewarm cream, paprika, parsley, salt, and sugar. Stir and pour over chicken and cover dish with dough. Brush dough with beaten egg. Bake in a (preheated) hot oven for half an hour.

Cobie Penning de Vries
The Netherlands

Baked Chicken

1   kg chicken
1 1/2 c (8-12 oz) plain yoghurt
2 1/2 tbsp tomato paste
2 1/2 tbsp lemon juice
1   medium yellow onion, minced
1 1/2 tbsp (1 1/2 inches) minced ginger root
6-8   cloves garlic, minced
2 1/2 tsp ground coriander
1 1/4 tsp ground cumin
1 1/4 tsp garam masala
1 1/4 tsp salt
       Big pinch of sugar
1/4   c (2 oz) vegetable oil
1 1/2 c cornflake crumbs

In a large bowl, combine all ingredients except chicken and cornflake crumbs and mix well. Add chicken pieces and rub them well with spice mixture. Cover bowl with plastic wrap and refrigerate at least overnight, preferably for 24 hours. Turn chicken several times and baste with the marinade.

Preheat oven to 350 °F. Line a baking sheet with aluminum foil. Remove chicken pieces from marinade and dip in cornflake crumbs to coat lightly. Place chicken in prepared pan, meat side up. Place pan in the center of the oven and bake chicken for 1 hour, or until tender and golden. Place a piece of foil over chicken if it begins to brown too much. The chicken may be served hot with rice (kitchuri or pullao).

Kumari Pingali
India

Teriyaki Chicken

2   chicken thighs, deboned
2   tbsp oil

Sauce
6   tbsp soy sauce
1   tbsp saké (Japanese wine)
2   tbsp mirin
1 1/2 tbsp sugar

Pierce chicken thighs using a fork. Heat oil in a pan. Fry chicken on each side until golden brown. Drain oil from frying pan.

Mix sauce ingredients and pour into the pan; simmer until chicken is tender and well coated with sauce. When cool, slice chicken into 1-cm pieces and serve.

Ritsuko Ikeda
Japan

Satay (Barbecued Chicken with Peanut Sauce)

2	tbsp coriander seeds
2 1/2	tsp cumin
12	shallots
1/2	tsp turmeric powder
4	cloves garlic
3	stalks lemongrass
1	tsp salt
1	tsp dark soy sauce
3	tbsp sugar
4	tbsp oil
1/2	kg chicken, deboned, cut into cubes

Roast coriander seeds and cumin till fragrant. Grind into a powder. Pound the next 4 ingredients into a smooth paste.

Add salt, soy sauce, sugar, and oil to paste. Mix thoroughly and marinate chicken in this mixture for 2 hours. Thread the meat on skewers. Grill over a charcoal fire, occasionally basting with water-oil mixture. Serve barbecued chicken with peanut, cucumbers, and onion cut into wedges.

Harmit Wasan
Singapore

Tandoori Chicken (Charcoal-Barbecued Chicken)

1	small chicken
1	tbsp calamansi juice
1	tsp salt

Marinade

4	cloves garlic, pounded
1	tbsp calamansi juice
2-3	tbsp yoghurt
1/2	tsp curry powder
1/2	tsp black pepper
1	tsp turmeric powder
1	tsp ground cumin
1	tsp cayenne pepper
1	tbsp salad oil

Rub chicken with calamansi juice and salt, then marinate and refrigerate overnight. Bake at 350 °F for 30 minutes and then broil for 5-10 minutes. Remove from oven before it becomes too brown.

NOTE: If roasted over charcoal, brush with butter while turning.

Harwant Khush
India

African Harmattan Chicken

1/4 kg onion, sliced
1   tbsp curry powder
     in melted butter
1   tsp ground ginger
1   tsp crushed garlic
1   tbsp powdered chili
1   tsp white pepper
1   kg chicken, cut into serving pieces
1/4 c water
6   hard-boiled eggs, sliced
3-5 tbsp grated cheese (optional)

Cook onions in a little water for 5 minutes; then add butter with curry powder. When' all water has evaporated, add ginger, garlic, chili powder, and white pepper, stirring constantly. Cool spices for about 10 minutes. Add chicken and water. Cook till chicken is done (10-15 minutes), then add eggs and top with grated cheese. Serve with bread, cooked yam, coco yam, plantain, or rice. Good for 6 servings.

Mekdes A. Dua
Ghana

Chicken Curry

1   kg chicken
4   medium-size onions
1/2 can tomato paste or 6 tomatoes
1   big green chili
1   tsp grated ginger
4-6 cloves garlic, crushed
2   tbsp oil
1/2 tsp cumin seeds
2   cardamoms
2   cloves
2   tsp coriander powder
1/2 tsp turmeric powder
1/2 tsp chili powder
1/2 tsp garam masala
     Salt to taste

Remove skin of chicken. Cut meat into medium-size pieces. Wash and clean pieces, drain. Chop or grate onions fine. Make a paste with tomato paste, green chili, ginger, and garlic. If using tomatoes, boil, peel, remove pulp, and mash well.

Heat oil. Sauté onion, cumin seeds, cardamoms, and cloves. Add all spices and tomato paste and sauté till all ingredients form a paste and separate from the oil. Add chicken and salt, and mix well. Cover and cook on medium flame till chicken is done. Garnish with tomato slices and onion rings. Serve with rice or any kind of bread.

Usha Ladha
India

Chicken Adobo with Coconut Milk

3   lb chicken, cut up
1/2 c vinegar
1   tbsp salt
1/4 tsp pepper
1   small bay leaf
3   cloves garlic, minced
1   tsp grated ginger
1   hot banana pepper
3   tbsp cooking oil
1/2 c thick coconut milk

Place first 8 ingredients in a pot and simmer covered for 30 minutes or until chicken is tender. Drain and set sauce aside. Heat oil in a skillet, add chicken and sauté until brown. Pour off all fat from skillet. Add sauce again, and simmer uncovered until liquid is reduced to about 1/4 cup. Add coconut milk and cook stirring for 2-3 minutes more. Serve hot. Serves 6.

Vilma Garrity
Philippines

Chicken with Chili

2   kg or 4 lb chicken
4   slices of bread
1/2 c oil
     Onions
2   tsp minced garlic
6   chilies ground into paste
     Salt and pepper to taste
1/2 lb nuts, chopped
4   oz parmesan cheese, grated
2   c evaporated milk
6   yellow potatoes, boiled
     Olives
     Hard-boiled eggs

Boil chicken in salted water. Remove meat from bones. Remove crust from bread and soak slices in chicken broth. In a saucepan, heat oil and sauté the onion, garlic, and chili; add salt and pepper. Cook slowly for 10 minutes, then add chopped nuts, grated cheese, and chopped chicken. Add evaporated milk 2 or 3 minutes before serving. Decorate dish with halved potatoes, quartered eggs, and olives.

Cecilia Chujoy
Peru

Grilled Chicken with Basil and Garlic

1   medium clove garlic, finely minced
1/2 c fresh basil leaves
4   large chicken breasts with skin, deboned
     and halved

Seasoning sauce
1/2 c dry white wine
1/4 c olive oil
1/2 tsp salt
1   small head garlic,
     minced
1/8 tsp finely ground
     black pepper

Purée
1   c chicken stock
1   large head garlic,
     not peeled
2   tbsp whipped
     cream
     Salt and pepper to
     taste
1   tsp basil leaves for
     garnish

Slide 1/2 of minced garlic and all basil leaves under skin of each chicken breast and pour seasoning sauce over chicken. Refrigerate for 2 to 4 hours. Boil chicken stock; add garlic, cover, and simmer for 30 minutes. Make a purée of chicken stock, garlic, and basil. Add whipped cream and pepper and boil till sauce is thick. Grill seasoned chicken on barbecue grill until done. Pour thick sauce over grilled chicken and garnish with basil leaves.

Françoise Prot
France

Thai Chicken with Eggplant

1   kg chicken, with skin
2   coconuts, grated
1   tbsp hot sauce
1/2 c Thai eggplant, sliced (if not available,
     use round eggplant)
6   pc lemongrass or
1   tbsp Thai leaves, chopped

Curry-chili paste
4   pc dry chili
1   small clove garlic, crushed
1   small onion, shredded
2   tbsp calamansi juice
     Salt to taste

Cut chicken into small pieces. Mix 2 cups water and 1 grated coconut and squeeze the milk. Add 2 cups warm water to remaining coconut and squeeze milk. Put warm coconut milk aside.

Prepare curry-chili paste by grinding paste ingredients in a grinder. Boil the first 2 cups coconut milk for 10 minutes until it gets thick. Add curry-chili paste, and boil 10 more minutes. Add chicken, the remaining coconut milk, and 2 cups water. Cook on low heat for 30 minutes. Add eggplant, then cook on low heat for 10 minutes more. Add chopped Thai leaves or lemongrass before serving.

Nusrat Khan (Pakistan)
Thailand

Chicken Besquoise

6 tbsp oil
100 grams onion, chopped
2 cloves garlic, crushed
1 kg tomatoes, chopped
250 grams green pepper, seeded and
   chopped
   Salt and pepper to taste
6 pc chicken (1/2 kg chicken)

Heat oil in a pan. Add chopped onion and garlic; sauté till brown, then add tomatoes, green pepper, salt, and black pepper. Cook for 30 minutes on low heat. In another pan, fry the chicken; then add to onion-tomato mixture. Cook uncovered for 15 minutes on low heat until done.

Claudie Arraudeau
France

Indonesian Fried Chicken

1.5 kg chicken
3/4 c tamarind water
1 1/2 tbsp soy sauce
2 tsp ground ginger
1 tsp ground garlic
1 tsp ground coriander powder
1/4 tsp turmeric powder
   Chili powder (according to taste)
   Salt to taste
   Oil for frying

Cut chicken into serving pieces; wash and dry pieces very well. Mix all spices with tamarind water. Marinate chicken in the mixture for 2-3 hours. Turn the pieces 3-4 times. Remove the pieces from the mixture; shake each piece very well. Deep-fry a few pieces at a time. Place in a platter and serve hot.

Ikke Sunari
Indonesia

Chicken with Touco

1 kg chicken parts-legs, thigh, breast
2 tbsp vegetable oil
1/3 c sliced onion
1 tbsp touco (salted yellow beans) ground
   into paste
2 tsp ground garlic
2 tsp dark soy sauce
1 tsp ground ginger
1/2 c tamarind water
1 c water
1 tsp brown sugar
1/2 tsp chili powder (or according to taste)

Wash and dry chicken pieces. Heat oil in a pan, add onion and sauté until soft. Stir in touco paste and garlic. Add chicken, mixing pieces thoroughly with touco. Add the rest of the ingredients. Cover and cook on low heat for about 45-50 minutes. Then cook uncovered for 5-10 minutes on medium heat to reduce the gravy. Serve hot with rice.

Ikke Sunari
Indonesia

Chicken Tikka

1   kg boneless chicken, cut into small
        pieces
1 1/2   tsp garam masala (or less)
8   tbsp cooking oil
2   large onions, shredded
        or ground
6   medium pieces garlic
1-2   tbsp ground ginger
1   tsp coriander powder
8   tbsp cooking oil
1/2   tsp chili powder or as per taste
3/4   c yoghurt
1   tsp salt

Seasoning sauce (garam masala)
2   tsp black pepper, whole
1   pc clove
1   small stick of cinnamon
1   pc black or green cardamom

Grind all dry spices for seasoning sauce
and store in an airtight, dry jar.

Cut chicken into tiny pieces. Make
marinade by mixing the onions, garlic,
ginger, and coriander powder. Marinate
chicken overnight or at least 4 hours
before cooking.

Heat oil and fry seasoned chicken on
medium flame till moisture has
evaporated. Fry chicken for 10 more
minutes, sprinkling water every now and
then to prevent burning. Add seasoning
sauce, and cook till the chicken browns.

NOTE: More cooking oil can be added if
      chicken pieces stick to the pan.
      Spices can be increased as per
      taste.

Nusrat Khan
Pakistan

Pancit Guisado

1   big onion, sliced
4   segments garlic, macerated
1/2   c pork, sliced into long narrow strips
1/2   c shrimps (optional)
2   c boiled flaked chicken (optional)
3-5   tbsp soy sauce
        Pepper and salt to taste
1 1/2-2 c chicken stock
1   c cabbage, sliced into narrow strips
1/2   c baguio beans, sliced
1   c carrots, sliced into narrow strips
1/4   c kinchay, cut into 1-inch pieces
1   kg bihon (rice noodles)
3-4   pc calamansi

Sauté garlic and onions till light brown.
Add pork, shrimps, and chicken; cook for
5 minutes. Add soy sauce, salt, pepper,
and chicken stock. Cook till pork is
tender. Set aside a fourth of this for
garnish.

Add vegetables and let boil once. Add
bihon and stir continuously till noodles are
cooked and almost dry. Arrange in a
platter and garnish. Serve with calamansi.

Lucy Bonman
Philippines

Burmese Noodles with Coconut Milk Curry

2 kg chicken
4 coconuts
10 eggs
2 c vegetable oil
1/4 kg dried noodles
1 kg wet noodles
1 tsp monosodium glutamate
1 kg onions, sliced
5 tbsp chili powder
1 c yellow split bean powder
2 c water
1 tbsp sugar
1 tbsp salt

Boil chicken till done. Debone and cut the meat into cubes. Set aside. Extract coconut milk; boil it, and then set aside. Boil eggs, slice crosswise, and set aside. In 1 cup oil, fry dried noodles till crispy; keep in an airtight container. Boil wet noodles till half-done. Add 1/2 cup oil to the noodles with a pinch of MSG for seasoning and set aside. Spread noodles in a tray to dry. Pound sliced onion with chili powder and set aside. Mix yellow split pea powder with water. Heat remaining oil, sauté onion till it becomes golden brown and crispy. Add chicken cubes, coconut milk, and split pea powder mixed with water. Stir gravy till it starts boiling, then add remaining MSG, sugar, sliced eggs, and salt. Pour gravy over wet noodles. Put crispy noodles on top of this gravy. Makes 10 servings.

Lily Khin Win
Myanmar

BEEF

Meat Pie

125 grams short crust pastry
30 grams butter
2 small onions, finely chopped
250 grams minced steak or substitute
2 eggs
1 c milk
1/2 tsp salt
1/2 tsp dry mustard
1/2 c grated tasty cheese
    Pinch of cayenne pepper
    Salt and pepper

Line 8- to 9-inch pie plate with pastry. Melt butter in frying pan, add onions and minced steak or substitute. Stir over medium heat till brown, season to taste. Cool slightly, then spread over base of pastry. Beat eggs, milk, salt, mustard, cayenne pepper, and 1/4 of cheese. Pour over meat mixture. Sprinkle rest of cheese on top. Bake in oven at 200 °C (400 °F) for 10 minutes. Reduce heat to 150 °C (300 °F) and bake for 25 minutes or till set and firm. Serve with green salad and tomatoes. Individual pies may be made using small square foil pans. Top mixture with short crust pastry; join to bottom pastry. Serve with tomato sauce (ketchup).

NOTE: Can substitute TVP (texturized vegemeat or tinned protein).

Marlene Quick
Australia

Beef-filled Red Pepper

20 red chilies, big
1   lb ground beef
4   egg yolks (reserve white)
2   cloves garlic, minced
4   green onions, minced
1   tbsp parsley, chopped
1   tbsp lemongrass
1/4 tsp ginger powder
1   tsp coriander powder
1/2 c bread crumbs
    Salt to taste
    Oil for frying

Slit chilies lengthwise, remove seeds, and set aside. Mix ground beef with egg yolks, garlic, and onions. Add parsley, lemongrass, ginger, coriander, and salt. Mix well. Stuff this mixture into chilies. Beat egg whites and coat tops of beef-filled peppers. Sprinkle with fine bread crumbs. Deep-fry; drain on paper towels. Serves 8-10.

Faiza Pervaz
Indonesia

Hachee (Savory Beef and Onion Stew)

2   large onions, sliced thin
1/4 c flour
1/4 c margarine
2   c stock or water and meat cubes
3   bay leaves
5   cloves
1   tbsp vinegar
1/2 lb leftover beef, diced
2   tbsp corn flour
    Pepper
    Worcestershire sauce

Brown onions and flour in margarine in a saucepan. Add stock gradually, stirring all the time. Add bay leaves, and cloves and simmer, covered, for 5 minutes. Add vinegar and beef, and simmer for one hour. To thicken sauce, dissolve corn flour in some water and add to stew. Stir continuously for 5 minutes. Add pepper and worcestershire sauce to taste. Serve stew with mashed potatoes and green beans.

Kathy HilleRisLambers
The Netherlands

Flemish Stew

500 grams beef (for stewing)
    Salt and pepper
1   heaping tbsp flour
25   grams butter
50   grams bacon fat
1   big onion, shredded
1   bay leaf
    Pinch of thyme
1   small bottle of light beer
1   thick slice white bread without crust
1   heaping tbsp mustard

Cut beef into pieces and sprinkle with salt, pepper, and flour. Fry till golden brown in butter and bacon fat on high heat. Add shredded onion and sauté with beef until golden yellow. Add thyme and bay leaf.

Stir in the beer (it ought to be at room temperature); don't worry if it foams a lot. Simmer the beef for 3 hours. After 2 hours, cover the slice of bread on both sides with mustard and put in the pot. Stir after a while. When stew is done, the bread ought to be totally dissolved in the sauce. The sharp taste of the mustard will have disappeared. Serve with crumbly boiled potatoes, carrots, and cabbage or Brussels sprouts.

Cobie Penning de Vries
The Netherlands

Beef Bourguignon

1/2 tbsp oil
5   medium onions, sliced
2   lb lean beef, cut into 1-inch cubes
1 1/2 tbsp flour
1/4 tsp marjoram
1/4 tsp thyme
1/2 tsp pepper
1 1/2 tsp salt
1/2 c bouillon
1   c dry, red wine (can be omitted but add more water)
1/2 lb fresh mushrooms, sliced (for canned mushrooms)

In heavy skillet, cook onions in oil until tender. Remove onions from skillet. In same pan, sauté beef cubes until brown; sprinkle with flour and seasoning. Add bouillon and wine, stir well, and simmer slowly for 1 1/2 hours. Add more bouillon and wine as necessary to keep beef barely covered. Return onions to the stew and add mushrooms. Cook, stirring, 30 minutes longer, adding more bouillon and wine if necessary. Sauce should be thick and brown. Enough for 8 servings.

Judy Buresh
USA

Shredded Beef with Sweet Pepper

1/2 kg beef tenderloin
2   tbsp soy sauce
1   tbsp corn oil
1/2 tbsp cornstarch
2   tsp wine
     Salt to taste
2   medium-size green peppers
1   spring onion
1   small ginger root
1/2 tsp sugar
3/4 c corn oil

Cut beef into long thin strips. Mix with soy sauce, wine, corn oil, cornstarch, and salt.

Marinate at least one hour. Cut green peppers lengthwise. Slice onion and ginger lengthwise. In a pan, fry beef on high flame. Keep stirring for a few seconds. Remove beef from pan. Pour 1 tsp oil in pan, and sauté ginger, onion, and sweet pepper; add sugar and salt. Keep stirring. Add beef and mix well. Remove from fire and serve with rice.

Nancy Chang (Taiwan)
China

Tenderloin Tips Delight

1   c beef tenderloin, cut into strips
1   egg white
1   tbsp cornstarch
1   tsp sugar to taste
1   tbsp oyster sauce
1/4 c cooking oil
1   onion, chopped
     Salt and pepper

Marinate tenderloin in egg white, cornstarch, sugar, and oyster sauce. Heat oil; add onion, pepper, and salt. Lower heat. Add marinated tenderloin and cook for 10 minutes. Remove from heat and serve hot.

Lucy Bonman
Philippines

Seco (Dry Beef)

1 1/2 kg meat
       Salt and pepper
1   tsp paprika
1   tsp chili, ground
1   c wine
       Corn oil
2   onions, finely chopped
1   tsp garlic, crushed
1   tsp chopped fresh coriander leaves
1   c peas
6   potatoes, peeled

Cut meat into medium-size squares; marinate in salt, pepper, paprika, and chili with wine. Sauté onions, garlic, coriander, then add pieces of meat with liquid in which they were marinated. As soon as meat is done, add peas and potatoes. Cook for 10 more minutes. Serve with rice.

Cecilia Chujoy
Peru

Almondigas (Meatballs)

1   lb ground meat (e.g., mixture of beef, pork)
1   spring onion, finely chopped
1/2 tsp salt
1   tbsp oil
1   medium onion, finely chopped
2   cloves garlic, crushed
1/2 tsp Chinese shrimp sauce
3   c hot water and pepper
1/2 c misua (fine wheat noodles)

Combine meat, spring onion, and salt. Mix well and form into balls the size of a large marble. Heat oil and sauté onion and garlic gently until golden brown. Add shrimp sauce and water and bring to a boil. Drop a few meatballs one at a time, so that the water keeps boiling. Simmer until meatballs are cooked. Drop in the misua and remove from heat. Cover and let stand for 5 minutes before serving.

Alice Flinn (Australia)
Philippines

Sweet and Sour Beef with Lettuce

8   oz tender beef
2   tbsp oil
2   tbsp vinegar
2   tbsp sugar
2   cloves garlic
2   tbsp water
2   tsp corn flour
1   head lettuce
1   tomato, sliced

Clean and cut beef into paper-thin strips. Heat oil; sauté beef and set aside. Mix vinegar, sugar, garlic, water, and corn flour. Boil for 3 minutes, stirring constantly. Remove from flame and add beef to sauce. Spread lettuce leaves on a platter; pour beef mixture on top of lettuce leaves. Garnish with tomatoes. Serve with rice.

Tham Aurin
Vietnam

Beef Rendang

1   kg beef
1   coconut, grated
      Water
8-12 dried chilies (long, red kind)
8   peppercorns
1/2-inch pc ginger
1/2-inch pc turmeric
5   cloves garlic
10   shallots
4   stalks lemongrass
4   candlenuts
4   tbsp oil
      Salt

Cut beef into cubes. Add enough water to the grated coconut to squeeze out 4 cups of coconut milk. Pound together all other ingredients except oil and salt. Heat oil in pan over medium heat and saute pounded ingredients until fragrant, stirring constantly. Add meat and fry 2-3 minutes. Add coconut milk one-half cup at a time, waiting for liquid to be absorbed before adding more. Simmer over low heat until meat is tender and curry is dry. Stir often to prevent browning. Add salt to taste. Serve hot with plain rice.

Siew-Fing Wong
Malaysia

Beef Stew

1   kg boneless beef, cubed
1/4 c oil
2   onions, sliced
4   cloves garlic
1/2 kg ripe tomatoes
     Salt and pepper
1   tsp grated ginger
2   c water

Clean beef and boil till tender. Heat oil, sauté 1 onion, and add garlic. Add cooked beef, reserving broth. Fry beef till brown. Set aside.

Blend tomatoes, pepper, and ginger with 1 cup water. Heat oil in pan; add 1 sliced onion and blended tomatoes. Stir continuously till cooked. Add beef and broth. Cook for 30 minutes. Serve with rice.

Djokoto
Ghana

Kalbee (Beef Spareribs)

12   beef spareribs

Barbecue sauce
1   tbsp sugar
3   tbsp grated pear
1   tbsp sesame oil
2   scallions, sliced
    Salt and pepper to taste
1   tbsp roasted sesame seeds
4   cloves garlic
4   tbsp soy sauce

Remove film covering from meat; slice meat halfway down the bones. Mix ingredients for barbecue sauce. Pour sauce over spareribs in a large bowl. Meat should be coated and covered with sauce. Set aside for 15 minutes. Bake both sides of ribs on preheated grill for half an hour or till done.

Sue Ahn
Korea

Frikkadels

1   tbsp butter
1   small onion, finely chopped
1   lb minced steak
1/2   c soft white bread crumbs
1 1/2   tsp salt
1/2   tsp ground black pepper
1/2   tsp dried dill weed
1/4   tsp ground cinnamon
1/4   tsp ground cloves
1   clove garlic, crushed
1/2   tsp finely grated fresh root ginger
2   tsp worcestershire sauce
2   tsp lemon juice
1   egg, beaten
1/4   c dry bread crumbs
1   c oil

Heat butter in a small frying pan and gently sauté onion until soft. Combine with minced steak, soft bread crumbs, salt, pepper, dill, cinnamon, cloves, garlic, ginger, worcestershire sauce, and lemon juice. Mix thoroughly and form into small balls (approximately 2.5 cm or 1 inch in diameter). Dip into beaten egg and coat with dry bread crumbs. Deep-fry in hot oil until golden brown. Drain on absorbent paper before serving.

Olga Ponnamperuma
Sri Lanka

Shiftas

1/4 kg finely ground beef
8 small cloves garlic, crushed
2 medium-size onions, very finely chopped
3 tbsp chopped celery leaves
1/2 c brown flour
2 tbsp tomato paste
1/4 tsp turmeric powder
1/2 tsp chili powder
1 tsp salt
1/4 c oil
2 tomatoes, sliced
1 cucumber, sliced
3 tbsp mint leaves, chopped
Ketchup

Mix very well all ingredients, except last five, mashing for about 5 to 10 minutes. Take small amounts of beef and form a ball. Flatten the ball round or oblong and press in the palms of your hands until shiftas are thin and neatly shaped.

Fry in oil on low fire until both sides are light brown. Add oil slowly as needed. Serve hot with sliced tomatoes, lettuce, cucumbers, mint leaves, and ketchup.

NOTE: Ingredients can be decreased or increased according to taste.

Nusrat Khan (Pakistan)
Iraq

Beef Stroganoff

1 lb lean beef round
Salt and pepper
1/2 lb mushrooms, sliced
3 tbsp oil
1 onion, sliced
3 tbsp flour
2 c beef bouillon
2 tbsp tomato paste
1 tsp dry mustard
Pinch of oregano
1/4 tsp dill weed
2 tbsp sherry (optional)
1/3 c low-fat yoghurt or sour cream

Remove all fat from meat and cut into thin strips, about 2 inches long. Sprinkle with salt and pepper and let stand in a cool place for 2 hours.

In a heavy skillet, sauté mushrooms in oil until tender. Remove from skillet, and sauté onions in same oil until brown. Remove from skillet.

Brown meat quickly on all sides until rare. Remove from pan and set aside.

Blend flour into oil in skillet and gradually add bouillon, stirring constantly until smooth and slightly thick. Add tomato paste, dry mustard, oregano, dill weed, and sherry. Blend well. Combine sauce, meat, mushrooms, and onions in top of a double boiler. Cook for 20 minutes. Blend in yoghurt 5 minutes before serving. Serves 6; 275 calories per serving; 375 with 1/2 cup rice or pasta.

Judy Buresh
USA

Hardi (Pot Kebab)

1	kg beef
3-4	tbsp yoghurt
	Oil
2 1/2	tsp ground ginger
1 1/2	tsp ground garlic
1	tbsp ground onion
	Chili powder to taste
	Salt to taste
1/2	c thinly sliced onions
1/2	tsp cumin
4	cloves
3-inch	pc cinnamon stick
4	pc cardamoms
1/4	tsp mace powder
1	tsp nutmeg powder
1	tsp coriander powder

The cooking is usually completed in two sessions about 24 hours apart.

Day 1. Cut beef into 1-inch strips, or bite size. Wash and marinate in yoghurt for at least 1 hour. Heat oil in a frying pan and add ground ginger, garlic, onion, chili powder, and salt. Sauté for 2-3 minutes, then add beef. Stir for a while then cover pan. Cook slowly until meat is half-done. When it cools, keep the whole pan in the refrigerator.

Day 2. Fry onion in deep oil until it turns golden brown; remove from oil. Cool, and mince. In same oil, fry cumin, cloves, cinnamon, and cardamom lightly. Drain then grind spices. In a small frying pan, heat 2 tsp oil, and then remove pan from flame. Add mace, nutmeg, and coriander powder. When meat is tender and only some gravy is left, add all spices and cook over low heat for 10-15 minutes. The meat should be moist when done. A little water can be added if the beef dries up before cooking is finished. Serve with rice or paratha.

Fauzi Bhuiyan
Bangladesh

Fried Beef and Eggs

3	eggs, hard-boiled
1	egg, beaten
6	slices beef tenderloin
1	tsp flour
1 1/2	c oil
	Salt and pepper

Shell hard-boiled eggs. Sprinkle salt and pepper on beef. Roll 2 beef slices around each boiled egg, and set aside. Combine flour and beaten egg. Dip roll in egg and deep-fry until light brown. Serve hot.

Shi Xiaorong
China

Sheesh Kebab

50   grams onion, finely sliced
1/2 kg finely ground beef
1   small pc ginger, finely crushed or ground
75   grams oil or butter
1/4 tsp ground cinnamon
1/4 tsp ground black cumin seed
3/4 tsp ground caraway seeds
1/4 tsp ground cloves
1/2 tsp chili powder
1/4 tsp ground cardamom
1/4 tsp ground nutmeg
75   grams oil or butter
1   tsp meat tenderizer
50   grams onion, shredded
     Salt to taste
     Thin iron rods

Sauté sliced onion in oil until golden brown. Add all other ingredients except salt to ground beef and set aside for 1 hour. After an hour, add salt. Take some beef and wrap it around the iron rod (handle of a tablespoon can be used). With wet hands press ground beef tightly around the rod so it would not fall off. Grill beef over charcoal-fire or in medium-hot oven. Brush some butter on the kebabs while they are being grilled or baked. Serve with fresh tomatoes, cucumber, round sliced onions, and lettuce.

NOTE: The kebabs can also be fried. Just after shaping them around the rod, remove rod and cook beef in oil over low fire.

Nusrat Khan
Pakistan

Shammi Kebab

1/2 c yellow split peas
1/2 kg ground beef or ground mutton
10   peppercorn
1   stick cinnamon
3   black cardamoms
1/2 tsp chili powder
1   tsp shredded ginger
2   large onions, sliced
2   c water
1   potato
3   eggs
1   green chili, chopped
1   onion, finely chopped
1/4 c oil
     Salt to taste

Soak yellow split peas for half an hour. Set aside. Put ground meat, peppercorn, cinnamon, cardamoms, chili powder, ginger, and sliced onions with 2 cups water in a pan. Drain split peas and add to meat mixture. Boil mixture on low heat till meat and peas are done. Boil potato; peel and mash. Add to cooked beef mixture. Grind mixture in a grinder. The mixture should look like hard dough. Add 1 egg, chopped green chili, chopped onion, and salt to taste. Mix well. Form walnut-size balls with this mixture, flatten them and set aside. Beat 2 eggs and set aside. Heat oil in a frying pan on medium heat. Dip each kebab in egg and fry on each side till golden brown. Serve hot with mint or tomato chutney.

Suriya Akbar
Pakistan

Pork Chops with Barbecue Sauce

12	pork chops
3	onions, sliced into rings
2	c tomato juice
2	tbsp vinegar
1	tbsp worcestershire sauce
1/2	c chopped onions
1	tsp dry mustard
1/2	tsp chili powder
1/2	tsp salt and pepper

Brown pork chops. Put in a baking dish and cover with onion rings. Combine the rest of the ingredients and simmer, uncovered for 10 minutes. Pour sauce mixture over the chops. Cover and bake at 325 °F for 25 minutes. Uncover and bake for 15 more minutes.

Ilse Zandstra
Canada

Pineapple Spareribs

3	lb pork spareribs, cut up
	Cornstarch
	Soy sauce
1/3	c vinegar
1/4	c brown sugar
1	can (20 oz) pineapple chunks, drained

Coat spareribs with cornstarch (easily done in a paper bag). Place on oiled baking sheet and sprinkle with soy sauce. Bake at 375 °F for 40 to 50 minutes. Turn ribs two or three times during baking. One hour before serving, heat vinegar, brown sugar, and pineapple juice. Remove from heat and add spareribs. Cover and let sit, stirring once in a while. Heat over medium heat 15 to 20 minutes. Add pineapple chunks and heat for 2 to 3 minutes. Serve.

Ilse Zandstra
Canada

Barbecued Pork

500	grams pork, sliced thin
3	cloves garlic
1	tsp salt
1/2	tsp fresh ginger, finely grated
1	tbsp light soy sauce
1	tbsp honey
1	tbsp sherry
1/2	five-spice powder

Combine all ingredients and marinate pork slices 3-4 hours. Skewer slices on barbecue sticks and broil over charcoal.

Alice Flinn
Australia

Pork Vindaloo

1/2 kg pork, cut into cubes
1/4 c vinegar or lemon juice
1/2 tsp chili, crushed
1/2 tsp cumin seed powder
2   tbsp butter
1   large onion, chopped
1   tsp root ginger, grated
1   tsp coriander powder
2   cloves garlic, chopped
1/4 tsp turmeric powder
1/4 tsp cinnamon powder
1/4 tsp sugar
2   tomatoes, chopped

Mix pork with vinegar, chili, cumin, and salt. Marinate 2-3 hours. Drain meat and reserve marinade.

Heat oil and fry pork for 5 minutes. As soon as meat gets brown, remove from pan. Combine onion, ginger, garlic, turmeric powder, coriander, paprika, cinnamon, and sugar. Sauté all together until onion is soft. Add chopped tomatoes to the mixture. Add pork and fry for a few minutes. Cover and cook on low heat until pork is done. Add marinade and simmer for 10 minutes. Remove from fire and serve with rice.

Kumari Pingali
India

Sauerkraut and Pork

400 grams sauerkraut
400 grams pork
1   apple
1   potato
40   grams margarine
1   onion, finely chopped
1   tbsp flour
     Salt

Add sauerkraut to 1/2-l cup boiling water. Wash meat and add to kraut. Wash and peel apple and potato, grind finely and add to kraut. Heat margarine in frying pan and fry onion. Add flour, stir, then add to kraut while stirring well. Bring once more to a boil. Add salt to taste.

Marie Kürschner
Germany

Hawaiian Pork Chops

4-5   pork chops
2   tbsp brown sugar
1   tsp salt
1/4   tsp pepper
2   tbsp tomato sauce
1/3   tsp curry powder
8-oz can crushed pineapple

Brown pork chops, then transfer to a baking dish. Combine and mix well the rest of the ingredients. Spoon mixture over chops. Bake at 350 °F for 1 hour.

Caren Hill
USA

Sweet and Sour Pork

1	lb pork tenderloin	1/2	tbsp cornstarch
3	slices pineapple	1	egg yolk, beaten
1	green sweet pepper	3/4	c corn oil
1	red sweet pepper		

Seasoning sauce

3	tbsp vinegar	4	tbsp tomato catsup
1/2	tbsp soy sauce	1	tsp salt
4	tbsp sugar	1	tsp sesame oil

Cut pork tenderloin into 1-inch cubes. Marinate in seasoning sauce for 1 hour.

Cut pineapple and green and red peppers into cubes. Dip pork cubes in cornstarch, then in beaten egg yolk, and again in cornstarch. Fry in hot oil for 5 minutes. Drain on paper towels.

Heat 2 tbsp oil in a frying pan; add peppers, and pineapple, stirring constantly. Add seasoning sauce from pork. Stir-fry until sauce has thickened. Add pork and serve immediately.

Nancy Chang
Taiwan, China

Pork Fillet

12	oz pork fillets	200	grams dried bread crumbs
2	eggs		
4	tbsp water	60	ml vegetable oil
1	tbsp salt		Pepper to taste
1	tsp rosemary		

Beat eggs, salt, rosemary, pepper, and water. Dip meat pieces in egg mixture, then coat with bread crumbs. Repeat to make double layer. Chill for 30 minutes. Heat oil and fry meat for about 10 minutes until brown and tender. Serve with garlic rice and vegetables.

NOTE: This can also be served with potato salad, boiled or fried potatoes.

Uschi Neue
Germany

Pork and Vegetables in Catsup

300 grams pork tenderloin,
cut into bite-size pieces
Salt and pepper
All-purpose flour for coating
Oil for deep-fat frying
1 tbsp oil
1 onion, cut into quarters,
then each quarter into two
1 carrot, cut into 1/6-inch-thick
rectangular pieces
5 pc Chinese dried mushrooms,
reconstituted in warm water, cut into
quarters
20 grams butter
1 onion, minced
3 tbsp all-purpose flour

Soup ingredients
1 1/2 c warm water
1 chicken stock cube
1/3 c tomato catsup
1/2 tsp prepared mustard
1/3 tsp salt
2 tsp rice wine (saké, if available, or dry
sherry)
2 tsp sugar
Dash of pepper

Sprinkle pork with salt and pepper.
Dredge in flour, then deep-fry until crisp
and golden. Set aside.

Over medium heat sauté onion, carrot,
and mushrooms in 1 tbsp fat until onion is
somewhat translucent. Be careful not to
brown them. Set aside.

Mix soup ingredients in a bowl. Melt
butter over low heat and sauté minced
onion until soft, about 10 minutes. Add 3
tbsp flour and continue frying for 3
minutes. Add soup ingredients, pork, and
vegetables. Cook for a couple of minutes
or until soup is heated through. Serves 4.

Ritsuko Ikeda
Japan

Pork Adobo

1 kg pork, cut into pieces about 2 inches
long and 1 1/2 inches thick
1 clove garlic, peeled and pounded
2 c water
1/2 c vinegar or
1/4 c calamansi juice
1 tbsp lard (optional)
1 tsp black pepper

Place pork in a saucepan. Add all other
ingredients. Cover saucepan and cook
slowly till meat is tender and about 1/4 of
the broth has evaporated.

Lucy Bonman
Philippines

Creamed Pork Tenderloin

1/2 kg pork tenderloin
    Pepper and paprika to taste
    Few bacon strips
6   cloves garlic
1   medium-size onion
1   big bell pepper
1   c chicken broth
1/2 c cream

Wash and clean pork and cut into strips. Chop onion, mince garlic, and cut bell pepper into pieces. Set aside. Wrap each pork strip with a piece of bacon and fasten with a toothpick. Sauté garlic, onion, and bell pepper; add pork and cook until brown. Add salt and chicken broth. Simmer for 15 minutes. Remove from fire and stir in cream. Serve hot.

NOTE: To thicken the sauce, you may add 1 tbsp tomato paste.

Heidi Graf
Switzerland

MUTTON

Kashmiri Rogunjosh

2   tbsp oil (mustard, preferably)
1   tsp cumin seeds
3   big black cardamoms
3   cloves
4   bay leaves
1   kg mutton (thigh pieces)
2   tsp red chili powder
    Salt to taste
1   tsp garam masala (curry powder)
2   c water

Pour oil in a pressure cooker. (If using mustard oil, heat it till the steaming point.) Fry cumin seeds, cardamoms, cloves, and bay leaves. Add mutton and cook on low flame for 10 minutes, sprinkling with water from time to time. Add chili powder and sprinkle some more water. Mix well to produce an even, red color. Cook for 2 minutes. Add salt and 1/2 tsp garam masala. Mix and stir for 2 more minutes.

Add 1 1/2 cups water and cover cooker; cook for 10 minutes. Remove from heat, sprinkle with 1/2 tsp garam masala, and serve hot.

NOTE: This dish can also be prepared using beef.

Shashi Raina
India

Kashmiri Kabargah

1 kg mutton (breast pieces)
2 c milk
1 c water
1 tsp cumin seeds
1 tsp garam masala
3 cardamoms
4 cloves
2 big black cardamoms
Salt as per taste
1 c yoghurt
Oil for deep frying
2 tsp coriander leaves, finely chopped

Mix mutton with all other ingredients except the last three. Put all in a pressure cooker and cook for 15 minutes. Set aside for 15 minutes. Take out every mutton piece, shaking off the clinging masala. Mix yoghurt with salt and a pinch of garam masala. Dip pieces, one at a time, in yoghurt mix and then deep-fry till brown. Garnish with coriander leaves and serve hot.

Shashi Raina
India

Yakhini

1 kg mutton, breast and thigh pieces
3 tsp anise seed
3 tsp ginger powder
Salt to taste
3 c water
3 c yoghurt
2 tsp chick-pea flour
2 tbsp corn oil
1/2 tsp cumin seeds
2 cloves
3 cardamoms
1 tsp garam masala (curry powder)

Mix mutton with anise seed, ginger powder, salt, and 2 cups water. Cook in a pressure cooker for 10 minutes. Turn off heat. Let off steam slowly by using a spoon to lift the weight. Uncover cooker slowly. Blend yoghurt and chick-pea flour in 1 cup water. Turn on flame and pour the blended ingredients little by little over the mutton, stirring constantly. Cook for another 10-25 minutes.

Heat 2 tbsp oil in a pan; saute cumin seeds, cloves, and cardamom. Add spices to cooking mutton, and mix well. Remove cooker from fire. Sprinkle mutton with garam masala, and serve hot.

Shashi Raina
India

Mutton with Kidney Beans

1/2 c kidney beans
1/2 kg mutton
1 tsp grated fresh ginger
2 sticks cinnamon
   Salt to taste
3 c water
1/4 c corn oil
3 big onions, minced
1/2 tsp turmeric powder
3 cloves garlic, minced
4 tomatoes, chopped
3 tsp coriander powder
2 tsp curry powder
1/4 tsp chili powder

Wash beans and soak overnight. Cook mutton and beans in a pressure cooker with ginger, cinnamon, and salt in 3 cups water for half an hour. More water can be added if meat and beans are not yet done.

Heat oil in a skillet, add minced onion and sauté till golden brown; add turmeric powder, garlic, and 1/4 cup water. Cook for 10-15 minutes; then add tomatoes, coriander powder, curry powder, and chili powder. Cook very well till sauce is like a thick paste. Add mutton and beans to this sauce, reserving broth. Stir on high heat for 10 minutes; add broth. Let boil for 5 minutes on high heat, then leave on low heat for 15 minutes. Serve with rice.

NOTE: This recipe can be made with beef or pork.

Indu Virmani
India

Lamb with Lettuce

1 kg lamb
1 c butter
2 onions, minced
1 tbsp corn flour
   Salt and black pepper
1 tbsp chopped parsley
1/4 tsp dill
2 green onions
4 lettuce heads, quartered
2 lemons

Cut meat into pieces of equal sizes. Boil for 5 minutes and let cool in the broth. Remove from pan and drain. Saute onions in butter; add meat and flour, stirring constantly. Be sure that the flour does not brown too much. Add 1/2 cup water, salt, black pepper, parsley, and dill. Simmer for 15 minutes. Boil green onions and lettuce for 5 minutes in another pot. Remove meat from sauce and put on one side of a dish with lettuce on the other side. Purée the meat sauce and pour over the lamb and lettuce. Garnish with lemon slices. Serves 6.

Vivi Moridis
Greece

Lampries Curry
(Mixture of Beef, Mutton, Chicken, and Pork)

1   lb chunk steak
1   lb mutton
5   tsp salt
8   cardamom pods
20   peppercorns
1   lb chicken pieces,
     breasts or thighs
1   lb pork shoulder, diced
1   tbsp ghee (butter)
2   tbsp oil
4   medium-size onions, finely chopped
8   cloves garlic, finely chopped
1   tbsp finely chopped fresh ginger root
2   tsp ground curry leaves
1/4 tsp fenugreek seeds (optional)
4   tbsp Ceylon curry powder
1   tsp ground turmeric
2   tsp chili powder
3   1-inch pc cinnamon sticks
1   tsp ground cardamom
6-8 pc dried rampe leaf (optional)
12   strips dried lemongrass (optional)
2   tbsp lemon juice
5   c coconut milk
     Extra salt

Place steak and mutton in a large saucepan with cold water. Add 2 tsp salt, cardamom, and peppercorns. Cover pan and simmer for 30 minutes. Add chicken pieces and simmer for 15 minutes. Allow to cool slightly, strain, and reserve stock for boiling rice. Dice mutton and steak into small pieces.

Heat butter and oil in a large saucepan and gently sauté onion, garlic, ginger, and curry leaves until onion is soft and starts to turn golden. Add fenugreek seeds and sauté 1 minute longer. Add curry powder, turmeric, chili powder, cinnamon stick, ground cardamom, rampe leaf, and lemongrass, if used. Add remaining 3 tsp salt, lemon juice, pork, and half the coconut milk. Stir well. Cover and cook over low heat for 30 minutes, stirring occasionally. Add parboiled steak and mutton and remaining coconut milk. Cover and simmer for approximately 1 1/2 hours, or until meat is tender and gravy is reduced. Add extra salt to taste if necessary. Remove cinnamon stick, rampe leaf, and lemongrass before serving.

Olga Ponnamperuma
Sri Lanka

Shrimp Fritters

25 grams butter
1 tbsp oil
2 medium-size onions,
1 kg shrimps, shelled and chopped
1 lemon
 Parsley
 Salt and pepper
1 egg, beaten
1 c bread crumbs

Cream
2 egg yolks, beaten
3 tsp cornstarch
1 1/2 c water

Dough
4 c water
4 tbsp butter
4 c flour

Prepare cream by mixing egg yolks, cornstarch, and water well and cooking over low heat till thick.

Melt butter and oil in a saucepan; add onions and sauté, stirring occasionally until lightly browned. Add shrimps, and cook until all liquid has evaporated. Add lemon juice, chopped parsley, pepper and salt as desired, and cream. Allow to cool slightly.

To prepare dough, place water and butter in a saucepan and bring to a boil. Add flour all at once. Beat well with a wooden spoon until mixture leaves the sides of the pan. Remove from heat and allow to cool for about 3 minutes. Roll out half of the dough to about 5 mm (1/4 inch) thick. Using a 7-cm (3-inch) cutter, cut into rounds. Put 1 tsp cooked shrimp mixture in center of round and press edges with fingers to seal. Dip the fritters in egg and then in bread crumbs and fry in deep oil until golden brown.

Fatima Lamb
Portugal

Shrimp with Cashew Nuts

1/2 kg shrimps, shelled
1 egg white
2 tsp cornstarch
2 tsp wine
1/2 tsp sesame oil
 Salt to taste
3/4 c oil
3 green onions
 Small ginger root
1/2 c cashew nuts, fried

After cleaning shrimps well, mix with egg white, cornstarch, wine, sesame oil, and salt. Marinate at least 1 hour.

Heat oil, fry shrimps for a minute; remove from pan. In the same oil, sauté green onions and ginger; add shrimps and sauce and stir very well over high heat. Add cashew nuts and serve with rice.

Nancy Chang
Taiwan, China

Stuffed Squid

4	medium-size squid, cleaned
2	fl oz olive oil
2	cloves garlic, crushed
14	oz fresh tomatoes, peeled and roughly chopped
2	fl oz dry white wine
1/2	tsp rosemary spines

Stuffing

3	tbsp fresh bread crumbs
2	tbsp chopped parsley
6	tbsp grated parmesan cheese
2	cloves garlic, chopped
1	beaten egg
	Pinch cayenne pepper
2	tbsp olive oil
	Juice of 1 lemon
	Salt and pepper
	Squid tentacles, chopped

Combine stuffing ingredients (makes quite a moist mixture). Stuff squid and sew up ends. Don't fill too full as stuffing will expand when cooked. You may prepare in advance to this point, keeping the stuffed squid in the refrigerator until it is time to cook them.

Sauté garlic in olive oil in a large pan or casserole. Brown squid on all sides. Add tomatoes, wine, and rosemary and reduce heat. Simmer for about 30 minutes, turning occasionally.

Kate Kirk
UK

Stuffed Squid

1	kg large squid
250	grams mussel, shells removed
4	stalks green onions
250	grams shrimps
200	grams butter
500	grams rice
1	lemon, sliced
	Parsley
1/3	c ouzo

Clean and wash squids. Separate body from the head and tress. Chop head and tress fine. Sauté onions, finely cut, in butter. Add shrimps, mussels, squid head and tress, rice, salt, and pepper; sauté for 5-10 minutes. Add ouzo. Stuff squid bodies, and place them in a pan with a little water. Bake for 25 minutes in 375 °F. Before serving, decorate with lemon slices and parsley.

Vivi Moridis
Greece

Prawn Blachan

1   c dried prawn powder
1/2 c desiccated coconut
2   tsp chili powder (to taste)
2   medium-size onions, chopped
1   tsp salt (to taste)
3   cloves garlic, sliced
1   tbsp ginger root, finely chopped
2/3 c lemon juice

Place prawn powder in a dry frying pan and heat for a few minutes, stirring continuously. Turn onto a large plate. Place desiccated coconut in the same pan and heat, stirring constantly, until it turns a rich brown color. Turn out onto a plate to cool. Place remaining ingredients into blender container, cover and blend until smooth. Add prawn powder and desiccated coconut, cover and blend again, adding a little water if necessary to bind ingredients together. Scrape down sides of container with a spatula from time to time. Turn onto a plate and form into a round, flat cake. Serve with rice and curries.

Olga Ponnamperuma
Sri Lanka

FISH

Half-fried Fish

500 grams seer fish
1   tsp black pepper
1/2 tsp turmeric powder
1   tsp chili powder
2   tbsp vinegar
3   tbsp oil
3   big onions, chopped
6   green chilies, chopped
2   tsp lime or calamansi juice
     Salt

Cut fish into 2- x 2-cm pieces and sprinkle with pepper, turmeric powder, and some salt. Add some water and bring to a boil on low heat. Drain excess water from fish and add chili powder and vinegar.

Heat oil in a pan, add onions and green chilies, stir for a while to mix well. Boil 3-4 minutes then add boiled fish, lime or calamansi juice. Simmer on low heat till fish is done.

Tilaka Senanayake
Sri Lanka

Fish Loaf

1	kg fish
4	slices of bread
2	tsp ground ginger
1	tsp ground garlic
1/4	c cubed onions
1	tsp coriander powder
1/2	tsp cumin powder
2	tsp green chili (can be adjusted according to taste)
1/2	tsp black pepper
	Salt to taste
1-2	tbsp oil
2	hard-boiled eggs (cut into cubes, reserve one egg yolk for garnish)
	Oil for frying

Debone fish and ground meat. Soak bread slices in water, then mix with ground fish. Add the rest of the ingredients to fish. Make 2 round loaves. Wrap the loaves in cheese cloth and tie both ends tightly. Boil loaves in water for half an hour or until done. Cool, then unwrap.

Heat oil in a frying pan and fry loaves till they are a light color on the outside. Slice loaves and garnish each slice with tomato sauce and egg yolk crumbs.

Fauzi Bhuiyan
Bangladesh

Baked Fish with Tomatoes

2 1/2	lb whole fish or a large piece
1/2	lb tomatoes
1	oz clarified butter
1/2	tsp ground
4	fenugreek seeds
4	cloves garlic (2 sliced, 2 minced)
1	inch green ginger, sliced
1	tbsp cumin, coarsely ground
1	tbsp fresh coriander leaves
1 1/2	tsp turmeric powder
4	tbsp double cream
1/2	pint yoghurt
1	tsp paprika, roasted
1/4	tsp cayenne
1	tbsp vinegar
1	lemon or lime

Clean fish after removing head and tail. Peel tomatoes, remove the seeds, and sieve the pulp. Sauté the fenugreek seeds in butter over low heat. Add sliced garlic and ginger when seeds are light brown; drain, and remove spices; set aside. To leftover butter add ground ginger and minced garlic with 3/4 pint water. Add cumin, coriander, turmeric, and tomatoes. Beat yoghurt and cream together very well; add this mixture and paprika to the spices. Then add sauteed fenugreek, garlic, and ginger. Bring to a boil and simmer until liquid is reduced to less than half.

Place the fish in a baking dish, and dust with salt and cayenne. Sprinkle with vinegar on both sides, then bake in hot oven (400 °F) until all liquid has evaporated. Pour sauce over the fish and continue baking in medium heat (350 °F) until done (about 35 minutes). Arrange thin, round slices of lemon or lime on top of fish. Continue baking in a very hot oven until the lemon slices soften. Serve hot with rice.

Roopa Dewan
India

Rellenong Bangus (Stuffed Milkfish)

1   whole milkfish
1   tbsp soy sauce
2   tsp lemon juice or calamansi juice
2   tsp sugar
4   c water plus 1 tsp lemon juice

Stuffing
2   tbsp cooking oil
1   clove garlic, minced
1   small onion, chopped
1   medium tomato, chopped
1/4 c frozen peas
1   tsp salt
2   tbsp raisins
1   tsp salt
2   tbsp sweet pickle relish
1/4 c grated carrot
1/8 tsp pepper
2   eggs, slightly beaten

Pound the fish body gently until it is soft. Break the spine near the tail and just below the head, and carefully pull it out through the head opening. Turn fish shell inside out carefully. Remove as much flesh as possible from shell without breaking the skin. Return shell to right position; marinate in soy sauce, lemon juice, and sugar. Set aside.

Boil water and lemon juice mixture; drop meat and bones in boiling water. Bring to a boil again. Remove pot from heat and let stand covered for about 5 minutes, or until meat becomes firm. Drain, pick over fish meat to remove all bones.

Prepare stuffing. Sauté garlic, onion, and tomatoes in hot oil, add peas and cook until done. Add fish meat and all other stuffing ingredients except eggs; sauté for about 1 minute. Let cool. Add eggs to stuffing mixture, and stuff drained fish shell.

Fry in hot oil until brown on both sides, or brush fish all over with oil and bake at 375 °F for 45 minutes in a pan lined with aluminum foil, turning fish once to brown evenly. Brush with more oil to prevent drying up. Slice when slightly cooled. Serves 4-5.

Vilma Garrity
Philippines

Salmon Mousse

1   envelope unflavored gelatin
1/2 c clam juice (or water)
2   tbsp minced fresh dill or
1   tsp dried dill weed
2   tbsp grated onion
1   tbsp lemon juice
1   tsp salt
    Dash of tabasco sauce
3/4 c plain yoghurt
1/2 c sour cream (or mayonnaise)
1/2 c celery, finely chopped
2   cans (7 3/4 oz each) red sockeye salmon,
    drained

In a small saucepan, sprinkle gelatin over cold water or the clam juice. Let stand 5 minutes until soft. Warm over medium heat until dissolved. Cool to room temperature. Stir in dill, onion, lemon juice, salt, tabasco, yoghurt, sour cream, and celery. Refrigerate until just beginning to set. Remove skin and bones from salmon. Mash with a fork. Add to gelatin mixture. Spoon into a 4-cup mold; cover and refrigerate until firm (at least 3 hours). Unmold and surround with melba toast or fresh vegetables.

Ilse Zandstra
Canada

Mustard Fish

500 grams fish
3-4 tsp mustard
3-4 green chilies
3   tbsp mustard oil or any cooking oil
1/2 tsp cumin seed
1-3 tomatoes
1/2 tsp turmeric powder
    Salt to taste

Fry fish lightly. Grind the mustard and green chili into a paste, adding a little amount of water (1 cup). Again put some cooking oil in the frying pan. Add cumin seed, and tomatoes; wait for 15 seconds, then add fried fish, liquefied mustard paste, turmeric, salt, and 1 cup water. Cover pan and let the mixture boil. Add 1 tsp mustard oil before removing from fire. Serve with rice.

Supti Mallik
India

Fish Curry with Cauliflower

1	kg cauliflower, separated into florets
200	grams potatoes, sliced
1/4	c cooking oil
500	grams fish
1	tsp ginger
2	tsp cumin powder
3-4	tomatoes, chopped
4-5	green chilies
1/4	tsp sugar
1	tsp turmeric powder
1	tsp salt
1	tsp butter or ghee

Sauté cauliflower and potato. Remove from pan. Deep-fry fish in cooking oil. Put oil in another frying pan, then add ginger, cumin powder, tomato, chili, sugar, turmeric powder, and cauliflower; saute all for a while. Add enough water and salt to taste. Next add fried potato and fish and cover pan. Bring to a boil and cook for 10 minutes. Add ghee. Serve with rice.

Supti Mallik (Bengal)
India

Fish Cutlets

1/2	lb fish (tanigue)
3	tbsp butter
2	cloves garlic, minced
1-inch	piece ginger, minced
2	green chilies, sliced thinly
2	onions, minced
1	tsp salt
1	tsp sugar
2	tbsp chili powder
1	tbsp cumin powder
3	potatoes, boiled and mashed
1	tbsp flour
2	tsp garam masala
1/2	c bread crumbs
1	egg, slightly beaten
1/2	c cooking oil for deep-frying

Steam fish until cooked. Cool and scrape off meat, discard bones. Mash meat. Heat butter in pan. Sauté garlic, ginger, green chilies, and onions till fragrant. Add fish, salt, sugar, chili powder, and cumin powder. Stir and mix thoroughly. Mix fish mixture thoroughly with mashed potatoes, flour, and garam masala. Take a handful of the mixture, roll into a ball, and flatten slightly. Coat with bread crumbs and dip in egg. Roll in bread crumbs again. Heat cooking oil and deep-fry cutlets until golden brown. Serve while hot with chutney or chili sauce.

Harmit Wasan
Singapore

Gratin de Fruits de Mer (Baked Fish and Seafoods)

3   bay leaves
2   onions
     Salt to taste
     Pepper
3   liters water
300 grams fish
     (lapu-lapu, any
     other boneless
     fish)
200 grams shrimps
100 grams mussels
200 grams mushrooms
     (whole)
100 grams crab

Sauce
30   grams butter or
     oil
40   grams flour
1/2   liter milk
1   tbsp tomato paste
     or
1/2   tin of bisque
     (cream)
100 grams swiss
     cheese

Boil bay leaves, onion, salt, and pepper in water for 5 minutes. Add fish and boil for 5 minutes. Remove fish from broth. Boil shrimps, mussels, and mushrooms in the broth for 5 minutes. Add crabs, boil for 10 minutes. Sauté all with salt and pepper for 5 minutes.

Melt butter; add flour, mixing slowly. Add milk, stirring constantly. Add tomato paste and salt and pepper to taste. Mix sauce with fish and seafoods and place all in a baking dish. Sprinkle with grated cheese and bake for 10 minutes at 350 °F.

Claudie Arraudeau
France

Macchi-Methi (Fish with Fenugreek Leaves)

50   grams refined cooking oil
1/2   tsp methi seeds
1/2   kg tomato, chopped
250 grams onion, chopped
10   cloves garlic
1   kg methi (fenugreek) leaves, chopped
1/2   tsp chili powder
2   tsp coriander powder
500 grams fish (carpa, tanigue, etc.), sliced
1/2   tsp turmeric powder
1   tsp dried mango powder
2   green chilies
1   bunch coriander leaves
     Salt

Heat oil in a pan. Add methi seeds and onion; sauté until light brown. Add garlic and tomato and sauté for another 5 minutes. Add chopped methi leaves, chili powder, coriander powder, and salt. Mix thoroughly for about 2 minutes, then pressure cook about 5-7 minutes. Remove lid and let steam out. Cook over high flame, uncovered, till half the water dries up. Place fish pieces one by one in the pan, add turmeric powder and dried mango powder. Cover pan and simmer over low flame. Turn fish pieces once and cook for 10 minutes or till the water dries up. Remove from flame and garnish with green chilies and coriander leaves. Serve with rice.

Malvika Dadlani
India

Breads
Rolls

Breads and Rolls

Speedy Dinner Rolls

1/2   c warm water
2   tbsp yeast
1   c water or milk
1/3   c sugar
3 1/2 c flour
1   tsp salt
2   eggs
1/3   c margarine or butter

Soften yeast in 1/2 cup warm water. Mix together remaining 1 cup milk or water, sugar, and softened yeast. Then add 1 tsp salt and 1 cup flour. Beat. Add eggs and butter; beat. Work in remaining flour and mix until smooth. Cover and let stand for 20 minutes. Form into rolls. Let rise until double. Bake for 12-15 minutes at 375 °F.

Judy Buresh
USA

Ugali

1   kg flour (corn, rice, sorghum, millet, or cassava flour)
2   liters water

Boil water; add flour little by little (to avoid formation of balls) until the mixture becomes thick; keep on stirring until it is well cooked. Serve with beef stew or chicken stew, or fish.

Eva Kanyeka
Tanzania

Ulmer Klosse

5   buns (3-4 days old)
50 grams smoked bacon
1   onion, finely chopped
    Parsley
2   eggs
1   tsp salt
    Pinch of paprika and nutmeg

Soak buns in cold water. Cut bacon in small cubes, and fry. Add onions and parsley. Squeeze water out of the buns and tear them into small pieces. Place in a bowl, add the bacon/onion mixture, eggs, and spices. Mix well with hands. Form balls (klosse) and drop them in boiling salted water. Let the klosse simmer for about 5 minutes. Serve with any dark meat dish or with tomato sauce and salads.

Marie Kürschner
Germany

Frank's Pizza (Vegetarian)

Dough

1	tbsp yeast	1 3/4	c flour
1/2	tsp sugar	1/4	tsp salt
5/8	c warm water		

Dissolve sugar and yeast in warm water. Stir and let it sit in a warm place until the yeast begins to work (about 5 minutes). The yeast mixture is ready when it begins to get foamy.

Add 1 1/2 cups flour to the yeast and mix to form dough. Turn the dough onto a board that has been floured with the remaining 1/4 cup flour. Knead the dough about 10 minutes. During kneading, use flour to keep the dough from sticking to the board or to your hands. The dough is ready when it is "rubbery," that is, when it stretches instead of tearing when you pull on it.

Put dough in an oiled bowl and cover with a clean towel. Let rise about 30 minutes while you make the sauce.

Sauce

4-5 cloves garlic, minced
1 onion, chopped
1 can tomato sauce (8-oz can)
   Salt and pepper to taste
1/2 tsp oregano
1/2 tsp sugar
1/2 tsp fennel
   Pinch of hot pepper

Sauté garlic and onions in a little oil until soft. Add the remaining ingredients and simmer for 20-30 minutes, or until the sauce is thickened.

Topping

2 chopped onions, sautéed
2 c chopped olives
2 sliced green pepper
1/2 c shrimp
1 c mushrooms
1/4 c drained pineapple chunks
2 hard-boiled eggs, sliced

The best cheese to use is mozzarella. One-half pound is required.

A heavy cast-iron skillet is best for baking the pizza. Oil the skillet and spread the dough evenly on it with your hands. Make a ridge around the edge so the topping won't spill out. Spread sauce over the dough. Arrange toppings on the sauce and sprinkle cheese over them. Bake in a hot oven 425 °F for at least 20 minutes, or until the pizza top is bubbly and the cheese is turning brown. This recipe makes one 12-inch pizza.

Rae Bourquein
USA

Naans

2 1/2 c all-purpose flour
2   tsp sugar
2   tsp baking powder
2   tsp salt
2   eggs
1/2 tbsp yeast
3   tbsp butter or cooking oil
1/4 c yoghurt
1/2 c milk or water
2   tbsp poppy seeds (optional)
4   tbsp butter or
2   egg yolks

Sift flour, sugar, baking powder, and salt into a big bowl. Warm yoghurt and milk or water. Then add yeast, butter or cooking oil, and egg. Mix to combine thoroughly. Make a depression in the center of flour mixture and pour in yeast mixture. Mix very well. Knead for 15 minutes till smooth and spongy. (If dough is sticky or soft, a little more flour can be added. If it is hard, a little more warm water can be added.) Cover; leave in a warm place to rise until double.

Divide dough into 10 balls, using dry flour on hands. Set aside for another 15 minutes. Flatten each ball and roll out to 1/3 inch (8 mm) thick. Place on a greased cookie sheet. Brush top with melted butter or beaten egg yolks. Make small cuts on a few places on the naan. Sprinkle with poppy seeds. Bake for 10 minutes at 450 °F or 230 °C. Then grill for 3-5 minutes or until top is lightly browned. Serve hot with curry.

Nusrat Khan
Pakistan

Lebanese Bread

1   tbsp dry yeast
1   tsp sugar
2 1/2 c warm water
7   c all-purpose flour or
925 grams brown flour
2   tsp salt
2   tbsp oil

Dissolve yeast and sugar in 1 cup warm water; let stand for about 5 minutes. Mix flour, salt, and oil in a large bowl. Add yeast mixture. Add remaining warm water, mix well, and knead for at least 15 minutes until smooth. Put in warm, oiled bowl, turning dough over to coat surface with oil. Cover bowl with dry cloth. Put in warm place to rise until double, about 2 hours. Punch dough down. Make a big ball, then cut into 4 pieces. On a lightly floured board, roll out each piece into a circle, then roll out with rolling pin to make it thin. Cut out circles with a small cup. Place on dry cloth and let rise in a warm place for 1 hour. Bake 6-8 minutes in a preheated oven on a preheated baking sheet, 500 °F or 260 °C.

Katia Sayegh
Lebanon

Cinnamon Raisin English Muffin Bread

6	c flour
1/2	c raisins
2	tbsp yeast
1	tbsp sugar
2	tsp salt
1 1/2	tsp cinnamon
1/4	tsp baking soda
2	c milk
1/2	c water
	Cornmeal or flour

Combine 3 cups flour, raisins, yeast, sugar, salt, cinnamon, and baking soda. Set aside. In a saucepan, combine milk and water. Heat on low fire until warm (120-130 °F). Gradually add to dry ingredients and beat well. Stir in remaining flour to make a stiff batter. Spoon into 2 loaf pans that have been greased and coated with cornmeal or flour. Cover and let rise 45 minutes. Bake 400 °F or 200 °C for 25 minutes. Remove from pan immediately; cool.

Judy Buresh
USA

Nature Bread

2	tbsp yeast
2 1/4	c warm water
1	c raisins
3/4	c wheat germ
3/4	c shredded carrots
2/3	c nonfat dry milk
1/3	c molasses
1/3	c oil
3	tbsp sugar
1	tbsp salt
2 1/2	c whole wheat flour
3 1/2-4	c all-purpose flour or white flour
	Melted butter or oil

Dissolve yeast in water in a large bowl. Stir in raisins, wheat germ, carrots, dry milk, molasses, oil, sugar, salt, whole wheat flour, and 1 cup white flour. Beat vigorously with wooden spoon for 1 minute. Stir in about 1 1/2 cups white flour to make a stiff dough. Turn out on floured surface. Knead until smooth, about 10 minutes. Place in a well-oiled bowl, brush top with butter. Cover, let rise in warm place until double in bulk, about 2 hours. Punch down, divide into two portions. Roll each into an 8- × 12-inch rectangle. Roll up, starting at short end. Turn ends under and seal. Place in two greased loaf pans. Cover; let rise until double in bulk, about 1 1/2 hours. Bake in moderate oven 350 °F for 30-40 minutes until loaves sound hollow when tapped. Remove from pans and cool on wire racks. Brush top with butter while still hot, if desired. Makes 2 loaves.

Judy Buresh
USA

Butter Crescents

2   tbsp yeast
2   c warm water
2   c butter, melted
1   c sugar
6   eggs, beaten
1 1/2 tsp salt
9   c flour

In a large mixing bowl, dissolve yeast in warm water. Add 1 cup melted butter, sugar, eggs, and salt; stir well. Gradually add flour, mixing well. Cover and let rise in a warm place (85 °F) for 4 hours. Divide dough into 4 equal parts. Turn each part out onto a lightly floured board. Knead 4 or 5 times. Roll into 12-inch circles and brush with remaining melted butter. Cut each circle into 12 wedges. Roll up each wedge, beginning at wide end, and place on lightly greased cookie sheets. Let rise 1 hour in a warm place. Bake for 10 minutes at 400 °F or until light brown. Yield: 4 dozen rolls.

Judy Buresh
USA

No-Knead Whole Wheat Bread

2   tbsp molasses
1/3   c butter
2 1/2 c buttermilk
4   c whole wheat flour
1 1/2 c oatmeal
2   eggs
2   tbsp yeast
1 1/2 c white flour

Heat together molasses, butter, and buttermilk until warm. Add this to whole wheat flour and oatmeal. Add 2 eggs and yeast. Beat. Stir in white flour. Let rise until double (about 25 minutes). Punch down. Shape and place in greased loaf pans. Let rise until double (about 25 minutes). Bake for 35-40 minutes at 375 °F. Sunflower seeds or nuts can be added.

NOTE: To make buttermilk, add 2 tbsp juice or vinegar to each cup of milk and let stand for 5 minutes.

Judy Buresh
USA

Pizza

Dough

1	tbsp yeast
1	c warm water
2 1/2	c white or whole wheat flour
1	tsp salt
2	tbsp oil
1	tsp sugar

Sauce

1	c tomato sauce
2	tsp oregano
1 1/4	tsp salt
1/8	tsp garlic powder
1/8	tsp black pepper

or

1	c tomato sauce
1	onion
3	cloves garlic
1/2	c water
	Pinch of sugar
1/2	tsp red pepper (optional)
1/2	tsp oregano
1	tbsp oil
1/4	c parmesan cheese
1/2	c mozzarella cheese

Dissolve yeast in warm water. Stir in remaining ingredients; beat vigorously in 20 strokes. Let rest for about 5 minutes. Dough makes 2 11-inch circles or one deep dish crust for 9- × 13- × 9-inch pan.

Combine ingredients in a saucepan. Bring to a boil; simmer for 20 minutes. Grease pans. Spread out dough. Spread sauce over dough. Sprinkle with parmesan cheese. Then add whatever toppings you like: hamburger, onions, green pepper, tuna, sausage, mushrooms, olives, etc. Sprinkle grated mozzarella cheese on top. Bake for 20-25 minutes at 425 °F, or until cheese is lightly browned.

To prepare ahead for use on the same day
Make pizza dough. Cover with foil or plastic wrap and store in refrigerator up to 4 hours. Do not put pizza sauce or cheese on dough until just before baking.

To prepare ahead for use within 7 days
Make pizza dough. Bake at 425 °F for 7-8 minutes or until light golden brown. Cool thoroughly. Pour on sauce and other ingredients. Freeze until sauce is hard. Cover with foil and store in freezer. Bake from a frozen state (uncovered) in a preheated oven at 500 °F or 260 °C for about 10 minutes.

Judy Buresh
USA

Dal Puri

1 tsp ginger, minced
1 tbsp onion, minced
  Green chili, minced
1/2 c lentil (or any other dal)
  Shortening for frying
3 c flour
1 tsp salt
3 tbsp oil
1 c onion, thinly sliced
1 tsp roasted, ground cumin seed
  Chili powder

Mix ginger, onion, green chili, and enough water to cook the dal. After cooking, stir for sometime, then allow to dry completely. Mix flour with salt and oil. Add water little by little until dough is easy to handle. Knead it very well on a lightly floured surface. Cover and let stand for about 30 minutes.

On medium heat, fry onion in deep oil until it turns golden brown (it should be crispy). Cool and grind it. Mix the dal with ground onion, cumin, chili powder, and salt.

Divide dough into 18-20 balls and the dal into 18-20 portions. Take a ball, and flatten it into a circle with the palm. Stuff with dal and then seal. Do this with all the balls.

Roll out each ball carefully into a circular disk (dust it with flour, if necessary). Fry (not deep-fry) each piece separately in a small amount of oil in a heavy skillet.

NOTE: Do-ahead tip. Instead of frying in oil, warm both sides in a heavy skillet until the color changes. Cool and wrap balls, 2-3 pieces together, before freezing. Before using them, thaw completely and fry in oil the usual way.

Fauzi Bhuiyan
Bangladesh

Dutch Fried Puffs

3/4 c milk
1/2 c sugar
1/2 c oil
2 eggs
3 tsp baking powder
1/2 tsp salt
1/2 tsp ground mace
2 1/2 c flour
1/2 c raisins
1/4 c sugar
1/2 tsp ground cinnamon
  Oil for deep-frying

Mix the first 6 ingredients in a bowl. Beat on low speed for 30 seconds, scraping the bowl constantly. Beat on medium speed for 2 more minutes. Stir in the next 3 ingredients. Heat oil on high flame. Drop batter by teaspoonfuls in hot oil. Turn puffs as they rise, and fry until golden brown on each side. Drain on paper towels. Combine sugar and cinnamon, and roll puffs in the mixture. Makes 30 puffs.

Joan Hagerman
USA

Paratha

2   c flour
1/2 tsp baking powder
1/2 tsp baking soda
1/4 tsp salt
1/4 tsp sugar
2   tbsp oil
1/2 c water
     Shortening

Sift flour very well with the next 4 ingredients. Add oil and mix well. Slowly add water little by little until the dough is easy to handle. Turn the dough onto a lightly floured surface and knead it very well until it is smooth. Cover with a wet cloth and set aside for about 30 minutes.

Divide the dough into 6-8 balls. Roll out each ball into a thin circle, dusting with flour if necessary. Spread shortening on top and dust it with flour. Make one cut from the center to the edge. Start rolling the dough lightly from one side while keeping your thumb in the center. The dough will be in the shape of a cone. Press the cone with the hand. Cover cones with a towel.

Take out one piece at a time and roll into a 1/8-inch-thick disk. Warm both sides of the paratha carefully on a hot griddle for a few minutes. Add 1/2 tsp oil, then fry both sides till light golden-brown. Serve with curried meat or vegetable dishes.

Do-ahead tip: instead of frying in shortening, heat both sides till the color changes. Cool; wrap before freezing. Before using, thaw and fry in shortening.

Fauzi Bhuiyan
Bangladesh

Cranberry Walnut Muffins

2   c all-purpose flour
3/4 c granulated sugar
1   tbsp baking powder
1/2 tsp baking soda
1/2 tsp salt
1 1/2 c chopped fresh (or 1 c frozen) cranberries
1/2 c chopped walnuts
2   eggs
1   c milk
1/4 c butter or margarine, melted
1   tsp vanilla

Combine first 7 ingredients in a mixing bowl. Stir well to blend. Beat last 4 ingredients together, and add all at once to dry ingredients. Stir just until all ingredients are moistened. Fill well-greased muffin cups 3/4 full. Bake at 375 °F for 20 to 25 minutes or until top springs back when lightly touched. Remove from pan and cool on wire racks. Makes 2 dozen muffins.

Ilse Zandstra
Canada

Pancake

1 c cottage cheese
3 eggs
1/4 c flour
2 tsp sugar
2 tsp vegetable oil

Beat all ingredients together. If batter is too thick, add 1-2 tsp milk. Fry small 2- or 3-inch pancakes.

NOTE: These pancakes can be frozen and reheated.

Marge Litsinger
USA

Desserts

Desserts

Agar-Agar

30 grams agar-agar, cut in small pieces and soaked in 1 liter water
220 grams sugar
1/2 tsp salt
400 ml coconut milk
6 screw pine leaves (pandan leaves) tied in a knot
4 drops red food color

Press agar-agar lightly to fill one cup. Boil the water and pandan leaves in a saucepan. Add the agar-agar and boil until dissolved. Add sugar and continue to boil, until sugar is dissolved. Add coconut milk and salt. When mixture is about to boil remove from heat. Add food color. Pour into a dish. Set on a flat surface and allow to cool. Chill. Cut before serving.

NOTE: Do not shake or move the tray of agar-agar until the mixture is well set.

Harmit Wasan
Singapore

Strained Beans

1/2 kg black beans
1/2 can evaporated milk
2 lb sugar
1/2 cup water
1 tsp cloves, ground
1 tsp toasted sesame seeds

Soak beans overnight. Boil them next morning until cooked. Rub through a sieve, together with the milk. In a saucepan make a syrup with the sugar, water, and cloves. Pour syrup over the bean purée. Simmer mixture, stirring constantly until done (when you can see the bottom of the saucepan). Put in a bowl and sprinkle with toasted sesame seed. Serve cold.

Cecilia Chujoy
Peru

Chocolate Fudge Pudding

1 c self-rising flour
1/2 c sugar
2 tbsp cocoa
1/2 c milk
2 oz butter
1/2 c brown sugar
1 1/2 c hot water

Mix flour, sugar, and 1 tbsp cocoa in a bowl. Melt butter in milk, then add to dry ingredients and mix. Put into a well-greased ovenproof dish. Mix brown sugar and remaining cocoa and sprinkle on top. Pour hot water on batter. Do not stir or mix—have faith. Bake at 350 °F for 1/2 hour until the top is cake-like, with sauce underneath. Delicious with whipped cream or ice cream.

Karen Moody
USA

Burmese Pudding

7 eggs
4 pints milk
1 c sugar
1/2 c flour
3 tbsp butter

Beat eggs thoroughly. Boil milk, then add sugar and flour; mix well. Add eggs and butter; mix well. Pour mixture into medium-size curry bowls with covers. Place bowls in a large pot with 10 pints water and steam for 1 hour.

Lily Khin Win
Myanmar

Quick Trifle

Crumble sponge cake into a bowl. Sprinkle liberally with sherry (optional). Add a can of raspberries and enough juice to moisten. Top with custard (homemade or from a can). When cool, cover with whipped cream. Decorate with chopped nuts, glace cherries, or chocolate vermicelli.

Mary Greenland
UK

Buco Lychee Sherbet

8-10 buco (young coconut), grated
1 can lychees, cut into small strips
4 c buco juice (water from buco)
1 c lychee syrup
1 c white sugar

Mix all ingredients in a bowl and freeze overnight. To serve, use an ice pick to break up the buco-lychees into small bits. Scoop and serve in small cups or glasses.

Cheli Banta
Philippines

Leche Flan

2 c milk
8 egg yolks, slightly beaten
1 c sugar
1 tsp vanilla
2 tbsp brown sugar
1/4 c water

Scald milk in a double boiler for 15 minutes. Add egg yolks, sugar, and vanilla and mix till sugar is dissolved. Using a strainer, pour into a mold lined with caramelized sugar. Place this in a bigger pan half-filled with water. Bake until firm. Cool before removing from mold. Refrigerate before serving.

To caramelize sugar, dissolve brown sugar in water and cook over moderate heat until the sugar browns, or caramelizes. Line a suitable mold with 3/4 of the caramelized syrup. Use remaining syrup when serving flan.

Lucy Bonman
Philippines

Buco Pie

1/4 c cornstarch
1 1/4 c sugar
1/4 tsp salt
2 c buco water
1/2 c evaporated milk
2 eggs, well beaten
1 tsp vanilla
2 tbsp butter
2 c buco meat, coarsely chopped
Pastry for 2-crust pie

Mix cornstarch, sugar, and salt. Combine buco water and milk; add gradually to the cornstarch mixture. Cook on medium heat till thickened. Add eggs and cook for 1 more minute; add vanilla and butter. Pour on prepared pie shell with the layer of buco meat in between cream sauce. Adjust top crust. Bake at 350 °F for 30 minutes or until golden brown.

Adela Reyes
Philippines

Lazy Marie (Marshmallow Squares)

1 pkg unflavored gelatin
1 c boiling water
2 c cold water
1/2 c sugar
2 c grated fresh coconut

Put gelatin in a bowl and add boiling water. Stir, add cold water. Mix in sugar and beat with mixer until contents thicken.

Butter a 9- × 13-inch pan, pour mixture into it. Cool for 1 hour. Cut into small squares and roll in fresh coconut.

Neiares Singh
Brazil

Shrikhand

1 liter fresh milk (or 1 kg yoghurt)
Powdered sugar
1/2 tsp saffron (or yellow food coloring)
1/2 nutmeg
1/4 tsp cardamom powder
3 almonds, diced
5 pistachios, diced

Prepare yoghurt from 1 liter fresh milk (or use yoghurt). Put yoghurt in cheesecloth and drain water to make cheese. Weigh

the cheese. Mix an equal quantity of powdered sugar and cheese (by weight). Let stand for 1 hour. When sugar dissolves, add saffron. Decorate with almonds, pistachios, and spices. Serve cold.

Smita Gadgil
India

Sweet Potato Casserole

3   c cooked and mashed sweet potatoes
1/2 c sugar
2   eggs
1   tsp vanilla
1/2 c butter, melted
1/3 c milk

Topping
1   c brown sugar
1   c chopped nuts
1/3 c flour
1/3 c butter, melted

Mix first 6 ingredients, beating well. Put into a baking dish. Mix ingredients for topping and sprinkle on top of sweet potatoes. Bake at 350 °F for about 25 minutes.

Judy Buresh
USA

Ribbon Jello

2   3-oz pkg red jello
2   3-oz pkg lime jello
2   3-oz pkg lemon jello
2   3-oz pkg orange or peach jello
1/2 c evaporated milk

First layer: Pour 1 cup boiling water in a bowl. Sprinkle 1 package red jello over the water. Stir to dissolve; add 1/2 cup cold water. Chill and allow to set.

Second layer: Pour 1 cup boiling water in a bowl. Sprinkle another red jello package over the water. Stir to dissolve.

Cool to room temperature. Add 1/2 cup evaporated milk. Chill until slightly thickened, then pour on top of fruit layer. Repeat with other colors adding slightly thickened mixture when preceding layer has set.

NOTE: This is a very attractive but time-consuming dessert to make.

Judy Buresh
USA

Pineapple Dessert

1/2 c butter
1/2 c sugar
4 eggs
5 slices bread (dried and crushed)
1 can crushed pineapple or pineapple pieces

Cream butter and sugar. Beat in eggs one at a time. Stir in pineapple and bread. Put in greased 1 1/2-quart casserole. Bake at 350 °F for 1 hour or until done.

Judy Buresh
USA

Halo-Halo

1 tbsp sweetened langka (jackfruit)
1 tbsp ube jam
1 tbsp sweetened kaong (sugar palm seeds)
1 tbsp sweetened garbanzos (chick-pea)
1 tbsp leche flan
1 tbsp sweetened macapuno
1 tsp toasted pinipig (crispy rice)
Sugar to taste
Shaved ice
Milk
Vanilla ice cream (optional)

Combine the first 8 ingredients in a tall glass. Fill the glass with shaved ice. Pour milk over ice. Top with vanilla ice cream. Serve immediately.

Lucy Bonman
Philippines

Cassava Cake

3 tbsp shortening
2 eggs
1 c sugar
1 1/4 c coconut milk
120 grams cassava powder
1 c buco, cut into strips
4 tbsp grated cheese

Melt shortening. Beat eggs; add sugar, melted shortening, and coconut milk. Add cassava powder, buco strips, and 2 tbsp cheese; mix well. Line a greased mold or pie pan with wax paper. Pour in mixture. Bake at 350 °F for 50-60 minutes. When almost done, brush with butter, and sprinkle top with sugar and remaining cheese. Continue baking until golden brown.

NOTE: Sweetened macapuno may also be used as a topping.

Lucy Bonman
Philippines

Pavlova

4-5	egg whites	1	tsp cornflour
	Pinch of salt	1	tsp white vinegar
1 1/4	c castor sugar	1	tsp vanilla

Line a cookie tray with greaseproof paper. Draw an 8- to 9-inch circle. Scald bowl and beaters; dry with clean towel. Pour egg whites into warm bowl; add salt. Beat with an electric mixer on high speed. While beating, add castor sugar slowly (about 3 minutes). Fold in cornflour, vinegar, and vanilla.

Pile mixture onto prepared tray, within the circle, and surround with a greased springform ring or greased foil collar. Spread out evenly, keeping mixture to 1 1/4 to 1 1/2 inch deep. Bake in a preheated, slow oven (250 °F) for 1 to 1 1/4 hours, or until surface is crisp and dry. Slide the pavlova and greaseproof paper onto a cake cooler. Remove foil collar or ring while still hot. Let cool. Invert pavlova onto a flat serving dish and peel off paper. Cover with whipped cream, strawberries, kiwi or other fresh fruit. Sprinkle with nuts. The pavlova should have a crisp thin outer shell and a delicious, soft center. Pavlovas without filling can be frozen.

Alice Flinn
Marlene Quick
Australia

Yoghurt Cake

1	8-oz carton plain yoghurt
2	cartons sugar
4	c flour
1	carton oil
2	eggs
2	tsp baking powder
1 1/2	tsp grated lemon

Empty yoghurt into a large bowl and use empty carton as a measure. Combine all ingredients and mix well. Pour into a greased pan. Bake at 350 °F for 45 minutes (or until tester inserted into center comes out clean).

Françoise Prot
France

Pumpkin Chiffon Pie

1   envelope Knox gelatin
1/2 c dark brown sugar
1/2 tsp salt
1/2 tsp nutmeg
1/2 tsp cinnamon
1/4 tsp ginger
2   eggs, separated
1/4 c dark brown sugar
1   c evaporated milk
1/2 c cold water
1 1/4 c canned pumpkin (small can)
1/2 c heavy cream, whipped (optional)
     Baked 9-inch pie shell

Combine gelatin, 1/2 cup brown sugar, salt, and spices. In double-boiler top, beat egg yolks; stir in milk, water, pumpkin, then gelatin mixture. Cook over boiling water, stirring, for 10 minutes (longer if you use double recipe). Refrigerate, stirring occasionally, until as thick and syrupy as unbeaten egg white. Beat egg whites until fairly stiff; gradually add 1/4 cup brown sugar, beating until very stiff; fold in pumpkin mixture. Turn into baked pie shell. Refrigerate until set. Serve with whipped cream.

NOTE: Fresh pumpkin, cooked and mashed, can be used.

Caren Hill
USA

Date Pie

8   oz dates, chopped
1/2 c raisins
1   tbsp golden syrup
3/4 c water
     Dough for 2-crust pie

Mix all ingredients and cook till mushy and most of the water has been absorbed (about 10-15 minutes). Pour mixture on pie shell and adjust top crust. Bake at 420 °F for 40 minutes or till top crust becomes crispy.

Isabel Way
UK

Clafoutis (Fresh Fruit Cake)

7   tbsp flour
2   tsp baking powder
3   tbsp sugar
2   tbsp oil
2   tbsp milk
2   pc fresh fruits (apple, pear, banana)
2   tbsp rum
     Pinch of salt
2   eggs

Mix all ingredients. Pour in a greased pan. Bake in 350 °F oven 30-45 minutes.

Françoise Prot
France

Carrot Halwa (Sweet Carrots)

2   kg carrots, grated
2 1/2   c fresh milk
1   tin condensed milk
6   cardamoms
1   c butter
1/4   c sugar
3/4   c dried fruit, sliced and roasted almonds,
        sliced pistachios and cashews

Boil carrots and milk together; add pounded cardamom. Boil mixture till milk dries. Add 1/4 cup butter before it sticks to the bottom of the pan. Stir again on low heat for about 5 minutes. As soon as it gets dry, stir for 5 more minutes, add remaining butter, and stir constantly for 15 minutes more. Add sugar and leave on low fire for 15 minutes more. Mix and stir well till carrots turn red. Remove from fire and garnish with dry nuts.

NOTE: This can be cooked in advance and kept in the freezer for a long time.

Indu Virmani
India

Bread Custard Pudding

5-6   slices stale bread
1   c raisins or mixed fruits
1   tsp grated orange rind
1   tsp powdered cinnamon
3   eggs
1/2   c sugar
1/4   tsp salt
3   c diluted evaporated milk
1   tsp vanilla essence
      Jelly or jam for glacing (optional)

Cut off crust from bread slices; cut each slice into squares and butter on one side. Grease ovenproof dish with butter. Mix orange rind and cinnamon with dried fruit. Scatter some dried fruit on bottom of dish and place over them some pieces of bread, buttered side up. Spread more mixed fruits on bread slices, then a layer of bread pieces. Continue to do this till dish is three-fourths full. Beat eggs, add sugar, salt, milk, and vanilla essence and strain through a sieve over the bread and fruit in the dish. Allow to stand for 1/2 hour for bread to absorb custard mixture. Bake in a moderate oven about 1 hour or until set. Brush top with jelly or jam that has been heated. If top of pudding is not sufficiently brown, put dish under grill till golden.

Harmit Wasan
Singapore

Passion Fruit Jelly

8	eggs, separated
200	grams sugar
1 1/3	bags passion fruit juice
1	tbsp gelatin
	Some calamansi juice

Dissolve gelatin in 1/2 cup cold water. Let soak for 10 minutes, then heat till gelatin dissolves. Combine egg yolks with 6 tbsp hot water in a blender, add 3/4 of sugar and blend till creamy. Stir in passion fruit juice and warm gelatin slowly. Cool, then refrigerate. As soon as the cream is sufficiently chilled (try to "create a road" in it), beat egg whites until stiff, gradually adding the remaining sugar. Fold in the egg white into the cream. Add some calamansi juice if desired. Fill glasses with cream, and decorate.

Annemarie Lampe
Germany

Gulab Jamun (Milk Balls)

3	c Nido powder
1	c all-purpose flour
2	tsp baking powder
	Pinch of soda
2	tbsp ghee (melted butter)
3/4	c fresh milk
4	c oil for frying

Syrup

7	c water
5	c sugar

Mix all dry ingredients and butter; make a dough by adding fresh milk. Form pingpong-size balls. Heat oil (but do not boil); drop balls, a few at a time; fry on low heat till light brown. Remove and cool. Mix sugar and water to make syrup; boil till thick. The syrup should be lighter than maple syrup. Drop balls in syrup. May be served with ice cream.

Indu Virmani
India

Buttermilk-Pineapple Sherbet

1	can (16 oz) crushed pineapple, drained
2	c buttermilk
	Sugar substitute equal to 3 tbsp sugar

Combine ingredients and freeze until slushy. Beat on high speed with an electric mixer, then refreeze before serving. 6 servings, 81 calories each.

Marlene Smith
USA

Rasgulla

2	liters milk
3-4	tbsp vinegar
3	c sugar
2 1/2	c water
30-35	pc crystal sugar
1/2	tsp crushed cardamom seeds for flavoring (optional)

Boil milk. When it starts to boil, add vinegar. Let boil until whey and cheese separate. Strain with muslin. Hang the cloth for 1-2 hours so that water drips and the cheese forms a lump. Unwrap cheese and knead till smooth. Divide into 30-35 portions. Insert a piece of crystal sugar in each portion and make a smooth ball.

Make a thin syrup with water and sugar; divide into two parts. To one part add the balls and cook till syrup is almost dry. Remove from fire and add other half of syrup. Cool and add the crushed cardamom seeds. Serve cold.

Usha Ladha
India

Baked Fudge Dessert

1/2	c flour
1/2	c cocoa
2	c sugar
4	eggs, beaten
1	c melted butter
2	tsp vanilla
1	c nuts

Preheat oven to 350 °F. Mix flour, cocoa, and sugar. Add eggs. Stir in butter and vanilla. Beat well. Fold in nuts.

Pour batter into a 9-inch square pan. Set in a 9- × 13-inch baking pan and add 1/4 inch water. Bake for 1 hour. Serve warm with a scoop of ice cream or whipped cream.

Marlene Smith
USA

Kashmiri Shufta

1/2   kg fresh cheese (homemade cheese)
1/4   c finely sliced dry coconut
1/4   c almonds, soaked overnight and peeled
1/4   c cashew nuts
1/4   c raisins
3   c sugar
2 1/2 c water
5   cardamoms

Cut fresh cheese into small square pieces. Deep-fry cheese and dried nuts till light brown. Boil sugar in water till it dissolves. Add fried cheese, dried nuts, raisins, and cardamom. Boil till mixture is thick, but has a flowing consistency. Serve cold, but not refrigerated.

Fresh cheese
2   liters milk
3-4 tbsp vinegar

Boil milk. As soon as it starts boiling, add vinegar. Let boil until whey and cheese separate. Strain and wrap in muslin. Hang for 1-2 hours, so that water drips and cheese curdles. Unwrap when done.

Shashi Raina
Kashmir, India

Mango Brown Betty

2   tbsp butter
2/3 c bread crumbs
2   c half-ripe mango slices
1   tsp cinnamon
3/4 c brown sugar

Melt butter, add bread crumbs. Place layer of crumbs in oiled baking dish. Add layer of mangoes, sprinkle with sugar and cinnamon, add another layer of crumbs, then mangoes and then crumbs mixed with cinnamon and sugar. Bake at 350 °F, about 45 minutes.

Marlene Smith
USA

Candied Bananas

2   tbsp butter
1/4 c brown sugar, firmly packed
     Dash of cinnamon
1   tsp grated lemon rind or
1/2 tsp lemon flavoring
1   tbsp lemon juice
     Dash of nutmeg
3   medium-size, firm bananas

Melt butter in a heavy skillet. Add the next 5 ingredients. Cook over low heat, stirring constantly, until bubbly. Peel bananas, and slice in half lengthwise. Place in skillet; cook over low heat for 2-3 minutes, turning once. Serve warm.

Judy Buresh
USA

Cherry Cheesecakes

3   8-oz pkg cream cheese, at room temperature
1 1/2 c sugar
3   eggs
1   tsp vanilla
1   tbsp lemon juice
    Vanilla wafers
1   can cherry pie filling

Combine cream cheese, sugar, eggs, vanilla, and lemon juice and beat at medium speed until smooth. Put one vanilla wafer (flat side down) in each cupcake paper. Fill paper cup 1/2 full with batter. Bake at 350 °F, 12-15 minutes or until edges begin to brown and crack. Cool and top with cherry pie filling.

Marlene Smith
USA

Bread and Butter Pudding

4   thin slices buttered bread
1/3 c currants or sultanas
1   tbsp castor sugar
1 3/4 c milk
2   eggs
1/8 tsp ground nutmeg

Cut bread into strips and arrange, buttered side up, in layers in an ovenproof dish. Sprinkle each layer with some currants and sugar. Heat milk, but do not allow it to boil. Whisk eggs lightly and pour warm milk onto them, stirring all the time. Strain mixture over the bread and sprinkle some nutmeg on top. Allow to stand for 15 minutes. Bake at 350 °F for 30-40 minutes until set and lightly browned. Serves 4-6.

Kate Kirk
UK

Passion Fruit Chiffon Pie

4   eggs, separated
1/2 c passion fruit juice
1/2 tsp salt
3/4 c sugar
1   tbsp unflavored gelatin
2   tbsp water
1   tsp grated lemon rind
1   baked 9-inch pie shell
1/2 c heavy cream, whipped and sweetened

Beat egg yolks until thickened. Stir in juice, salt, and 1/4 cup sugar. Cook over low heat, stirring constantly until mixture thickens. Soften gelatin in water; add to hot mixture, stirring until gelatin is dissolved. Stir in rind; chill until mixture begins to congeal. In small bowl or electric mixer, beat egg whites until soft peaks form. Gradually beat in the remaining 1/2 cup sugar until stiff peaks form. Fold in gelatin mixture. Pour into pie shell and chill until firm. Top with cream before serving. Makes 8 servings.

Karen Moody
USA

Butter Tart

1/2 c raisins
1/4 c butter
1/2 c light brown sugar
1   c corn syrup
2   slightly beaten eggs
1   tsp vanilla
1   tsp lemon juice
     Pastry for 15 medium-size muffin cups

Pour 1 cup boiling water over raisins. Let stand 5 minutes and drain. Set aside. Preheat oven to 375 °F. Stir butter and sugar together and blend in rest of the ingredients. Add drained raisins. Line muffin cups with pastry. Do not prick pastry. Fill cups 2/3 full. Bake 15-20 minutes or until pastry is golden. Do not allow to bubble.

NOTE: To prevent butter tarts from bubbling over, stir as little as possible.

Ilse Zandstra
Canada

Cakes and Cookies

Banana Cake

1/2   c butter
1   c sugar
3   ripe bananas, mashed
1   egg
1 1/2 c self-rising flour
1   tsp baking soda dissolved in 3 tbsp hot milk

Cream butter and sugar. Add egg and beat well. Mix in mashed bananas; add sifted flour. Stir in the baking soda-milk mixture. Bake in a greased 8-inch cake tin for 1 hour at 150 °C or 325 °F.

Mary Greenland
UK

Quick Pineapple Upside-down Cake

1/4   c margarine, melted
1/2   c firmly packed brown sugar
1 1/2 c crushed pineapple
1   c sifted cake flour
1/2   tsp salt
3/4   c white sugar
1/4   c oil
1/2   c skim milk
1 1/2 tsp baking powder
2   egg whites, unbeaten
1/2   tsp vanilla extract

Pour melted margarine into an 8-inch square pan. Sprinkle with brown sugar and line bottom of pan with crushed pineapple. In a mixing bowl, sift together flour, salt, and sugar. Add oil and 1/2 of milk. Stir until flour is moistened, then beat 1 minute. Stir in baking powder, remaining milk, egg whites, and vanilla. Beat for 2 minutes. Pour batter over the crushed pineapple and bake 35-40 minutes in a preheated oven at 350 °F or 180 °C, or until a toothpick inserted in the cake comes out clean. Remove from oven, cool slightly, and invert onto a serving plate. 9 servings, 290 cal/serving.

Judy Buresh
USA

Cornmeal Cake

3   eggs
3   c sugar
1 1/2 tbsp shortening
4   c milk
1 1/2 c parmesan cheese
1   tbsp flour
1 1/2 c cornmeal
1 1/2 tsp baking powder

Beat eggs, sugar, shortening, milk, and cheese. Add flour, cornmeal, and baking powder. Pour into a greased pan and bake at 350 °F for 1 hour.

Neiares Singh
Brazil

Boterkoek (Butter Cake)

2	c flour	1	small egg, beaten
1	c butter (not	2	tbsp milk
	margarine)	1	tsp ginger powder
1	c sugar		

Keeping some of egg and milk mixture for decorating, combine all ingredients and knead into a smooth paste. Butter an 8-inch-diameter pie pan. Press dough onto the pie pan. Brush top with leftover egg and milk mixture and form squares with back of knife. Bake in a moderate oven (350 °F or 180 °C) for 30 minutes or until golden brown. Press down the middle while still hot and allow to cool. Turn out of pan when firm to touch. This cake should be soft on the inside and hard on the outside.

Kathy HilleRisLambers
The Netherlands

Coconut Carrot Cake with Coconut Cream Frosting

2	c flour
2 1/2	tsp baking soda
2	tsp cinnamon
1	tsp salt
1	c oil
2	c sugar
3	eggs
225	grams can crushed pineapple with syrup
2	c grated carrots
1 1/3	c coconut
1/2	c chopped nuts
1/2	c raisins

Mix flour, baking soda, cinnamon, and salt. In another bowl, beat oil, sugar, and eggs. Add flour mixture and beat. Add pineapple, carrots, coconut, nuts, and raisins. Pour into greased 9- × 13-inch pan. Bake at 350 °F (180 °C) for 50-60 minutes. Cool 10 minutes. Remove from pan and cool. Frost with coconut cream.

Coconut cream frosting

1	c coconut
3	oz cream cheese
1/4	c butter
3	c confectioners' sugar
1	tbsp milk
1/2	tsp vanilla

Toast coconut. Cool. Cream cheese with butter. Alternately add confectioners' sugar, milk, and vanilla. Beat until smooth. Add half of the toasted coconut. Frost cake and sprinkle the rest of the coconut on top.

Judy Buresh
USA

Yoghurt Cake with Chocolate Glaze

1	c butter	1 c brown sugar
1 1/2	c sugar	Cinnamon
3	eggs	
	Lemon peel, grated	
3	c self-rising flour	
1 1/2	c yoghurt	
1	c walnuts, cut into pieces	

Cream butter and add sugar gradually. Add eggs, one at a time, and lemon peel, mixing rapidly and well. Add flour and yoghurt, mixing lightly. In separate bowl, combine walnuts, brown sugar, and a little cinnamon. Put 1/3 of the batter in a 37- × 23-cm (15 × 9 inch) well-buttered and floured baking pan. Sprinkle with half of walnut mixture. Repeat once more and cover with remaining batter. Bake at 375 °F (190 °C) for 40 minutes. Cool and cover with chocolate glaze.

Chocolate glaze

1/4	c butter	4 tbsp milk
50	grams semisweet chocolate	2 c sugar

Melt together chocolate, butter, and milk over boiling water. Gradually add sugar and beat until smooth.

Vivi Moridis
Greece

Mayonnaise Cake

1	c sugar
2	c flour
2	tbsp baking soda
	Dash of salt
3-6	tbsp cocoa
1	c mayonnaise
1	c water

Sift together dry ingredients. Add mayonnaise and water. Mix well. Pour into a greased and floured 9- × 13-inch pan. Bake for 25 minutes at 350 °F.

Marlene Smith
USA

Gratias (Golden Bars)

1/3	c shortening or margarine
2	c brown sugar
2	eggs, beaten
1	tsp vanilla
1 1/2	c flour
1/2	tsp salt
2	tsp baking powder
3/4	c chopped nuts

Cream shortening and sugar; set aside. Beat eggs and vanilla; add to creamed mixture. Stir in the sifted dry ingredients and nuts. Spread in greased 9- × 13- × 2-inch pan. Sprinkle with powdered sugar. Bake 5 minutes or until golden (up to 10 minutes, if necessary).

Caren Hill
USA

Fruit Cake

1/2 c + 1 tbsp salted butter, softened
3/4 c sugar
3 eggs
1 c + 3 tbsp flour
2 tsp baking powder
1 small glass of rum or tea
1/2 c raisins
1/4 c dried fruits

Soak raisins and dried fruits in rum or tea for about 1 hour. In a big bowl cream butter and sugar. Add eggs, one at a time, mixing well after each addition. Sift together flour and baking powder, and add to creamed mixture. Sprinkle raisins and dried fruits with a little flour, then fold into the batter. Line a loaf pan with foil, and butter and flour it. Pour mixture into the pan. Bake in a preheated oven at 400 °F (200 °C) for 8 minutes. Then make zigzag cuts on the cake to produce a lattice design. Reduce oven temperature to 300 °F (150 °C) and bake cake about 40 minutes more.

Claudie Arraudeau
France

Lamingtons with Chocolate Icing

1/2 c + 1 tbsp butter   1/2 tsp salt
2/3 c sugar   1/3 c milk
2 eggs   1/2 tsp vanilla
2 c self-rising flour

Chocolate icing
2 1/2 tbsp butter   1/3 c cocoa
1/2 c boiling water   1/2 tsp vanilla
3 c icing sugar   2 c desiccated
                             coconut

Cream butter and sugar until light and fluffy. Add eggs, one at a time, beating well after each addition. Sift flour and salt. Add alternately with milk to creamed mixture. Add vanilla. Blend well but do not overbeat. Add a little more milk, if necessary to form batter with a dropping consistency. Spread evenly in a greased and floured 31- × 25-cm (12- × 10-inch) cake pan that has been covered with wax paper. Bake in a moderate oven (350 °F or 180 °C) 25-35 minutes or until done. Turn out on a cake rack and cool. Cut into 30 squares. Dip each square in chocolate icing and roll in desiccated coconut.

Melt butter in 1/4 cup boiling water. Sift icing sugar with cocoa. Add liquid, mixing well. Add vanilla. Icing must be thin so that squares of cake can be readily coated. Add more boiling water if needed to reach that consistency. Dip each square in icing, then roll in coconut. Leave to dry on cake rack. Makes 30 lamingtons.

Alice Flinn
Marlene Quick
Australia

Engadiner Nusstorte (Nutcake from Engadin, Switzerland)

Pastry

275 grams all-purpose flour	1 egg
1/4 tsp salt	1-2 tbsp heavy
175 grams margarine	cream
125 grams sugar	

Filling

150 grams sugar, heated	25 grams
1 qt heavy cream	almonds,
125 grams chopped	chopped
gently to light	1 tbsp honey
brown nuts	

Combine flour, salt, margarine, and sugar. Add egg and heavy cream and prepare dough. Let stand in the refrigerator or cold place for 30 minutes. Roll out 2/3 of the pastry dough and line a 9- or 10-inch-diameter greased cake pan, pressing the pastry carefully over the bottom and around the side. Heat sugar for a short time, stirring constantly. Pour in 1 quart heavy cream and cook till slightly thick. Stir in honey. Add chopped nuts. Cool. Spread filling on crust and top with 1/3 of roll-out dough. Wet dough edges with water and press firmly with a fork. Bake in a preheated moderate oven (180 °C or 355 °F) about 55 minutes. Remove from pan while still warm.

Heidi Graf
Switzerland

Rose Cake

400	grams flour
4	eggs
1	egg white
2	liters vegetable oil or lard
	Blackberry marmalade
	Icing sugar

Mix flour and eggs well to form a firm dough; allow to rest for 30 minutes. Cut round pieces with diameter of 4, 5, 6, and 7 cm (make about 20 of each size). See illustration.

Stack 4 pieces of different sizes together, starting with the biggest, using egg white as glue (only on center). Deep-fry for about 5 minutes. After frying, the cakes look like roses. Put 1 tsp blackberry jam in the center of each rose and sprinkle with icing sugar.

NOTE: Should be eaten immediately, while still warm and crisp.

Marie Kürschner
Germany

Best Chocolate Cake

2	c flour	1/2	c buttermilk
2	c sugar	2	eggs, beaten
3	tbsp margarine	1	tsp soda
4	tbsp cocoa	1	tsp vanilla
1	c water	1	tsp salt

Mix flour and sugar. Set aside. In a saucepan melt margarine; add cocoa and water. Bring to a boil, then pour this mixture over flour and sugar. Mix with spatula or wooden spoon. Add buttermilk, eggs, soda, and vanilla. Mix well and pour on greased and floured 11- × 16-inch pan or 9- × 13- × 2-inch pan. Bake at 400 °F for 20 minutes.

Frosting

1/4	c margarine	1	tsp vanilla
6	tbsp buttermilk	1	c chopped nuts
4	tbsp cocoa		(optional)
1	box powdered sugar		

Melt margarine in a saucepan. Remove from fire; add cocoa and buttermilk. Stir into powdered sugar and mix well. Add vanilla and nuts. Spread on cake while hot.

NOTE: Prepare frosting about 5 minutes before cake is done.

Caren Hill
USA

Dream Bars with Orange Butter Frosting

1/2	c margarine
1/2	c brown sugar
1	c flour
2	eggs, beaten
1	c brown sugar
1	tsp vanilla
2	tbsp flour
1/2	tsp salt
1	tsp baking powder
1 1/2	c grated coconut
1	c chopped nuts

Mix and bake the first 3 ingredients at 375 °F for 10 minutes. Set aside to cool. Beat eggs, sugar, and vanilla together. Mix flour, salt, and baking powder and sprinkle over the coconut and nuts mixture. Pour egg-sugar mixture over this.

Spread over baked layer and bake for 20 minutes. Cool slightly. Cut into 3/4- x 2-inch bars. Spread with orange butter frosting.

Orange butter frosting

1/4	c soft margarine	1/2	tsp vanilla
2	c powdered sugar	1	tsp grated orange
2	tbsp orange juice		rind

Cream margarine and sugar. Add vanilla, orange rind, and orange juice for spreading consistency.

Caren Hill
USA

Mango and Coconut Bars

1   pkg dried mangoes, snipped

Crust		Topping	
1	c wheat germ	2/3	c whole wheat flour
1	c whole wheat flour	1	tsp baking powder
1/3	c honey or 1/4 c brown sugar	1/2	tsp salt (optional)
1/4	c butter	3	eggs
1/4	c oil	1/2	tsp almond extract
		3/4	c desiccated shredded coconut

Drop mango bits into 1 1/2 cups boiling water. Simmer about 10 minutes or until soft. While mangoes simmer, mix wheat germ and flour; add honey and stir. Cut in butter, then add oil. Mix well, using hands. Press 2 cups of mixture into 7- × 11-inch (18 × 28 cm) or 9- × 9-inch (23 × 23 cm) baking pan. Set the rest aside. Bake crust at 350 °F (180 °C) for 10 minutes. For topping, mix flour, baking powder, and salt. In another bowl, beat eggs and almond extract; stir in flour mixture, coconut, and cooked mango. Spread mixture over baked crust. Sprinkle reserved crust mixture over the top, pressing it in lightly. Bake for another 25 minutes. Cool and cut into 18 bars.

NOTE: May use 2 eggs and 1 cup freshly shredded coconut instead of 3 eggs and 3/4 cups desiccated coconut.

Yokiko Vaughan
UK

Salted Nut Bars

1   box yellow cake mix (plain)
1/3   c margarine
1   egg
3   c miniature marshmallows

2   tsp vanilla
2   c salted peanuts
2   c rice krispies

Mix first 3 ingredients and pat firmly into a 9- × 13-inch greased and floured pan. Bake at 350 °F (180 °C) for 12-15 minutes. Take out, cover with marshmallows then bake another 2-3 minutes until marshmallows puff. Cool.
    Mix the following ingredients:
1/4   c margarine or butter
2/3   c corn syrup
2   c Reese's peanut butter chips or 1 c peanut butter and 1 c marshmallows

Put the mixture on top of the fluffy marshmallows. Cut into squares. Cool, then place in refrigerator.

Judy Buresh
USA

Deluxe Fudgy Brownies

4   squares unsweetened chocolate
1/2   c butter
4   eggs
2   c sugar
1   c flour
1   tsp vanilla
1   c coarsely chopped nuts

Melt chocolate and butter in a saucepan over low heat; cool slightly. Beat eggs lightly; then gradually beat in sugar and continue beating for 2-3 minutes. Blend in chocolate mixture. Stir in flour; then add vanilla and nuts. Spread in greased 9- × 13-inch pan. Bake at 325 °F (160 °C) about 30-35 minutes. Cool in pan; then cut into squares.

Judy Buresh
USA

Danish Apple Bars

2 1/2   c flour
1   tsp salt
1   c shortening
1   egg yolk and enough milk to make 2/3 c with the egg yolk
1   c crushed cornflakes
8-10   apples or 2 cans apple slices (5 cups) or
2   cans apple pie filling
1   c sugar (if using raw apples; 1/2 c if using canned apples; no sugar if using pie filling)
1   tsp cinnamon or more to taste
1   egg white
1   c powdered sugar
1/2   tsp vanilla
1/2   tbsp water

Combine flour and salt and cut in shortening. Add milk and egg yolk mixture and blend to form dough. Roll out 1/2 of the dough to fill a 10 1/2- × 15 1/2- inch cookie sheet. Sprinkle with crushed cornflakes. Peel and slice apples. Place on dough. Sprinkle apples with sugar and cinnamon. Cover with the remaining dough. Pinch edges together. Beat egg white until stiff and brush over crust. Bake at 400 °F (200 °C) for 60 minutes or until apples are done (less time is needed for canned apples - around 30 minutes). While warm, frost with powdered sugar moistened with 1 tbsp water and vanilla.

Judy Buresh
USA

Princeregenten Torte

1	c butter or margarine
4	eggs
1 1/2	c sugar
1 1/2	tsp vanilla
	A little salt
1 1/2	c flour
1/2	c cornstarch
1	tsp baking powder

Cream butter well. Add eggs one at a time; add sugar, vanilla, and salt and beat. Sift together flour, cornstarch, and baking powder and add to the butter-egg mixture. Bake 8 layers (8 thin layers or 6 or 7 thick layers) at 350 °F (180 °C) for 7-15 minutes. Each layer is made with 2 tbsp dough in a greased springform pan or on the back of a cake pan. Remove carefully and put on a level place to cool.

Filling

Bring 3/4 cup + 2 tbsp butter to room temperature. Make a regular chocolate pudding to which has been added l tbsp cocoa. Let cool to room temperature. Then fold the pudding into the butter and mix well. If it should curdle, it is still good although it does not look nice. Put filling between the layers, ending with a layer of cake. Cover with icing.

Icing

Mix 1 1/2 to 2 cups powdered sugar, 2 tbsp cocoa, 2 tbsp melted butter, and 2-3 tbsp hot water (or as needed). Spread on top and sides of cake. Refrigerate cake, covered. The cake is best done a day ahead.

Sigrid Campbell
USA

Walnut Wonder Torte

1	c butter	2	c flour
1	c sugar	1	tsp baking powder
1	tsp vanilla	1	tsp baking soda
2	eggs	1/2	tsp salt
		1	c sour cream

Filling

1/3	c brown sugar	3/4	c chopped walnuts
1/2	c granulated sugar	1	tsp cinnamon

Beat butter, sugar, and vanilla until fluffy and light. Add eggs one at a time; beat after each addition. In a separate bowl, sift together dry ingredients. Add sifted mixture to creamed mixture alternately with sour cream, in thirds. Beat smooth after each addition. Grease and flour a 9- × 13-inch pan. Sprinkle with some filling, then alternate with batter to make 3 layers. Bake at 350 °F (180 °C) for 25-30 minutes.

Karen Moody
USA

Cassava Coconut Bars

1/2 c butter
1/2 c sugar
1 c grated fresh coconut
1 c grated cassava
1/2 tsp baking powder
1 tsp salt
1 tsp vanilla
1/2 c evaporated milk
2 eggs

Mix butter and sugar and blend in a blender. Add grated coconut and cassava. Beat eggs, then add to the batter with the remaining ingredients. Mix all very well then pour mixture in a well-greased loaf pan. Bake at 300 °F for 1 hour. Increase heat to 375 °F for at least 5-8 minutes so that the top portion would brown. Remove from pan. If cassava is old, use more milk; if cassava is very young, decrease milk.

Rhoda Tubman
Liberia

Chocolate Balls

1 can condensed milk
3 tbsp cocoa
1 tbsp shortening or margarine

Put all ingredients in a heavy saucepan or double boiler. Heat slowly, stirring constantly until thickened. When cool, form balls about 3/4-inch in diameter and roll in chocolate sprinkles. Makes 24 balls.

NOTE: Paper cups can be used for individual servings.

Neiares Singh
Brazil

Chips for Birthday Parties

3 c flour
1 tsp salt
2 tsp nutmeg
2 tsp baking powder
1/2 c butter
1 medium egg
1/2 c milk
1/2 c water
1/8 tsp vanilla

Sift flour into a bowl. Add salt, nutmeg, baking powder, and butter. Knead for 15 minutes, set aside. Beat egg, add milk and water. Pour mixture into the dough and blend thoroughly. Divide dough into 5 parts. Roll each piece and cut into small square pieces. Fry pieces till light brown. Roasted peanuts may be added.

Djokoto
Ghana

Chocolate Biscuits

6   oz butter
3/4 c sugar
1   egg, beaten
1 1/2 c self-rising flour
2   tbsp cocoa
     Walnuts or almond halves

Cream butter and sugar; add well-beaten egg. Mix in sifted flour and cocoa. Form into small balls and place on baking sheet.

Press a walnut or almond half on each ball. Flatten with fork. Bake 350 °F for 15 minutes.

Alice Flinn
Australia

Sugar Cutout Cookies

3   c flour   1/2 c shortening
1   tsp baking powder 2   eggs
1   tbsp cream of tartar 1 c sugar
1   tsp baking soda   1   tsp vanilla
1/2 c margarine

Mix together dry ingredients except sugar. Cut in margarine and shortening. Beat eggs, add sugar and vanilla and beat again. Add mixture to dry ingredients. Mix as for pie crust and wrap tightly in wax

paper. Put in a plastic bag and chill until cold (at least 3 hours). Roll out to approximately 1/16-inch (2 mm) thickness. Cut with cookie cutter and sprinkle with sugar (colored, if desired). Bake at 400 °F (200 °C) for 5-7 minutes or until light brown.

Caren Hill
USA

Lorna's Oatmeal Crackers

3   c quick-cooking oats   1   tbsp sugar
2   c flour   1   c water
1   c wheat germ (or   3/4 c salad oil
     1/2 c wheat germ, and 1   c sesame oil
     1/2 c wheat bran)   Coarse salt
1/2 tsp salt

Measure dry ingredients into bowl; stir well. Make a well in the dry ingredients and pour combined oil and water mixture into it. Knead with hands to blend. Form

into 3 balls. Roll out each ball thinly on cookie pans. Cut dough into squares and rectangles; sprinkle lightly with coarse salt. Bake at 350 °F for 20-25 minutes (edges cook faster). Remove from pan and cool.

Baby Duff (Philippines)
USA

Jam Poinsettias

1 1/2 c flour
2   tbsp sugar
3/4   c butter or margarine
1/4   c sour cream or yoghurt
1-2   egg whites
       Sugar and jam

Mix flour and sugar. Cut in butter until mixture is crumbly. Add sour cream and stir with fork until dough holds together. Wrap and chill several hours or overnight. Roll out half the dough into a 10- × 7-inch (25 × 18 cm) rectangle. Cut into twelve 2 1/2-inch (6-cm) squares. Transfer to ungreased cookie sheet 1 inch (2.5 cm) apart. Make cut 1 1/4 inches (3 cm) long from each corner of square toward center. Fold every other tip to center to make pinwheel shape. Press center down gently. Repeat with other half of dough. Refrigerate on cookie sheet 15 minutes. Brush each cookie with egg white. Sprinkle with sugar. Place 1/4 tsp jam in center. Bake in a preheated oven at 375 °F 12-14 minutes or until golden brown and slightly puffed. Remove from sheet to cool.

Judy Buresh
USA

Swiss Christmas Cookies

2 cubes of sweet margarine
1 c sugar
2 eggs
2 c flour
2 pinches of salt
2 egg yolks, beaten

Cream margarine and sugar. Add 2 eggs, and mix until smooth. Add flour and salt, then knead mixture slowly into a smooth dough. Let dough rest for an hour.

Roll dough about 1/4 inch thick. Cut out with cookie cutter. Brush with beaten egg yolks. Bake on greased cookie pan in 350 °F oven for about 15 minutes or until golden brown.

Heidi Graf
Switzerland

Pickles and Chutneys

Sweet and Sour Cucumber Pickles

500 grams cucumber
330 grams vinegar (spiced with tarragon)
500 grams sugar
2 sticks cinnamon
2 slices lemon peel
4 cloves garlic
250 grams water

Wash, peel, and clean cucumbers. Remove seeds. Cut cucumbers into 2-cm-long pieces and marinate in tarragon-vinegar mixture for 3-4 hours. Drain vinegar in a bowl. Add water, sugar, and last three ingredients. Boil till a thick syrup is formed. Add cucumber to syrup, and boil till cucumber becomes glossy. Cool, then put in a glass jar with cover.

Annemarie Lampe
Germany

Easy Refrigerator Pickles

1   c cucumber
1   c onions
1   c green pepper
1   tbsp salt
1   tsp celery seed
1   tsp mustard seed
1   c white vinegar
2   c white sugar

Peel cucumber and cut into thin slices. Slice onions. Chop green pepper very fine. Combine all dry ingredients, sugar, vinegar, and salt. Mix all together and put in a glass jar or tupperware. Keep in the refrigerator.

Judy Buresh
USA

Pickled Cucumber Sticks

1   large cucumber
2   red chilies
1/4 c vinegar
1/8 tsp shrimp paste
1/2 tsp salt
1/4 c water

Peel cucumber and slice into thin strips. Mix all other ingredients well; add cucumber strips. Serve with any Indonesian dish.

Faiza Pervaz (Pakistan)
Indonesia

Carrot Pickles

2   kg carrots
8   green chilies (optional)
2 1/2 c oil
       Pinch of asafoetida
1 1/2 c fresh mustard seed, ground
1/2   tbsp turmeric powder
1   tsp chili powder
3   tbsp salt

Peel carrots; cut into long strips. Slit green chilies. Heat oil; remove from fire, let cool for a while, then add a pinch of asafoetida. After a minute, add chilies, turmeric powder, mustard, and chili powder. Stir mixture, then add carrots and salt. Set aside to cool. Pour in bottles and cover.

NOTE: No need for refrigeration.

Indu Virmani
India

Mango Pickles

1   c corn oil
1   tbsp fenugreek seeds, crushed
1/4   c mustard seeds, crushed
4   tbsp anise seeds, crushed
3-4   tbsp chili powder (more
       if you like hot pickles)
4-6   tbsp salt
1-2   tbsp turmeric powder
6-8   cloves
4-5   cardamoms
2   bay leaves (optional)
       Few seeds of black pepper
1   kg green mangoes, unpeeled, cut into
       slivers

Heat oil. Fry fenugreek seeds. Remove pan from fire. Add all other spices and sauté. Allow mixture to cool. Add mangoes and mix well. Cool before putting in a preserving jar. Stir from time to time. The pickle will be ready in a week.

NOTE: There should always be enough oil to keep pickle from spoiling. Add more oil if needed. Always heat and cool oil before adding to the pickle.

Durga Pathak
India

Onion and Cucumber Pickles

3/4	c sugar
1/2	c salt
1	qt water + 1 qt vinegar
3	tbsp mixed pickling spices
30-40	medium-size cucumbers or
100	small onions

Combine sugar, vinegar, salt, and water. Tie pickling spices in a cheesecloth bag. Add to the vinegar mixture, and simmer 15 minutes. Pack onions or cucumbers in jars, leaving 1/4-inch headspace. Add 1 clove garlic, 1 bay leaf, 1/2 tsp mustard seed, and 1 piece hot red pepper in each jar. Pour boiling hot vinegar mixture over cucumber or onions.

Neiares Singh
Brazil

Radish Pickles

1	kg radish
1/4	c corn oil
	Pinch of asafoetida
1/2	tsp turmeric powder
	Salt and chili powder to taste
1	tbsp crushed garlic
1/2	c mustard seed
1/4	tsp citric acid or sour medium

Peel radish and cut into medium-size cubes or slices. Dry with paper towel. Heat oil well, then turn off heat. To oil add asafoetida, turmeric, chili powder, crushed garlic, mustard seeds, and salt. Stir and mix well. Add citric acid and stir for a while. Remove from heat and let cool. Add radish and mix well. Pour into jars and store in a refrigerator.

Durga Pathak
India

Chili Pickles

1/2	kg long green chilies
1	tbsp fenugreek seeds (methi), roasted and powdered
1	tsp onion seeds (calaunji) roasted and powdered
1/4	c brown mustard powder
1	tbsp mango powder
	Salt to taste

Cut chilies into 1-inch pieces and dry on paper towel. Heat oil. Add all spices and chilies and mix well. Pour into a jar.

Usha Ladha
India

Brinjal Pahi (Eggplant Pahi)

2	large eggplants
2	tsp salt
2	tsp ground turmeric
1	tbsp black mustard seed
1/2	c vinegar
1	medium onion, finely chopped
4	cloves garlic, sliced
1	tbsp finely chopped fresh root ginger
	Oil for frying
1	tbsp coriander, ground
2	tsp ground cumin
1	tsp ground fennel
1/2	c tamarind pulp
3/4	c hot water
3	fresh chilies, seeded and sliced
3-inch	piece of cinnamon stick
1	tsp chili powder (optional)
2	tsp sugar
	Salt to taste

Cut eggplants into thin slices; rub with salt and turmeric and place in a bowl. Let stand for at least 1 hour. Pour off liquid that collects and drain eggplant on paper towels. Heat approximately 2.5 cm (1-inch) oil in a frying pan and fry eggplant slices slowly until brown on both sides. Lift slices and place in a dry bowl. Reserve oil used for frying.

Place mustard seed and vinegar in blender container, cover and blend on high speed until mustard is ground. Add onion, garlic, and ginger; cover and blend again until smooth paste is formed. Set aside.

Place coriander, cumin, and fennel in a small dry pan and heat gently, until medium brown in color, stirring frequently. (If preferred, substitute 1 1/2 tbsp Ceylon curry powder for these ingredients.)

Squeeze tamarind pulp in hot water, strain and discard seeds, but reserve liquid.

Heat 1/2 cup of reserved oil and fry the blended mixture for 5 minutes. Add coriander mixture or curry powder, chilies, cinnamon stick, chili powder, if used, and tamarind liquid. Add fried eggplant slices and any oil that has collected in the bowl. Stir well, cover, and simmer for 15 minutes. Remove from heat, stir in sugar. Add extra salt to taste, if necessary. Cool thoroughly and store in clear, dry jars.

Olga Ponnamperuma
Sri Lanka

Lime Pickles

8	limes
1 1/2	tbsp salt
1/2	tsp turmeric powder
2	tsp garam masala (curry powder)
2	tsp chili powder
4	tbsp sugar

Cut each lime into four pieces. Mix all spices and cover lime pieces with the mixture. Put all in a dry jar. Stir from time to time. The pickle will be ready sooner if placed in the sunshine.

Usha Ladha
India

Tomato Pickles

500	grams ripe tomatoes
25	grams ginger
3	cloves garlic
50	grams green chilies
50	grams green peas
2	boiled eggs (optional)
25	grams white cheese (optional)
	Few fresh coriander leaves
1/2	tsp cumin powder
4	tbsp oil
1	tsp fenugreek seeds
1/4	tsp turmeric powder
1 1/2	tsp salt
1 1/2	tsp chili powder

Chop tomatoes; slice ginger, garlic, and chilies lengthwise. Soak peas overnight; drain; set aside. Slice boiled eggs; chop white cheese into cubes; chop coriander leaves and set aside. Heat oil in a pan on low flame; add fenugreek seeds; sauté till brown. Add ginger, garlic, green chilies, and peas; stir very well. Add turmeric powder, salt, chili, and cumin powder; stir again, and cook till light brown. Add tomatoes, and keep on stirring. Cover pan and cook 10-12 minutes. Remove from fire and either serve immediately or store for 24 hours. Garnish with 4 egg slices, 4 coriander leaves, and 4 cheese cubes. Serves 10.

NOTE: If frozen peas are used, there is no need to soak.

Sushila Pradhan
Nepal

Chicken or Pork Pickles

1	chicken or	100	grams anise seeds
1	kg pork	50	grams cumin seeds
200	grams ginger	20	grams onion seeds
50	grams garlic	50	grams black
3	c hot water		pepper
1/2	kg tamarind	10	grams cinnamon,
1	c vegetable oil		whole
1/4	tsp nutmeg or	200	grams vinegar
	mace powder		Salt to taste

Clean meat, remove skin, cut into cubes, and set aside. Grind garlic and ginger. Boil tamarind in hot water. Discard seeds and keep juice. Heat oil, fry meat for 10-15 minutes, add garlic and ginger. Fry again for a few minutes. Add all dry spices. Add tamarind juice, and cook till meat is almost done. Add vinegar and cook for a while. Remove from fire and allow to cool. Pour into bottles.

Satnam Taneja
India

Potato Pickles

200	grams green peas
1	kg small potatoes
200	grams brown sesame seeds
25	pc green chilies
1	tsp chili powder
1 1/2	tsp salt
	Juice from 20 pc calamansi
4	tbsp corn oil
1/2	tsp turmeric powder
1/2	tsp fenugreek seed

Soak green peas overnight; drain. Boil potatoes until well cooked; peel and cut into halves. Roast sesame seeds, then grind with a few drops of water. Cut green chilies. Put potatoes in a big bowl; add peas, sesame powder, chili powder, and salt. Mix thoroughly; add calamansi juice, little by little. Heat oil over medium flame; add fenugreek seeds and sauté till dark brown; add chilies, and turmeric powder. Stir well. Pour this mixture over potato mixture. Serve immediately, or else store for 12-18 hours.

NOTE: To serve as an appetizer, reduce potato and add cucumber and radish.

Sushila Pradhan
Nepal

Pineapple and Apple Chutney

1	fresh pineapple
1	apple
1/4	c vinegar
3/4	c sugar
	Salt to taste
2	cloves garlic
1	tbsp ginger powder
1/4	c raisins
4	whole dried red chilies
1/4	tsp cinnamon powder

Peel and cut pineapple into small cubes. Peel and dice apple. Boil vinegar with sugar, salt, cinnamon, ground ginger, chilies, and garlic. Add pineapple, apple, and raisins. Boil slowly, stirring again and again till the fruits soften. Remove from fire and cool. Put into bottles and cover. Serve with rice and curry.

NOTE: This chutney can be stored for months.

Avtar Singh
Malaysia

Coconut Chutney

1/2	coconut
1/4	c tamarind pulp
2	dry red chilies
1	tbsp oil
6	curry leaves
1/2	tsp mustard seeds
1/2-inch pc of ginger	
1/2	onion, minced
3/4	tsp salt

Grate coconut. Soak tamarind in some water and discard seed. Cut chilies into 4 pieces each. Heat a little oil. Toast chilies, curry leaves, and mustard seeds. Add grated coconut; toast till light brown. Grind the mixture with tamarind pulp and water, ginger, and salt while still warm. Sauté onion in 1 tbsp oil; add a few more curry leaves. Add coconut paste and mix well. Serve cold. This will keep for about a week.

Usha Ladha
India

Mango Chutney

1	kg green mangoes
2	pods garlic
1	tbsp cumin seeds
1	tsp sliced ginger
1	c vinegar
50	grams black currants
1 1/2	tbsp chili powder
1 1/2	c sugar
1	tbsp salt

Wash, dry, peel, and shred mangoes. Squeeze out the juice. Crush garlic and cumin seeds. Slice ginger fine and soak in 2 tbsp vinegar along with black currants. Boil the remaining vinegar in a large pot and add garlic, cumin seeds, and chili powder. After 5 minutes, add mango, sugar, and salt and cook on slow fire. When half done, add soaked ginger and currants together with the vinegar; stir constantly, until syrup is thick. Remove and cool. When completely cold, transfer to airtight containers.

Usha Ladha
India

Coriander Chutney

1	c coriander leaves
1/2	c chopped onions, preferably green
2	green chilies
3-4	cloves garlic
1/2-inch	pc ginger, chopped
1	tsp salt
1/2	tsp cumin seeds (optional)
	Juice of one lime

Mix all ingredients and blend, using minimum possible water. For those who like their chutney sweet, add 1 tsp sugar to the mixture.

NOTE: Coriander can be replaced with mint leaves, or the two can be mixed half and half. Mint chutney tastes better without sugar. One small raw mango can be used instead of lime juice.

Usha Ladha
India

Tamarind Chutney

4	oz tamarind
4	tbsp sugar
1/2	tbsp chili powder
1	tsp salt
1	tbsp raisins
1/2	tsp cumin powder
1/2	tsp garam masala (curry powder) optional

Soak tamarind in a cup of warm water for 15-30 minutes. Discard seed and mix pulp with all other ingredients.

NOTE: Amount of sugar can be varied according to taste.

Usha Ladha
India

Watermelon Peels Preserve

1	watermelon
1	tbsp lime water
1	liter water

Syrup

1	c water
2	c sugar

Pare watermelon and slice crosswise about one-third-inch thick. Remove the central part, but leave the rind with some red portion. Soak in lime-water mixture overnight. Wash and blanch for 10 minutes. Cook in syrup of 2 parts sugar and one part water for 30 minutes. Soak in syrup overnight.

Boil until syrup is thick. Roll watermelon slices into pinwheels and pack in 12-oz preserving jars. Pour syrup and remove air bubbles; refill with syrup. Half seal and sterilize jars for 25 minutes in boiling water. Seal completely.

Normita dela Cruz
Philippines

Kitchen Hints

Kitchen Hints

1. To reheat leftover rice, empty it into a large container. Cover, set over simmering water, and steam until fluffy and hot.

2. To remove excess salt from food that you are cooking, cut up a potato and cook it with the food. The potato will absorb a lot of the salt.

3. To completely thaw frozen bread loaves and rolls, wrap them in a brown paper bag and heat in the oven at 325 °F.

4. To keep bread fresh for a longer time, keep a rib of celery in the bread box.

5. To get rid of the smell of onion, fish or garlic, cut a lime in half and rub it onto the surface of your breadboard.

6. To keep onion fresh for a longer time, rub butter on the cut side of the onion.

7. To use leftover baked potato, dip them in water and rebake at 300 °F for about 20 minutes. It will taste like fresh baked potato.

8. To keep mashed potato from becoming soggy, sprinkle dry milk powder on top.

9. To make golden fried potatoes, sprinkle the slices with flour before frying.

10. To keep corn yellow, add 1 teaspoon of lemon juice while boiling the corn.

11. To keep crackers crispy, store them in the refrigerator. When you take them out at room temperature, they will still be crispy.

12. To make fried eggplant less oily, keep the slices in the refrigerator for a few hours before frying.

13. To store fresh ginger, keep in the freezer or in a screw-top jar in sherry in the refrigerator. It will stay fresh for months.

14. To prevent a vegetable salad from becoming soft when it has to stand for a few hours, place a saucer upside down at the bottom of the bowl before filling it. The moisture will run underneath and the vegetables will remain fresh and crisp.

15. To prevent icing from forming crystals, add a pinch of salt to it.

16. To make a substitute for cake flour, take out 1 tbsp all-purpose flour from each cup of the required amount and replace it with 2 tsp cornstarch.

17. To make self-rising flour, mix well 2 cups unsifted all-purpose flour, 2 1/2 tsp baking powder, and 1 1/2 tsp salt.

18. To open a clogged drainage pipe, pour a cup of salt and baking soda into the drain and then pour in hot water.

19. To strengthen and refresh sponge, soak it overnight in baking soda and salt and water.

20. To clean the inside of a tea kettle, fill it with equal amounts of vinegar and water overnight, then bring to a boil.

21. To clean a meat grinder and remove any unpleasant smell, run a piece of bread through it before washing it.

22. To get rid of cockroaches, mix 1 kg boric acid powder with 1/2 cup sugar. Add 2 tsp of milk, a little at a time, until the mixture can be formed into small balls the size of your fingernails. Stick the balls in the back cover of drawers and cabinets where they will harden. The cockroaches will go away or die.

23 REHYDRATION DRINK. To replace electrolytes in the system of people who have been dehydrated because of diarrhea or vomiting, this drink is recommended by WHO (World Health Organization).
Dissolve the following in one liter of boiled water:

1/4	tsp salt
1/4	tsp baking soda
2-3	tbsp honey
2	tbsp lemon or calamansi juice

Abbreviations

tsp = teaspoon
tbsp = tablespoon
c = cup
kg = kilogram
pc = piece

oz = ounce
lb = pound
ml = milliliter
qt = quart

Basic Measures and Equivalents

A pinch = 1/8 tsp
60 drops = 1 tsp
3 tsp = 1 tbsp
2 tbsp = 1 fluid oz
4 tbsp = 1/4 c or 2 oz

1/2 cup = 8 tbsp or 4 oz
1 c = 16 tbsp or 8 oz
2 c = 1 pint or 16 fluid oz
2 pints = 1 qt or 4 c
4 qt = 1 gallon

Metric Measures and Equivalents

1 tsp = 5 grams, or 5 ml
1 tbsp = 15 grams, or 15 ml
6 2/3 tbsp = 100 grams
1 c = 225 grams, or 1/4 liter
2 c (1 pint) = 454 grams
4 c (1 qt) = 907 grams
4 1/3 c = 1 liter or 1000 grams
1 c and 1 tbsp = 250 ml

1/4 c = 62 1/2 ml
1 liter = 2.1 pint
1 liter = 1.06 qt
1 liter = 0.26 gallon
1 pint = 0.45 liter
1 qt = 0.95 liter
1 gallon = 3.8 liters

Liquid Measures

		oz	grams	ml
1/16 c	= 1 tbsp	1/2	14	15
1/4 c	= 4 tbsp	2	60	59
1/2 c	= 8 tbsp	4	115	118
1 c	= 16 tbsp	8	225	236
1 3/4 c		14	400	414
2 c	= 1 pint	16	450	473
3 c		24	685	710
4 c		32	900	946

Information that may be of Interest

1 British fluid ounce = 28.5 ml
1 American fluid ounce = 29.5 ml
1 Japanese cup = 200 ml = 7 British fl oz
1 British cup = 240 ml = 8 American fl oz
1 British pint = 570 ml = 20 British fl oz
1 American pint = 470 ml = 16 American
    fl oz

Common Equivalents

1 lb beef, uncooked	=	2 cups, ground
1 cup buttermilk	=	3/4 cup yoghurt plus 1/4 cup water
1 oz chocolate	=	1 square or 4 tbsp, grated
1 oz chocolate (unsweetened)	=	3 tbsp cocoa and 1 tbsp butter or fat
1 small clove garlic	=	1/8 tsp garlic powder
1 tbsp raw ginger	=	1/8 tsp ginger powder
1 lb or 1 1/4 cup lentils	=	5 cups cooked lentils
1 lb uncooked noodles	=	6 to 8 cups cooked noodles
1 cup uncooked noodles	=	1 1/4 cup cooked noodles (1-inch pieces)
1 tbsp mustard sauce	=	1 tsp dry mustard
1/2 cup raw rice	=	1 cup cooked rice
1 lb dry spaghetti	=	5-6 cups cooked spaghetti
1 cup dry spaghetti	=	1 3/4 cups cooked spaghetti (2-inch pieces)
1 pkg yeast (active dry)	=	1 tbsp granular yeast
1 tsp baking powder	=	1/4 tsp baking soda + 1 tsp cream of tartar

Glossary

A

Abura-age	Deep-fried tofu.
Ada	A thick pancake made by grinding different dals and rice.
Agar-agar	Gelatin made from seaweed.
Ajinomoto	A brand name for monosodium glutamate.
Ajwain	Carom seeds; also known as lovage.
Ampalaya	Bitter gourd.
Anarasa	Sweet, fried, rice patties.
Anise seeds	Similar to cumin seeds but are slightly lighter in color. They can be used for curries, snacks, and pickles. They are sometimes eaten with betel leaves after meals as a mouthwash and to aid digestion.
Arroz com feijao	Rice with beans.
Arroz con frijoles	Rice with beans.
Arroz con leche	Rice with milk.
Asafoetida	A gum resin with a very pungent smell. It is sold in the market as rock or powder.

B

Baare	Baked preparation with rice flour and sugar.
Basmati	A high-priced rice variety.
Besan	Chick-pea.

Bibingka	Philippine rice cake.
Bihon	Rice noodles.
Bisque	A rich, thick, cream soup, usually made from shellfish.
Blachan	Shrimp paste that comes in slabs. It is roasted before use.
Bonda	A South Indian snack of mashed potato, seasoned and formed into balls, dipped in batter, and then deep-fried.
Bringe	Rice with coconut milk.
Buco	Young coconut.
Burfi	A fudge-like sweet.
Buta-Niku No Catsup-Ni	Pork and vegetables in catsup.

C

Calamansi	A small lime-like fruit of the citrus family.
Calaunji	Onion seeds.
Caraway seeds	Similar to black cumin seeds but differ in flavor.
Cassava	A tropical spurge whose fleshy root stock yields a nutritious starch from which tapioca is prepared.
Chapati	Indian bread.
Chicharo	Snow peas.
Chivra	A mixture of nuts, fried pressed rice, fried lentils.

Cinnamon	The outer bark of the cinnamon tree. It has a sweet aromatic taste. This is also used for flavoring garam masala, meats, and rice dishes.
Clafoutis	Cake with fresh fruits.
Coriander	Seeds, powder, or fresh leaves. The seeds resemble peppercorn and are very aromatic. When crushed and ground into powder, it is mixed with curry powder and is used for all kinds of curries. Fresh coriander leaves are similar to parsley leaves, but are fragrant; they are used for garnishing and also in making chutneys.
Curry leaves	Curry patta or Kariwepillau from the plant called sweet neem in northern India and in South India. These leaves are used for flavoring or may be fried in oil until crisp. They are very popular in South India and are used in many dishes.
Curry powder	A blend of several spices such as turmeric powder, cumin powder, red chili powder, and coriander powder.

D

Dal or dhal	Split pulse or legume such as black gram (*Phaseolus mungo*), green mongo (*Phaseolus aureus*), gram dal or split Bengal gram, masoor dal or lentils with skin removed, tur dal or split pigeonpea, and urad dal or split black gram with skin removed.
Dalpuri	Flat bread stuffed with dal.
Dashi	Soup stock.
Dhakni	Sweet rice.

Dharodi	Sweet rice ball.
Dhokla	Steamed rice and bean cake.
Dosa	Pancake made with fermented batter of ground urad dal and rice; a specialty in South India.

E

Erwtensoep	Dutch pea soup.

F

Fennel	The small elongated green seeds of *Foeniculum vulgare.* They taste like anise seed and are used in curries. They are known to aid digestion and also are used as mouthwash.
Fenugreek	The leaves of the plant *Trigonella foenumgraecum;* they have a strong flavor and aroma. The seeds are very tiny and rock-hard with bitter flavor. The lightly roasted seeds are used in curries, vegetable soups, in cooking legumes, and in pickles.
Firni	A rice pudding.
Frikkadels	Dutch meatballs.
Fritters	Meat, fish, vegetables, or fruit dipped in batter and deep-fried.

G

Gabi	Yam.
Gado-gado	Cooked mixed vegetable salad with peanut sauce.

Garam masala	A ground mixture of these spices: cumin seeds, black peppercorn, cloves, black cardamoms, black cumin seeds, coriander, and cinnamon.
Ghee	Clarified butter.
Gomoke gohen	Rice cooked with slices of chicken and bits of various vegetables flavored with soy sauce.
Gram-flour	Flour prepared from ground black gram.
Gratin de fruits de mer	Baked fish and seafoods.
Guisado	Sauteed.
Gulab jamun	Fried milk balls in rose sugar syrup.
Gur	Unrefined cane sugar with crude but individual taste and quality. It is also known as jaggery.

H

Hachee	Savory beef and onion stew.
Half-and-half	Mixture of half cream and half milk.
Halo-halo	A Philippine concoction made of several kinds of sweets mixed with shaved ice, sugar, and milk.

I

Idli	Steamed plain rice cake.
Ilayappam	A rice flour preparation, wrapped in banana leaf and steamed.

J

Jaggery	Unrefined brown sugar, especially from palm sap.
Jal-Jeera	Spicy hot juice.

K

Kabargah	Roasted mutton dish from Kashmir (India).
Kangkong	Philippine spinach; Chinese spinach or kale.
Kanom Chan	Layer cake.
Kanom Tueoy Foo	Rice cupcake.
Kaong	Sugar palm seeds.
Kapyo	Dried gourd.
Kedgeree	Rice with fish and lentils.
Ketupat	Rice cooked in a shell of coconut leaves; a compressed rice cake eaten with a thick sauce; food with a thick gravy.
Ketuput pulut	Glutinous rice wrapped and cooked in banana leaf.
Khaskhus	Poppy seeds, generally added to special meat curries, such as Khorma; they give the curry a rich flavor.
Kheer	Sweet rice pudding.
Khichuri	Rice cooked with mongo.
Kikkoman	A brand of soy sauce.
Kimchee	Pickles made of cabbage and radish.

Kinchay	A variety of coriander.
Knorr seasoning	A trade name for a kind of flavor cubes.
Konyakku	Paste made from devil's-tongue.
Kozahakkhatta	A steamed pastry, with a crust made of rice flour. The filling can be either sweet (with coconut and brown sugar) or salty (with black gram, coconut, and spices).
Krupuk	Prawn crackers.
Kuch Lapis	A layered cake.
Kuskus (also khaskhus)	Poppy seeds.

L

Labuyo	Hot chili.
Laddoo	Any ball made of rice flour, or pea flour eaten with sugar syrup.
Lamington	Sponge cake cut into squares, dipped in melted chocolate, and sprinkled with desiccated coconut.
Lampries curry	Mixture of all kinds of meats, cooked together.
Leche flan	Egg custard.
Lemongrass	A tall grass that grows in clumps. The thick root is used. The outer layer is usually removed before use.

M

Macapuno	Sport coconut.
Maggi sauce	Seasoning similar to worcestershire sauce.

Mahashy	Stuffed eggplant with rice.
Masala	Curry powder.
Methi	Fenugreek seeds.
Mirin	A sweet wine made from steamed glutinous rice and used to flavor boiled food.
Misua	Fine wheat noodles.
MSG	Monosodium glutamate.
Mujaddarh	Rice with lentils.
Muri	Puffed rice.
Murrukku	Pretzels made of rice flour.
Mustard oil	Pungent salad oil; it contains vitamin D.
Mustard seeds	The seeds are black, yellow, and brown. Pungent in flavor, they contain manganese and vitamin D. They add flavor to curries, pickles, and chutneys.
Mutton	Goat's meat.

N

Naan	Flat baked bread.
Nangka (or langka)	Jackfruit.
Nasi goreng	Malaysian fried rice.
Nasi himpit	Malaysian rice cake.
Nata de coco	Gelatinous mold grown on a substrate of coconut.
Nimki	Salty fried biscuits.

O

Orze shara	Rice with vermicelli.
Ouzo	Anise-flavored, unsweetened Greek liqueur.
Oyako chicken rice	Bowl of rice topped with slices of chicken, onion, mushrooms, and omelet. It is seasoned with soy sauce, sugar, and sweet rice wine.

P

Pahi	Pickles.
Pakoras	Fritters.
Palitaw	Glutinous rice cake eaten with grated coconut, sugar, and sesame seed powder.
Palillo	Ground paprika.
Pancit	A Philippine dish made with noodles, slices of pork and chicken, shrimps, and vegetables.
Pandan leaves	Screwpine leaves, used for flavor and aroma, especially in Indonesian dishes.
Panocha	Hard brown sugar formed into a ball.
Pappardam	A crisp bread (like tortillas) made from pea flour. They can also be made with sago and rice flour.
Paratha	Flat fried bread.
Patis	A strongly salty fish sauce.
Patishapta pitha	Sweet rice crispy.
Pechay	Chinese cabbage.

Pindakas	Peanut butter.
Pinipig	Pressed or puffed rice.
Pitha	Special rice cake from Bangladesh.
Plantain	Cooking banana.
Pohe	Bombay cereal made of rice with peas and potatoes.
Pork vindaloo	Hot and sour curry.
Pulses	Legumes, rich in proteins.

R

Raita	Vegetables, raw or parboiled, mixed with beaten and seasoned yoghurt.
Rasgulla	Cream cheese balls in light syrup.
Reisauflauf	Baked rice pudding.
Rellenong bangus	Stuffed milkfish.
Rendang tok	A dried meat preparation served in Perak, Central Malaysia, during festive occasions.
Roganjosh	Mutton curry from Kashmir.
Rose water	An aromatic liquid used in sherbets and sweets.

S

Sabji-Bhaji	Mixed vegetables.
Saffron	A flavoring and coloring spice, grown in Kashmir. It is the dried stigmata of the saffron crocus.
Sago	Light granular starch, used in puddings.

Sake	Japanese wine made from fermented rice and water. It is used in cooking as a seasoning for soups and boiled dishes.
Sambal, sambol	Chili sauce; any hot or spicy relish.
Sambal ulek	Relish made of crushed chilies.
Sambbar	Hot lentil soup. Also a dish consisting of split pigeonpea with one or more vegetables, served with rice in South India.
Sambbar powder	Mixture of ground coriander seeds, cumin seeds, chick-peas, gram dal, asafoetida, cinnamon, black peppercorn, fenugreek seeds, red chilies.
Samosa	A thin pastry cone filled with boiled or spiced vegetables or meat, and deep-fried.
Sausagi	Bamboo leaf.
Seaweed sheets	Wrapper.
Shifta	Meat patties, Iraqi style.
Shiitake (dried noshi)	Flat dried Japanese mushroom, cultivated on oak logs.
Shoyu	A dark brown sauce made from fermenting steamed soybean and roasted wheat, and mixing with a special yeast in brine.
Shufta	A sweet dish made with cheese from Kashmir.
Srikhand	A sweet yoghurt-based dish with liquid removed by steaming and flavored with saffron and nuts.

Suji	Cream of wheat or farina.
Sushi	Vinegar rice. Various kinds of shellfish, fish, egg, or vegetables are mixed in or placed on the rice.

T

Tahini	Sesame seed paste.
Tamago-dofu	Egg custard.
Tamales	Square, stuffed preparation with meat and rice.
Tamarind	The sour fruit of the tamarind tree. The seed pod and the pulp are soaked in warm water to extract the acidic water pulp. Tamarind adds a sour taste to vegetables, dals, meats, and other food.
Taoco	Bottled, thick, brown liquid soybean concentrate.
Tempe	Fermented molded soybean.
Touco	Product from fermented soybean.
Trautamanndorf	Sweet rice pudding with gelatin and cointreau.
Turmeric	Dried fleshy root of a member of the ginger family. It gives the yellow color in all curries.

U

Ubi	Purple yam.
Ugali	African bread.
Upauma	Spicy fried farina.
Urad dhal	*See* Dal.

V

Vada	Fritters.
Vetsin	Monosodium glutamate.
Vevara	Rice cookies.
Vindaloo	A way of cooking that has a high proportion of green and red chilies.

W

Wansuy	Green coriander.

Y

Yakhini	Mutton with yoghurt.
Yaksik	Sweet rice cake.
Yaprakh	Rice stuffed in leafy vegetables.

Z

Zardah	Yellow sweet rice with saffron and nuts.

Selected References

Anonymous. 1990. A handbook of Korea. Korean Overseas Information Service, Seoul, Korea.

Bunge, F. M. 1984. Area handbook for Malaysia. The American University, Washington, D.C., USA.

Devi, E. M. 1971. Handy rice recipes. Singapore.

FAO (Food and Agriculture Organization). 1948. Rice and rice diets. FAO, Washington Nutritional Studies, No. 1.

Grist, D. H. 1975. Rice. 5th ed. Longman, London.

Hahn, E. 1968. The cooking of China. Time Life Books. Alexandria, Virginia, USA.

Hillman, H., Shilling, D. 1979. The book of the world's cuisines. Penguin Books, New York.

Kano, A. K. et al. 1968. Genetic and environmental variation in the quality of high yielding varieties. J. Post Graduate School, Indian Agric. Res. Inst. 6(2):148-156.

Singh, D. 1970. Indian cookery. Cox and Hayman, Great Britain.

Smith, H. H., Al-Any, W. N., Bernier, D. W., Bunge, F. M., Giloane, W., Jabbra, J. G., Kerr, P., Teleki, S. 1974. Area handbook for Lebanon, American University, Washington, D. C., USA.

Smith, H. H., Bernier, D. W., Bunge, F. M., Chadwickrintz, F., Shinn, R. S., Teleki, S. 1967. Area handbook for South Vietnam. American University, Washington, D.C., USA.

Smith, H. H., Cover, W. W., Folen, J. B., Meissenburg, M. L., Szentadorjany, J., Teleki, S. 1971. Area handbook for Iran. American University, Washington, D.C., USA.